Maya®

Professional Tips and Techniques

Maya®

Professional Tips and Techniques

Lee Lanier

WILEY PUBLISHING, INC.

ACQUISITIONS AND DEVELOPMENT EDITOR: Mariann Barsolo
TECHNICAL EDITOR: Keith Reicher
PRODUCTION EDITOR: Martine Dardignac
COPY EDITOR: Judy Flynn
PRODUCTION MANAGER: Tim Tate
VICE PRESIDENT AND EXECUTIVE GROUP PUBLISHER: Richard Swadley
VICE PRESIDENT AND EXECUTIVE PUBLISHER: Joseph B. Wikert
VICE PRESIDENT AND PUBLISHER: Neil Edde
MEDIA PROJECT SUPERVISOR: Laura Atkinson
MEDIA DEVELOPMENT SPECIALIST: Steve Kudirka
BOOK DESIGNER: Chris Gillespie, Happenstance Type-O-Rama
COMPOSITOR: Kate Kaminski, Happenstance Type-O-Rama
PROOFREADER: Nancy Riddiough
INDEXER: Ted Laux
ANNIVERSARY LOGO DESIGN: Richard Pacifico
COVER DESIGNER: Ryan Sneed
COVER IMAGE: Lee Lanier
Copyright © 2007 by Wiley Publishing, Inc., Indianapolis, Indiana

Published simultaneously in Canada

ISBN: 978-0-470-10740-9

Library of Congress Cataloging-in-Publication Data

Lanier, Lee, 1966–

Maya : professional tips and techniques / Lee Lanier.

p. cm.

Includes bibliographical references.

ISBN-13: 978-0-470-10740-9 (paper/cd-rom)

ISBN-10: 0-470-10740-5 (paper/cd-rom)

1. Computer animation. 2. Maya (Computer file). 3. Three-dimensional display systems. I. Title.

TR897.7.L37 2007

006.6@@sp96 — dc22

2006101053

Dear Reader,

Thank you for choosing *Maya Professional Tips and Techniques*. This book is part of a family of premium quality Sybex graphics books, all written by outstanding authors who combine practical experience with a gift for teaching.

Sybex was founded in 1976. More than 30 years later, we're still committed to producing consistently exceptional books. With each of our graphics titles we're working hard to set a new standard for the industry. From the paper we print on, to the writers and artists we work with, our goal is to bring you the best graphics books available.

I hope you see all that reflected in these pages. I'd be very interested to hear your comments and get your feedback on how we're doing. Feel free to let me know what you think about this or any other Sybex book by sending me an email at nedde@wiley.com, or if you think you've found an error in this book, please visit http://wiley.custhelp.com. Customer feedback is critical to our efforts at Sybex.

Best regards,

Neil Edde
Vice President and Publisher
Sybex, an Imprint of Wiley

To 3 of the 4 L's:
Lynn, Linda, and Luke

—Lee Lanier

Acknowledgments

My thanks go to the excellent editorial and production staff at Wiley, including my acquisitions editor, Mariann Barsolo; my production editor, Martine Dardignac; and my technical editor, Keith Reicher.

Special thanks to this book's special contributors: Michael Stolworthy, Matt Orlich, James Chandler, Kirk Buckendorf, Rocky Bright Jr., Joshua Perez, and Tim Kelly.

Special thanks to all the animators who have toiled before me and along with me. 3D animation is a wonderful, inspiring medium, particularly when so many pour their passion into the work.

Special thanks to my family and friends who supported my wild ambitions. And the biggest thanks go to my beautiful wife, Anita, who encouraged me all the way despite all those late, late 3D nights.

I'd like to point out that several of the photos in this book were provided by the photographers of Stock Xchng (www.sxc.hu). This is a wonderful site that provides royalty-free, restriction-free material simply out of love of the medium. Additional models were purchased from Turbo Squid (www.turbosquid.com), another excellent service.

Contents at a Glance

Contents

Introduction

I should stress that I am self-taught. In 1994, I sat down at a spare seat of Alias PowerAnimator 5.1 and started hacking away. After several years and various trials by fire, 3D became a livelihood, a love, and an obsession. Along the way, I was fortunate enough to work with many talented artists at Buena Vista Visual Effects and Pacific Data Images. In 2000, I switched from PowerAnimator to Maya and have since logged tens of thousands of hours with the subject of this book.

Due to the unusual combination of an informal and professional background, I do not profess to know everything there is to know about Maya. In fact, you may find a better, quicker, more-efficient way to achieve some of the tips and techniques described in this book. That's the beauty of Maya. There are probably a dozen ways to tackle every problem or challenge. If anything, I hope this book provides you with the theory, the background, and the basic approach needed for you to come up with *your own* creative solutions.

Who Can Benefit from This Book

Maya Professional Tips and Techniques is designed for anyone with a working knowledge of Maya. Specifically, this book was written with the following people in mind:

- Intermediate students who would like to learn unusual techniques not described in other books

- Hobbyists or amateurs who are self-starters and would like to refine their Maya skills

- Working professionals who have concentrated in specific areas of Maya but would like to expand their knowledge into other areas of the program

Although this book is very Maya specific, several sections touch upon Pixologic ZBrush, Adobe After Effects, Adobe Photoshop CS2, Photomatix Pro, and HDRShop. Although a working knowledge of these programs is by no means mandatory, it will help you get the most out of this book.

About This Book

Maya Professional Tips and Techniques is divided into 10 chapters. Each chapter contains 6 to 9 sections. Each section covers specific tips or techniques. The contents of each section vary from bullet-point lists of suggestions and specific step-by-step instructions to theoretical explanations. Many sections include sample scene files, which are included on the companion CD.

Since the sections are not dependent upon each other, feel free to skip to the sections that are of the most interest to you. A concentrated effort has been made to include useful tips and techniques that are somewhat obscure or that have been skipped by other books.

The Companion CD

The CD included in the back of this book is an important part of learning with *Maya Professional Tips and Techniques*. Sample scenes, shading networks, QuickTime movies, HDR files, and texture bitmaps are included to help you perfect your knowledge.

Please note that all scene files have been prepared with Maya 8.0. As such, you may not be able to read them with an older version. The various techniques have been tested with a beta version of Maya 8.5. Minor variations between version 8.0 and 8.5 have been noted.

As for Maya file locations, the traditional directory structure is used. For example, you'll be able to locate the files as follows:

Project_Files\Chapter_1\scenes holds scene files and shading networks.

Project_Files\Chapter_1\images includes background images and HDR files.

Project_Files\Chapter_1\movies is for sample QuickTime movies.

Project_Files\Chapter_1\textures holds texture bitmaps.

Project_Files\Chapter_1\mel contains MEL scripts.

Websites

Feel free to contact me at www.beezlebugbit.com. On the site, there's a forum set aside for this book and all its associated subjects. The public is invited to join for free. You can also find me at www.myspace.com/beezlbug.

If you have some cool-looking stills from an animation and you'd like to share them with the world, visit www.3d-motion-gallery.com.

If you're a fan of short films, or have made a short film and would like to find an audience, visit www.damshortfilm.org.

About the Author

Lee Lanier is an award-winning 3D animator and director. His short films have played over 200 film festivals, museums, and galleries worldwide. Before directing the shorts *Millennium Bug*, *Mirror*, *Day Off the Dead*, *Weapons of Mass Destruction*, and *13 Ways to Die at Home*, Lee served as a senior animator in the Modeling and Lighting departments of Pacific Data Images on *Shrek* and *Antz*. He got his start in 3D at Buena Vista Visual Effects at Walt Disney Studios, where he created visual effects for such films as *The Santa Clause* and *Mortal Kombat*. Lee currently lives in Boulder City, Nevada, where he serves as manager of BeezleBug Bit, LLC (www.beezlebugbit.com) and director of the Dam Short Film Festival (www.damshortfilm.org).

Customization and MEL Scripting

MAYA TAKES THE lion's share of high-end 3D work in the feature film and visual effects industry. You can trace this fact to one particular trait: the software is infinitely customizable. The customization is not restricted to multimillion-dollar productions, however. You can customize Maya to your own tastes and thereby work faster, more intelligently, and most important, more comfortably. The most thorough and powerful method of customization is the application of MEL scripting. MEL is the underlying language on which the entire program is built. Every single tool and function within Maya has one or more lines of MEL code associated with it.

This chapter's topics are organized into the following techniques:

- Resetting to Factory/Swapping *Prefs* Files
- Creating Custom Shelf Icons
- Building a Simple MEL Window
- Building an Intermediate MEL Window
- Creating an Autosave MEL Script
- Creating Your Own Paint Effects Brushes
- Creating Notes for Your Fellow Animators
- Passing Information to Files
- Industry Tip: Creating an "Expert Mode" MEL Script

Resetting to Factory/Swapping *Prefs* Files

There comes a time in every animator's life when it'd be nice to return to the past. That is, it's sometimes necessary to return Maya to either its "factory default" or to a state that is known to be productive.

To return the Maya user interface (UI) and global preferences to the factory default, choose **Window → Settings/Preferences → Preferences**. In the Preferences window, choose **Edit → Restore Default Settings** from the upper-left drop-down menu. This returns all the options in the Preferences window to default and redisplays any UI elements that were previously hidden. **Restore Default Settings** will not, however, restore individual tools to their default settings.

Every options window that is provided by a tool has an **Edit → Reset Settings** option in the upper-left drop-down menu. Unfortunately, **Reset Settings** does not provide a universal way to reset every tool.

You can force Maya to return to its original installation configuration by exiting the program, deleting the `prefs` folder, and restarting the program. If Maya discovers that the `prefs` folder is missing, but detects an older installation of the program, it displays a message window with two buttons. Choosing the Create Default Preferences button returns Maya to its installation configuration. Choosing the Copy Old Preferences button retrieves a copy of the `prefs` folder from the older installation.

The Maya startup preferences window

If the `prefs` folder is missing and no other installation exists, Maya automatically supplies a new, factory-default `prefs` folder. You can find the `prefs` folder in the following default locations with Maya 8.0:

Windows: `drive:\Documents and Settings\`*username*`\My Documents\maya\8.0\prefs`

Mac OS X: `Users/`*username*`/Library/Preferences/Alias/maya/8.0/prefs`

Linux: `~`*username*`/maya/8.0/prefs`

The `prefs` folder contains a series of subfolders and text files that store user settings. If you have Maya configured the way you like it, it's advisable to copy the entire `prefs` folder to a safe location. Should Maya wind up in a state you don't like, you can simply exit the program, delete the current `prefs` folder, and return your backup copy to its place. Saving and replacing the `prefs` folder is the perfect way to carry your preferences to machines that you are forced to share, such as those in a classroom. A description of default subfolders follows.

icons A folder that is available for user icon storage.

markingMenus A folder that contains custom marking menus. Each marking menu is saved as a separate file (for example, `menu_ChangePanelLayout.mel`).

shelves A folder that contains default and custom shelves. Each shelf is saved as a file (for example, shelf_Animation.mel). This folder is empty until a custom shelf is saved or Maya is exited for the first time.

The following files are created or updated when Maya is exited or the Save button is clicked in the Preferences window:

userHotkeys.mel Lists user-defined hot keys.

userNamedCommands.mel Lists commands that have user-defined hot keys assigned to them.

userRunTimeCommands.mel Stores user-defined commands. You can create your own commands with runTimeCommand. For example, you can create a command that displays the internal Maya time in a confirm dialog window by executing the following line in the Script Editor:

```
runTimeCommand -command ("confirmDialog
  -message `timerX`") WhatTime;
```

From that point forward, executing WhatTime in the Script Editor pops up a confirm dialog window with the system time.

> Many of the MEL commands discussed in this book are extremely long and thus must be printed on multiple lines. In reality, the Script Editor is indifferent to line breaks so long as the end of each command is indicated by a semicolon. You can open the Script Editor by choosing **Window → General Editors → Script Editor**. To execute a command in the Script Editor, you must press Ctrl+Enter after typing the command.

userPrefs.mel Stores global user preferences, including working units, performance settings, and Timeline options.

windowPrefs.mel Determines the default size and position of non-workspace windows (Hypergraph, options windows, and so on).

pluginPrefs.mel Lists all autoloaded plug-ins.

The following files are created or updated when custom UI colors are saved through the Colors window: userColors.mel, paletteColors.mel, and userRGBColors. userColors.mel stores user-defined colors defined in the Active and Inactive tabs of the Colors window. user-RGBColors.mel stores colors defined in the General tab of the Colors window. paletteColors .mel defines the colors that create the index palettes in the Active and Inactive tabs. You can change an existing palette by double-clicking on a palette swatch and choosing a new color through the Color Chooser window. The colors are written as RGB values with a 0 to 1 range. (If custom colors are never selected, these files are not created.) You can open the Colors window by choosing **Window → Settings/Preferences → Color Settings**.

If need be, you can edit any of the files in the prefs folder with a text editor. Perhaps the most useful file to edit by hand is userRunTimeCommands.mel, in which it's easy to delete custom commands that are no longer needed.

You can force Maya to update the files in the prefs folder by executing the savePrefs command in the Script Editor. The savePrefs command offers various flags, such as -uiLayout, that allow you to update specific files.

In addition, on each exit, Maya forces all tools that are not on a shelf to save their custom settings as optionVars. optionVars are specialized variables that survive multiple invocations of Maya. That is, if you exit Maya and open it later, the optionVars, with their correct values, remain accessible and readable (optionVars are written out to the disk). Aside from the option-Vars created by the Preferences window, however, optionVars are not accessible outside Maya. Nevertheless, you can create your own custom optionVars at any time and then retrieve the values with the -query or -q flag, as in this example:

```
optionVar -intValue "WorkOrderNumber" 57235;
```

```
optionVar -query "WorkOrderNumber";
```

Last, you can force Maya to save tool settings and update corresponding optionVars by executing the saveToolSettings command in the Script Editor.

Creating Custom Shelf Icons

Many Maya books have touched on the customization of shelves inside Maya. Nevertheless, they are so amazingly flexible that they are worth an additional look.

Maya comes from the factory with a set of ready-made shelves full of shelf icons (also referred to as shelf buttons). You can delete any of these by choosing **Window → Settings/Preferences → Shelf Editor**, selecting the Shelves tab, highlighting the shelf that is undesired, and clicking the Delete Shelf button. To make a new, empty shelf, click the New Shelf button.

There are several ways to populate a shelf with shelf icons. Pressing Ctrl+Alt+Shift and selecting a menu item, such as a tool, adds an icon to whichever shelf is visible at the time. Pressing Ctrl+Alt+Shift and selecting the options box of a tool also adds a shelf icon; in this case, clicking the icon opens the tool options window instead of applying the tool immediately with its prior settings.

You can also highlight and MMB drag any script lines you find in the Script Editor and drop them onto a shelf. A generic "mel" icon is created. When the icon is clicked, Maya runs through all the lines that were MMB dragged regardless of what they were. The shelf icon may be as simple as a single MEL line, such as performPlayblast true, which opens the Playblast options window. The icon may be as complex as the 200 lines necessary to create an entire skeleton. Once a shelf icon exists, you can edit the contained script lines in the Shelf

Editor. To do this, highlight the shelf name in the Shelves tab, select the icon name in the Shelf Contents tab, and make your changes in the Edit Commands tab. If you want to save your changes, press the keypad Enter key. To save all the shelves, click the Save All Shelves button (this exits the window).

    You can customize the look of a shelf icon by entering a name into the **Icon Name** field. The name is superimposed over the icon. You can also use your own custom icon by clicking the Change Image button. Maya is able to use a 32×32 BMP, XPM, or DIB file. XPM is a somewhat archaic ASCII image format supported by Maya and Silicon Graphics machines. DIB (Device Independent Bitmap) is a Windows variation of the standard BMP format. You can store your icon files in the `icons` folder found within the program directory or the `prefs` folder.

The Edit Commands tab of the Shelf Editor window

"mel" and other custom icons on a custom shelf. The custom icons are included in the Chapter 1 images folder on the CD.

    You can load a previously saved shelf by choosing Load Shelves from the Menu Of Items To Modify The Shelf shortcut arrow to the left of the shelves.

Building a Simple MEL Window

One of the most satisfying elements of MEL scripting is the creation of custom windows, or GUIs. If you're relatively new to the world of scripting, however, the MEL code can be very intimidating. With that in mind, this section boils down MEL windows into their most basic components.

    The following MEL script makes a simple window with two drop-down menu options, two buttons, and a short text message:

```
window -title "Simple Window" -menuBar true newWindow;

  menu -label "Options";

  menuItem -label "Save File" -command "file -f -save";

  menuItem -label "Exit Maya" -command "quit";

  columnLayout;

  button -label "Scale Up" -command "scale -r 2 2 2";

  button -label "Scale Down" -command "scale -r .5 .5 .5";

  text -label "Click me!";
showWindow newWindow;
```

This script is saved as `simple.mel` in the Chapter 1 mel folder on the CD. To use it, open the Script Editor, choose **File → Source Script**, and browse for the file. The MEL window pops up immediately. You can also paste the text into the work area of the Script Editor, highlight it, and MMB drag it onto a shelf to create a shelf icon.

You're free to use any command within the quotes after each `-command` flag, whether it is used for a menu item or a button. If you're wondering what commands are available, look no further than the Script Editor. Every single transform, operation, and tool within Maya has a MEL line associated with it. For example, if you transform a sphere, a line similar to this appears:

```
move -r -16.289322 8.110931 10.206124;
```

If you create a default sphere, this line appears:

```
sphere -p 0 0 0 -ax 0 1 0 -ssw 0 -esw 360 -r 1 -d 3 -ut
   -tol 0.01 -s 8 -nsp 4 -ch 1;objectMoveCommand;
```

Even though the `sphere` command has a huge number of option flags (a flag has a dash and several letters, such as `-p` or `-ax`), you do not have to use them all. `sphere` by itself will suffice. The same holds true for tools. For example, the Rebuild Surfaces tool prints out this:

```
rebuildSurface -ch 1 -rpo 1 -rt 0 -end 1 -kr 0 -kcp 0
   -kc 0 -su 4 -du 3 -sv 4 -dv 3 -tol 0.01 -fr 0
   -dir 2 "nurbsSphere";
```

With any tool, you can pick and choose the flags you need. For example, `rebuildSurface -su 12` will rebuild the surface with 12 spans in U direction with all the other settings left at default. Rest assured, memorizing what each and every flag does is close to impossible. Luckily, you can look up the flags and their functions by choosing **Help → MEL Command Reference** in the Script Editor. All Maya commands, including all tools, are listed with a detailed explanation of all possible flags. Keep in mind that flags have a short form and a long form. For instance, `-su` is the same as `-spansU`.

Commands used by buttons and menus are not limited to tools and such operations as `file -save` and `quit`. You can also launch Maya windows. For example, `HypergraphWindow` opens the Hypergraph window and `GraphEditor` opens the Graph Editor. To see the MEL lines associated with windows, choose **History → Echo All Commands** in the Script Editor. Note that MEL scripting is case sensitive.

Returning to the `simple.mel` script, the `columnLayout` command allows you to add as many buttons as you'd like to the layout. By default, they stack vertically. A layout command is mandatory for basic MEL windows. You have the choice of `rowColumnLayout`, `rowLayout`, or `columnLayout`, each of which organizes the window according to its name. You can add extra menu items by inserting additional `menuItem` lines. If you'd like more than one drop-down menu, add additional `menu` commands. The `text` command offers a simple way to add a message to a window. Whatever message you would like to appear should be inserted between the quotation marks after the `-label` flag.

On the first line of the script, the window command describes the GUI window. On the last line, showWindow newWindow launches the described window. A variation of the window command is mandatory if a pop-up window is desired.

If you write a new MEL script, or adapt an example, and the script fails to run, a red error message appears on the Command line.

```
                                        Error: Unterminated string.

Script Editor                                                    _|□|×|
File  Edit  History  Command  Help
};
// Error:              button -label "Scale Down" -command "scale -r .5 .5 .5;
//
// Error: Unterminated string. //
```

(Top) A red MEL error on the Command line. (Bottom) A MEL error message in the Script Editor. In this example, a quotation mark is missing before the ending semicolon.

If Maya has an issue with a specific part of the script, it will add a brief explanation to the Script Editor. Usually, broken MEL scripts are a result of a mistyping, a misspelling, or a missing semicolon, which needs to appear at the end of each command (except for those with an opening { or closing } curly bracket).

Building an Intermediate MEL Window

MEL scripting provides numerous ways to organize the look of a window and to control the way in which it operates. As an example, an intermediate MEL script named newcam.mel is included in the Chapter 1 mel folder on the CD. newcam.mel allows the user to create a 1-, 2-, or 3-node camera with the click of a button.

To use newcam.mel, open the Script Editor, choose **File → Source** Script, and browse for the file. newcam.mel is loaded into memory but will not run instantly. You must type **newcam** in the Script Editor work area and press Ctrl+Enter for the window to appear. To create a new camera, type a new value into the Focal Length field, press Enter, type a new value into the Far Clipping Plane field, press Enter, and click either the 1 Node, 2 Node, or 3 Node button. Ctrl+Entering newcam in the work area is required by the proc command. The script starts like this:

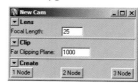

newcam.mel allows users to create camera with the click of a button.

```
global proc newcam () {
```

proc stands for *procedure*. A procedure is a group of MEL statements that can be used multiple times in a script. The start of a procedure is defined by an opening curly bracket {, which appears after the procedure name and double parentheses. The end of a procedure is determined by a closing curly bracket }. In the case of newcam.mel, the closing curly bracket is on the last line of the script.

A procedure is not activated until it is *called*. Executing the procedure name in the Script Editor work area is one way to call a procedure. This assumes that the procedure is *global*, which is determined by the inclusion of the word global. Once a procedure is global, you can call it from any part of a script that is not part of the procedure. That is, you can call global procedures from non-procedure parts of the script, from other procedures, or as a command listed by a button or menu item. If variables (symbolic names that hold values) are set up correctly within the script, the global option is not necessary and procedures become *local*. For a deeper discussion of global and local variables and when to use them, see Chapter 3.

Another feature of the newcam.mel script is the use of three collapsible frames (indicated by the down-pointing arrows on the left side of the window). To create a collapsible frame, code similar to the following is needed:

```
frameLayout -collapsable true -label "frame name"
  -width 250;
  rowLayout -numberOfColumns 3 -columnWidth3 100 100 100;
    [text, buttons, or fields go here]
    setParent ..;
  setParent ..;
```

The two setParent commands are necessary for the frame to function. You can place as many frames as you like in a window so long as each frameLayout command has two matching setParent commands. In addition, each frame must have its own layout command; in this example, rowLayout is used. The -numberOfColumns flag indicates the number of columns within the frame. The -columnWidth3 flag indicates the pixel width of each column; a pixel width of 100 is set by including 100 100 100 after the flag. Although these are optional flags, they make the results much cleaner.

Retrieving Values from Fields

One of the trickier aspects of MEL scripting is the creation of numeric fields in which users can enter new values. newcam.mel creates two of these: one in the Lens frame and one in the Clip frame. The following line creates the Lens field and establishes the size of the camera lens:

```
string $holdera =`intField -width 45 -value 25
  -minValue 25 -maxValue 250
  -changeCommand "int $cam_lens = `intField -query
  -value enteredValuea`" enteredValuea`;
```

The `intField` command creates an integer field. The `-width` flag sets the field width in pixels. The `-value` flag sets a default value that appears in the field. `-minValue` and `-maxValue` flags set lower and upper field limits. The `-changeCommand` flag executes a command when the value in the field is changed (and the Enter key is pressed). The command, appearing between quotes, is the declaration of a variable:

```
int $cam_lens = `intField -query
  -value enteredValuea`
```

A variable named `$cam_lens` is created. It's defined as an integer (a whole number with no decimal places) by including the `int` option. The variable is equal to everything within the single, back-facing quotes. In this case, `intField` is used again; this time, however, the `-query` flag forces it to output whatever the user entered into the field. Thus, if you enter 50, `$cam_lens` becomes 50. The `$cam_lens` variable is used again in each of the button commands, as in this example:

```
button -label "1 Node" -command "camera
  -focalLength $cam_lens -farClipPlane $far_clip;
  objectMoveCommand; cameraMakeNode 1 \"\"";
```

When the 1 Node button is clicked, it creates a camera with the `camera` command. The focal length of the camera is determined by the `-focalLength` flag. The focal length value is provided by the `$cam_lens` variable. `objectMoveCommand` is normally provided by Maya in order to keep the new camera selected and is necessary in this situation. Note that it is possible to have multiple commands within the button command quotation marks so long as they're separated by semicolons. The two backslashes at the end of the line are known as *escapes* and are necessary when there are quotes within quotes. If the escapes are not present, Maya becomes confused. To see what the 1-node camera command normally looks like in the Script Editor, choose **Create → Cameras → Camera**.

As demonstrated with this example, variables are often necessary in MEL scripting. Three simple types of variables exist: `int`, `float`, and `string`. While `int` rounds off a number to a whole value, `float` maintains all the decimal places. `string`, on the other hand, stores words and phrases, such as "hello there." A variable is always signified by the initial $ sign. For more complex examples of variables and variable use within expressions and MEL scripts, see Chapter 3.

Creating an Autosave MEL Script

One of the first features that users of Autodesk 3ds Max miss when switching to Maya is the autosave function. Although Maya has no autosave feature at this point, you can write one with a MEL script. This requires a MEL command that can sit in the background and wait for an opportune moment to save the file or to remind the user to save. `scriptJob` does just that.

scriptJob "triggers" a command when a particular event occurs. If the event does not occur, no action is taken. The easiest way to apply scriptJob is with the following line:

```
scriptJob -event "event_name" "command";
```

The -event flag offers a long list of events to choose from. Perhaps the most useful is "SelectionChanged", which triggers the command any time any object in Maya is selected or deselected. The following list includes other events:

"SelectTypeChanged" Triggered when the selection type is changed (for example, Select Surface Objects to Select Point Components).

"ToolChanged" Triggered when a new tool is selected (for example, switching from the Move tool to the Scale tool).

"timeChanged" Triggered when the Timeline moves to a new frame.

When scriptJob triggers the command, it outputs a job number. You can use the job number to kill the triggered scriptJob. This is often necessary to avoid multiple iterations of scriptJob running simultaneously. In order to capture the job number, you can use the following line:

```
$jobNumber = `scriptJob -event "SelectionChanged" "SaveScene"`;
```

In this example, Maya saves the scene file each time there is a selection change. To kill the job, you can use the following line at a different point in the script:

```
scriptJob -kill $jobNumber;
```

One way to avoid killing the job is to add the -runOnce flag to the scriptJob command, which allows the job to be triggered only one time.

Timing with *timerX* and Killing with *scriptJob*

Obviously, saving with every selection change is overkill. A second important element of an autosave script is thus an ability to track time. timerX provides that ability by serving as an internal stopwatch. You can note the current time, then derive elapsed time, with the following lines:

```
int $startTime = `timerX`;

int $totalTime = `timerX -startTime $startTime`;
```

If these two lines of code are placed within two different areas or procedures of a script, $totalTime becomes a value that represents the number of seconds Maya has been running. In actuality, timerX measures time in 10ths of a second; using an int variable, however, ensures that the value is rounded off to a whole second.

A working autosave script, named as.mel, is included in the Chapter 1 mel folder on the CD. To use as.mel, choose **File → Source Script** in the Script Editor. By default, it will pop up a save reminder window every 5 minutes.

With this script, you have the option to save the file with an incremental name (as.1.mb, as.2.mb, and so on), skip the save and exit the window, or kill the autosave job completely. You'll find additional customization notes at the top of the file. Keep in mind that this script is meant to demonstrate various MEL concepts and should not be considered a perfect example of MEL coding. That is, there are numerous ways to make the script "tighter" and take up fewer lines.

The save reminder window of the as.mel script

The scriptJob command has other uses beyond the creation of an autosave script. For instance, you can kill all MEL jobs currently running, regardless of their number, with the following line:

```
scriptJob -killAll
```

The -killAll flag won't affect protected jobs. To see what jobs exist and which ones are protected, use the -listJobs flag. The Script Editor lists all jobs with the job number to the left:

```
27: "-protected" "-event" "SelectionChanged"

  "objectDetailsSmoothness()"

4167: "-event" "SelectionChanged" "SaveScene"
```

If you're feeling adventurous, you can kill all the protected script jobs by adding the -force flag. Caution should be used, however, since Maya supplies a number of jobs that control the UI. You can also protect your own jobs by adding the -protected flag.

Creating Your Own Paint Effects Brushes

Paint Effects is a powerful system that allows you to paint geometry and other specialized strokes. With a few simple steps, you can create an entire forest, a raging fire, or a scruffy beard.

Paint Effects brushes are, in reality, short MEL scripts that live in the brushes folder in the Maya program directory (for example, C:\Program Files\Alias\Maya8.0\brushes\). Two basic brush styles exist: tube and sprite. Tube brushes grow primitive tube geometry into complex shapes. Sprite brushes paste bitmaps onto short tube segments.

To swap out a default sprite brush bitmap for your own:

1. Switch to the Rendering menu set, choose **Paint Effects → Get Brush**, and a select a brush that uses sprites, such a hands.mel in the flesh brush folder. Paint a stroke.

2. Select the stroke curve and open its Attribute Editor tab. Switch to the Paint Effects tab to the immediate right of the stroke tab. The Paint Effects tab is named after the brush type. In the Texturing section, click the file browse button beside the **Image Name** attribute and load your own bitmap. IFF, TIF, and BMP formats work. If you'd like transparency, choose an IFF file with an alpha channel. For a sprite to work, the **Map Method** attribute must be set to Tube 2D. (Tube 3D will work but will cause the image to disappear when the back side of the tube faces the camera.)

3. Render a test. Your bitmap image appears along the painted stroke.

If you'd like to permanently create a custom sprite brush, it's fairly easy to adapt an existing MEL file:

1. Open the Maya brushes folder. Open the flesh subfolder. Duplicate the hands.mel file. Rename the duplicated file custom.mel. Create a new subfolder and call it custom, as in this example:

```
C:\Program Files\Alias\Maya8.0\brushes\custom\
```

Move custom.mel into the custom folder.

2. Open custom.mel with a text editor. (Windows WordPad provides the proper formatting.) Change the second line to the following:

```
bPsetName "imageName" "custom.iff";
```

custom.iff is your custom bitmap. Maya assumes that all brush images are in the brushImages folder:

```
C:\Program Files\Alias\Maya8.0\brushImages\
```

Change the last line of the brush script to this:

```
rename (getDefaultBrush()) custom;
```

3. Save the file. Make sure that the file has the .mel extension or the brush will not work. Start or restart Maya. **Choose Window → General Editors → Visor**. Switch to the Paint Effects tab. The new custom folder is listed with all the original brush folders. Click the custom folder icon. The custom.mel brush appears with a generic "Maya" icon. Click the icon. The Paint Effects brush is activated. Click+drag the mouse in a workspace view. The Paint Effects stroke appears. Render a test frame. Your custom image is rendered along the stroke path.

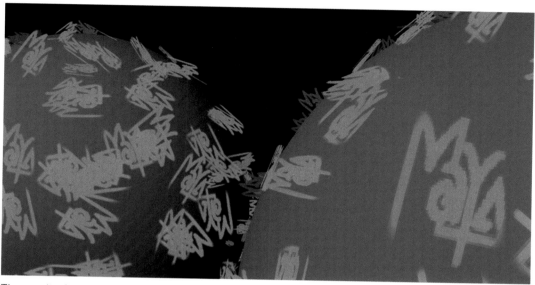

The result of a custom Paint Effects sprite brush. The brush is included as MayaBrush.mel in the Chapter 1 mel folder.

Customizing a Tube Brush

The main disadvantage of sprite brushes is the two-dimensionality of the resulting stroke. In addition, sprite strokes tend to create poor shadows. Tube strokes, on the other hand, can be quite realistic. Tube brushes are easily adapted with the Paint Effects Brush Settings window. To adapt an existing tube brush and save it out as a new brush:

1. Select a brush by choosing **Paint Effects → Get Brush**. Paint a stroke. Choose **Paint Effects → Template Brush Settings**. The Paint Effects Brush Settings window opens. The window contains all the settings of the brush that was last employed. Change as many attributes as is necessary to create a custom variation of the brush. Paint additional strokes to test your custom settings.

2. While the Paint Effects Brush Settings window remains open, choose **Paint Effects → Save Brush Preset**. The Save Brush Preset window opens. Select a **Label** name (this will be the brush's filename) and an **Overlay Label** (the text that appears on the icon). Choose a **Save Preset** option. The To Shelf option saves to the brush to the currently active shelf. The To Visor option permanently writes the brush to the disk in the folder determined by the **Visor Directory** field. Click the Save Brush Preset button.

It's possible to adapt the MEL script of a tube brush, although it's a bit more tricky. As an example, the first line of the `willow.mel` brush, found in the `trees` brush folder, looks like this:

```
brushPresetSetup();bPset "time" 1;

  bPset "globalScale" 0.3186736972;

  bPset "depth" 1; bPset "modifyDepth" 1;...
```

This is only a small portion of the first line. If printed out in full, it would fill an entire page. Fortunately, you can decipher it. Each item in quotes, such as `"depth"`, is an attribute. The number after the attribute is the attribute setting. Each attribute corresponds with an attribute in the Paint Effects Attribute Editor tab. For example, `"depth"` corresponds to the **Depth** check box in the Channels section. Digging deeper, `"color1G"` corresponds to the **Color G** channel of the **Color1** attribute in the Shading section. The following number, 0.6470588446, is the color value written for the 0-to-1 color range. As a third example, `"flowers"` corresponds to the **Flowers** check box in the Growth section. A 0 after `"flowers"` signifies that **Flowers** is unchecked.

Obviously, you would not want to write a tube brush from scratch. However, it's fairly easy to copy an existing brush and adapt it. If you're not sure what each attribute does, a detailed list can be found in the "brush node" Maya help file.

Creating Notes for Your Fellow Animators

Communication is important to professional animators, so there are a number of techniques available for making notes within Maya.

Every single node that can be loaded in the Attribute Editor has a Notes section. Anything you type into these sections is saved with the Maya scene file. On occasion, Maya uses these areas to add documentation notes that have not been included in the regular Maya help files. For example, the Make Motor Boats tool adds such a note.

You can create a 3D note by selecting an object, choosing **Create → Annotation**, and entering text into the Annotate Node window. The text appears in all the workspace views with an arrow pointing to the object's pivot point.

The Notes area for the Make Motor Boats tool

An annotation note and its position within the Hypergraph Hierarchy window

The annotation node is parented to a locator, which in turn is parented to the object. In reality, the arrow has a desire to point toward the locator. The annotation and locator nodes can be unparented and "freed" from the object or simply deleted if no longer needed. You can update the text at any time by opening the annotation node's Attribute Editor tab.

You can also use MEL scripting to create a note window that a user can launch from a shelf icon. For example, you can MMB drag the following text from the Script Editor work area to a shelf:

```
window -title "Notes" noteWin;

  rowColumnLayout;

  text -label "Note A: Try this.";

  text -label "Note B: Then this.";

showWindow noteWin;
```

When the new shelf icon is clicked, the note window opens. If you have the patience, you can make the window quite detailed.

In another variation, the text of the confirm dialog window is provided by an external file:

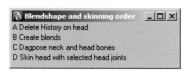

A custom note window

```
$fileRead = `fopen $fileName "r"`;

string $readText = `fgetline $fileRead`

confirmDialog -message $readText;
```

With this example, the script reads a binary file established by the `$filename` variable. You can create your own custom Maya binary files with the `fopen` command, which is discussed in the next section.

◼ Passing Information to Files

Maya allows you to write and read custom binary files. This is useful when a MEL script needs to call on a list or if the script needs to permanently record events (for example, a dynamic simulation). To write to a file, you can use this code:

```
$fileName = ( `internalVar -userWorkspaceDir`

  + "note.tmp" );

$fileWrite = `fopen $fileName "w"`;

fprint $fileWrite "Maya Rules";

fclose $fileWrite;
```

In this example, the written file, named note.tmp, is one line long and contains the text *Maya Rules*. The fprint command undertakes the writing. The fclose command frees the written file; if fclose is skipped, note.tmp will remain inaccessible to future fprint commands. The intenalVar variable, which is a permanent and global, establishes the directory to which the file is written. -userWorkspaceDir represents the current project directory. Other internalVar flags represent other default locations; for example, -userTmpDir represents the Maya temp directory and -userScriptDir represents the user script directory.

To read and print the line contained within note.tmp, use the following lines:

```
$fileName = ( `internalVar -userWorkspaceDir`

  + "note.tmp" );

$fileRead = `fopen $fileName "r"`;

string $readText = `fgetline $fileRead`;

print $readText; fclose $fileRead;
```

To write a longer file, you can create a script that contains these commands:

```
proc appendFile (){

  string $valueToWrite = ($test + "\n");

  $fileWrite = `fopen note.tmp "a"`;

  fprint $fileWrite $valueToWrite;

  fclose $fileWrite;

}
```

In this example, fopen, fprint, and fclose commands are contained within a procedure named appendFile. To append the file, fopen uses the a option instead of the w option. Each time appendFile is called, it writes $valueToWrite to a binary file named note.tmp. Since no directory path is declared, Maya assumes that note.tmp resides in the project directory. The $valueToWrite string is constructed from the variable $test, which is defined outside the procedure, and "\n". The \n instructs fprint to include an end-of-line code. This forces fprint to create a brand-new line the *next time* the procedure is called. If \n is not used, fprint will continually append to the same line. You can also use \n when creating the original file, like so:

```
fprint $fileWrite "Maya Rules\n";
```

fprint does not write to the disk each time it's called. Instead, it writes to a temporary software buffer. When the buffer is full or the fclose command is used, fprint writes all the information to the disk at one time. You can force fprint to write to the disk at any time by inserting the fflush command.

To read and print the contents of a file, one line at a time, you can use this code:

```
$fileRead = `fopen $fileName "r"`;

string $readLine = `fgetline $fileRead`;

while ( size($readLine) > 0) {

  print ( $readLine );

  $readLine = `fgetline $fileRead`;

}

fclose $fileRead;
```

Reading Text Files

As an alternative to fopen, the popen command allows you to read regular text files by piping a system function. For example, you can use the following code to read and print each line of a 50-line text file:

```
int $count = 0; int $lineNumber = 50;

$pipe = popen( "type note.txt", "r" );

if ($count < $lineNumber) {

  string $readLine = `fgetline $pipe`;

  string $line = ( $readLine );

  print $line;

  $count = $count + 1;

}

pclose ( $pipe );
```

With this code, the Windows command `type` prints out the contents of `note.txt`, which is found in the same folder as the script. The contents are "captured" by the `popen` command and made available for `fgetline` to read. `$lineNumber` establishes how many lines the text file contains. Each line is temporarily stored by the `$line variable`, allowing it to be printed with the `print` command.

As an additional working example, a MEL script named `video.mel` is included in the Chapter 1 mel folder on the CD. To use `video.mel`, choose **File → Source Script** in the Script Editor. This script randomly retrieves phrases from two text files and creates humorous video rental titles.

▉ Industry Tip: Creating an "Expert Mode" MEL Script

Some animators really enjoy creating custom MEL GUIs — so much so that they forgo the standard Maya UI elements in favor of their own custom windows. One example comes from Michael Stolworthy, an exhibit designer at GES. Michael has written `MDMwindow.mel`, which is designed to maximize the efficiency of a dual-monitor setup. The custom MEL window fills one monitor, while the Maya interface, with hidden UI elements, fills the other.

The script is included in the Chapter 1 mel folder on the CD. To run the script, see the `MDMReadMe.txt` file in the `MDMwindow` subfolder. The script works equally well on a single-monitor setup.

`MDMwindow.mel` is not a short script. In fact, at 19 pages and 27,000+ characters, it cannot be pasted into the Script Editor but can only be sourced. Nevertheless, like many MEL scripts, many of its components are fairly basic and are simply repeated numerous times. In terms of functionality, `MDMWindow.mel` carries several unique features, a few of which are discussed with their matching piece of MEL code:

Imbedded panels The right half of the MEL window is dedicated to standard Maya panels. You can set the panels to workspace views or windows such as the Hypergraph, Hypershade, and Graph Editor; simply choose a **Panels** menu option.

The following MEL code is used to imbed the Outliner panel at the script's start-up:

```
outlinerPanel; setParent..;
```

In order to arrange the panels, the `paneLayout` command is needed in the script:

```
paneLayout -configuration "right3";
```

`right3` signifies that there are three panes in the panel layout with two stacked on the right side. The panes are divided by moveable separator lines. A total of 16 pane layouts are available. You can find descriptions of each in the "paneLayout" Maya help file.

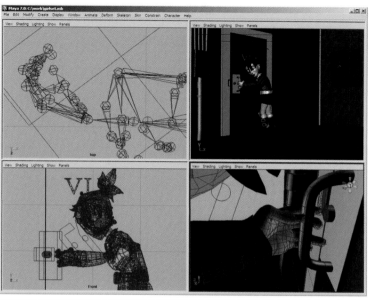

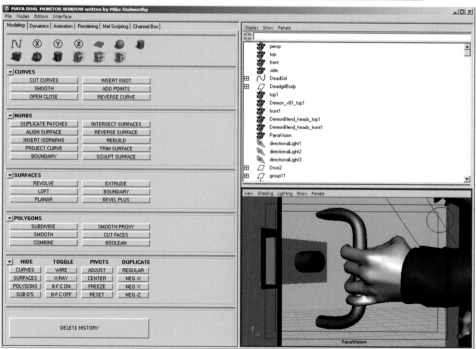

(Top) Maya interface with all UI elements hidden appears in monitor 1. (Bottom) `MDMwindow.mel` window fills monitor 2.

Imbedded shelf buttons Shelf buttons are freed from shelves and integrated directly into the layout. To create a single shelf button with a custom icon that creates a NURBS circle, the following line is used:

```
shelfButton -image1 "MDMcircleY.bmp" -width 32
   -height 32 -c CreateNURBSCircle;
```

Maya assumes that the custom icon BMP file is in the default icons folder. For example, the path might be as follows:

```
C:\Program Files\Alias\Maya8.0\icons\
```

Tab layout To maximize the number of buttons and windows, six tabs are included. Tabs are defined by the tabLayout command:

```
string $tabs = 'tabLayout -innerMarginWidth 3
   -innerMarginHeight 3';
```

The contents of each tab are preceded by the line similar to the following:

```
string $child1 = `columnLayout
   -adjustableColumn true`;
```

The tabs are finally constructed with the following code:

```
tabLayout -edit
   -tabLabel $child1 "Modeling"
   -tabLabel $child2 "Dynamics"
   -tabLabel $child3 "Animation"
   -tabLabel $child4 "Rendering"
   -tabLabel $child5 "Mel Scripting"
   -tabLabel $child6 "Channel Box"
   $tabs;
```

MICHAEL STOLWORTHY

After graduating with a degree in Media Arts and Animation, Michael served as creative director at Concept Design Productions, Inc., in Pasadena, California. Concept Design Productions specializes in the creation of retail store space, stage sets, trade show exhibits, and themed environments for public relations events. He has recently joined GES in Las Vegas, Nevada, as an exhibit designer. GES also specializes in trade show and event exhibition and has over two dozen offices in North America and Canada. To learn more about Michael's work, visit `www.ges.com` or `www.iaoy.com`.

Modeling

NUMEROUS MODELING TECHNIQUES exist, as well as many modeling formats. Box modeling, point modeling, edge loop modeling, and paint modeling are a few of the polygon modeling techniques. Polygon proxy modeling is a variation of subdivision modeling. NURBS surfaces, on the other hand, are a modeling system unto themselves. Although NURBS surfaces are used exclusively with only a small percentage of current feature film and visual effects projects, the format remains extremely efficient. More important, NURBS surfaces are used extensively in industrial design, manufacturing, and the automotive industry. Since NURBS surfaces tend to get little space in Maya books, the brunt of this chapter is dedicated to tips and tricks for modeling with them. Polygons, along with their importation remain a bedrock of 3D modeling and therefore get the remainder of the chapter.

This chapter's topics are organized into the following techniques:

- Breaking Up NURBS Surfaces
- Cleaning Up NURBS Surfaces with Attach and Detach
- Closing Holes in NURBS Objects
- Building a NURBS Gear
- Building a NURBS Eye
- Cleaning Up Imported Polygons
- Industry Tip: Building a Polygon Head by Extruding Edges
- Industry Tip: Adjusting the Maya Grid for Linear Units

Breaking Up NURBS Surfaces

It may seem that NURBS surfaces are inappropriate for complex models. Although NURBS are difficult to master when it comes to organic modeling, they are actually well suited for anything that is mechanical or man-made. The trick is to think in parts.

As an example, here is an instant coffee tin created with NURBS surfaces.

An instant coffee tin and a 3D facsimile

To replicate this model:

1. Choose **Create → CV Curve Tool** and draw a curve in the top workspace view that establishes the upper-right corner of the can. To ensure that the curve is truly square, temporarily click the Snap To Grids button on the Status line.

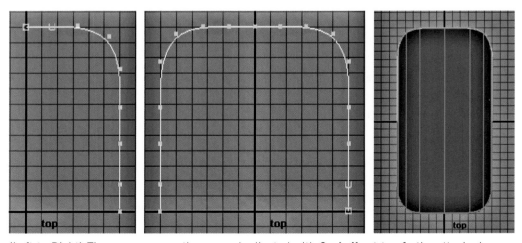

(Left to Right) The corner curve; the curve duplicated with **Scale X** set to −1; the attached curve duplicated with **Scale Z** set to −1 and the resulting curves lofted

2. Switch to the Surfaces menu set. With the curve selected, choose **Edit → Duplicate Special → ⬚**, set **Scale X** to –1, and click the Duplicate Special button. With the old and new curve selected, choose **Edit Curves → Attach Curves → ⬚**, set **Attach Method** to Connect, uncheck **Keep Originals**, and click the Attach button.

3. With the resulting curve selected, choose **Edit → Duplicate Special → ⬚**, set **Scale X** back to 1, set **Scale Z** to –1, and click the Duplicate Special button. With the old and new curve selected, choose **Surfaces → Loft**. The resulting surface forms the tin bottom. Select and delete the curves.

4. Shift+select the top and bottom edge isoparms of the surface (that is, choose the edges at the narrow ends). You can select edge isoparms by RMB clicking over the surface, choosing Isoparm from the marking menu, and clicking on an edge. Choose **Edit Curves → Duplicate Surface Curves**. Hide the bottom surface to make the new curves easier to see. With the new curves selected, choose **Edit → Delete By Type → History**. Select the new top curve, by itself, and choose **Edit Curves → Reverse Curve Direction**. Select both curves and choose **Edit Curves → Attach Curves**. If the Reverse Curve Direction tool is not applied, the attached curve will be twisted at the center. This is due to the duplicated curves possessing U directions running in opposite directions. In addition, the History delete tool is needed to prevent a gap from opening up in the curve when the Reverse Curve Direction tool is applied. If a small gap remains on one side of the curve, choose **Edit Curves → Open Open/Close Curves**.

5. With the curve selected, choose **Edit → Duplicate**. Scale the duplicated curve so that it no longer overlaps the original curve. Select the original curve again and make several more duplicates. Each time a duplicate is made, scale and transform the duplicate so that it doesn't overlap any other curve. Scale and transform all the duplicate curves so that they form the side of the can, the top and bottom metal lips, and the flat opening at the tin's top.

6. Select the curves in a logical order starting with the original bottom curve. Choose **Surfaces → Loft**. At

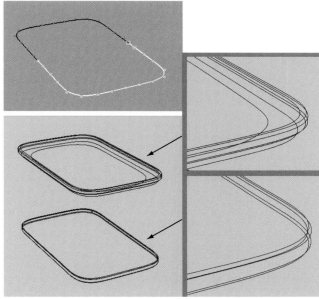

(Top left) Two curves duplicated off the bottom surface isoparms. (Bottom left) Duplicated curves transformed and scaled into position. (Right) Details of curves arranged to create top and bottom lips.

this point, the loft is quite ugly. The sides bow and the surface shoots too high through the top lip.

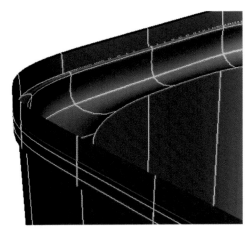

A bad loft

7. The NURBS model must be broken into smaller parts. Undo the loft. This time, select those curves that make up the bottom lip in logical order. Choose **Surfaces → Loft**. The lip forms cleanly. Choose all the curves that make up the top lip. Choose **Surfaces → Loft**. Once again, the surface is clean. Choose the two curves that establish the top of the bottom lip and the bottom of the top lip. Choose **Surfaces → Loft**. This creates the sides. As a last step, choose the two curves that form that flat opening at the top of the tin and choose **Surfaces → Loft**.

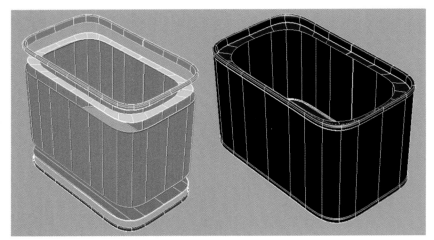

(Left) The five lofts that form the bottom lip, bottom, sides, flat opening, and top lip. (Right) A wireframe of the final model.

8. Unhide the bottom surface. Delete all the unneeded curves, name the surfaces appropriately, and group them together.

Important Rules for NURBS Modeling

Admittedly, the coffee tin is not a particularly complex model. Nevertheless, it demonstrates several techniques and traits that are important to any NURBS model, no matter what the complexity might be:

- Although it is a noble goal to limit the number of individual surfaces used on a NURBS model, no penalty exists for the existence of multiple surfaces. You can rig and animate a NURBS character, whatever that character might be, with multiple surfaces. You can texture a multi-surface object fairly efficiently. Although additional materials and maps may be necessary, the UV texture space of each NURBS surface is ready to go and requires no significant adjustment..

- You can speed up the NURBS modeling process by duplicating, mirroring, and attaching curves. In the tin example, you drew a single curve representing one corner. All other curves were duplicates. You can apply such a technique to a wide array of manufactured items in which symmetry exists at many levels.

- NURBS surfaces guarantee a high level of curvature with a minimal amount of geometry. The corner curve of the tin possesses only nine vertices, yet at no step of the process is it necessary to smooth out or rebuild the surface. If minor faceting should persist, you can temporarily increase the default NURBS tessellation by raising the **U Divisions Factor** and **V Divisions Factor** attributes in the Simple Tessellation Options section of the surface's Attribute Editor tab.

- Curves on a NURBS surface never go away. If you delete the curves that form a surface, you can retrieve them later by selecting an edge isoparm and applying the Duplicate Surface Curves tool.

For additional NURBS techniques, see the next four sections. (Polygon enthusiasts may want to skip to the last three sections of this chapter.) A finished version of the tin is included as tin_final.mb in the Chapter 2 scene folder on the CD.

Cleaning Up NURBS Surfaces with Attach and Detach

One frustrating aspect of NURBS modeling is the potential for isoparm discontinuity. When you need multiple NURBS surfaces, the odds that each surface will possess different isoparm counts and distributions is fairly great.

If care is taken while creating the original curves, you can avoid this problem. If two side-by-side NURBS surfaces are created from the same curve (or two curves that have an identical vertex count and placement), they will possess matching isoparms. If you've gotten to a point in the modeling process, however, where the NURBS surfaces already exist and the isoparms don't match up, you can apply the Attach Surfaces, Detach Surfaces, Duplicate Surface Curves, and Rebuild Surfaces tools to solve the problem. As a bonus, these tools are capable of removing any gaps that exist between side-by-side surfaces. As a working example, three NURBS surfaces sit side by side. The isoparms are poorly matched.

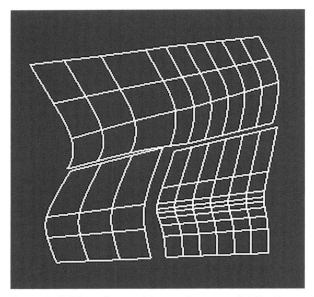

Three NURBS surfaces with poor isoparm distribution and gaps

Using this scene file, which is saved as `attach_detach.mb` in the Chapter 2 scene folder on the CD, you can follow these steps:

1. Select the two smaller surfaces at the bottom. Switch to the Surfaces menu set, choose **Edit NURBS → Attach Surfaces → ☐**, uncheck **Keep Originals**, and click the Attach button. The two surfaces blend together. For the moment, the isoparm distribution is rather ugly.

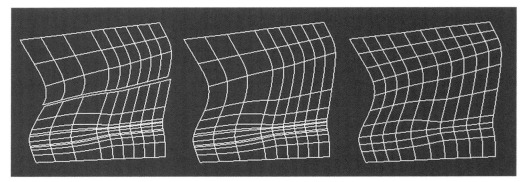

(Left) Bottom two surfaces are attached. (Middle) Top and bottom surfaces are attached. (Right) Resulting surface has the Rebuild Surfaces tool applied to it.

2. Select the bottom and top surface and choose **Edit NURBS → Attach Surfaces**. A single surface results. At this point, you should clean up the isoparm distribution. With the surface selected, choose **Edit NURBS → Rebuild Surfaces → ❏**, set **Number Of Spans U** to 10, set **Number Of Spans V** to 10, and click the Rebuild button. The resulting surface is cleaner. However, the isoparms remain bunched up at the bottom.

3. To fix the bunching, Shift+select the top and bottom edge isoparms of the surface. Shift+select seven evenly spaced, horizontal isoparm positions. Choose **Edit Curves → Duplicate Surface Curves**. New, evenly spaced curves are created.

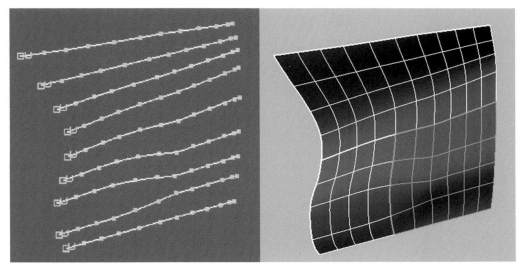

(Left) Evenly spaced curves are duplicated off surface isoparms. (Right) The lofted surface is resplit into three surfaces.

4. Delete the surface. Select the new curves in order (bottom to top) and choose **Surfaces → Loft**. The new surface has cleaner isoparm distribution. If you'd like to return the surface to the original three-patch configuration, select the central horizontal isoparm of the surface and choose **Edit NURBS → Detach Surfaces**. This splits the surface into two surfaces without opening a gap. Select the central vertical isoparm of the new bottom surface and choose **Edit NURBS → Detach Surfaces**.

This method of attaching, detaching, and rebuilding surfaces is ideal for a multi-surface NURBS model, particularly when time is limited and construction has to be rapid. Once you master this basic set of tools, their application becomes easy.

Closing Holes in NURBS Objects

Another potentially frustrating aspect of NURBS modeling is the closing of holes. This section steps through methods for sealing up the top of a cylindrical object, the top of the rectangular container, and a hole left by the Trim tool.

Capping a Cylindrical Object A generic cylindrical object is included as `cylindrical.mb` in the Chapter 2 scene folder on the CD. Open the file and select the edge isoparm of the opening at the top of the object. Choose **Edit Curves → Duplicate Surface Curves**. While the new curve is selected, choose **Edit → Duplicate**. Open the Channel Box. Scale the duplicated curve down to 0, 1, 0. The curve will become invisible. Select the edge curve and the scaled-down curve (you can select the scaled-down curve node in the Hypergraph Scene Hierarchy window). Choose **Surfaces → Loft**. A clean cap is created. If by chance you see a dark glitch at the center of the new surface, insert a new isoparm close to the new surface's center (once a new isoparm position is selected, choose **Edit NURBS → Insert Isoparms**). This will alleviate any rendering problem created by an unintentionally bent normal.

(Left) Duplicated edge curve. (Middle) Second duplicated curve scaled down to 0, 1, 0. (Right) Final loft.

Closing a Rectangular Container Using a variation of the tin model created in the first section of this chapter (`tin_open.mb`), select the edge isoparm that forms the inside of the top lip. Choose **Edit Curves → Duplicate Surface Curves**. With the new curve selected and the mouse pointer hovering over the curve, RMB click and choose Edit Point from the marking menu. Select the two edit points on the curve that are opposite each other and in the center of each wide end. Choose **Edit Curves → Detach Curves**. The curve is split into two. Select both curves and choose **Surfaces → Loft**. A clean surface closes the tin.

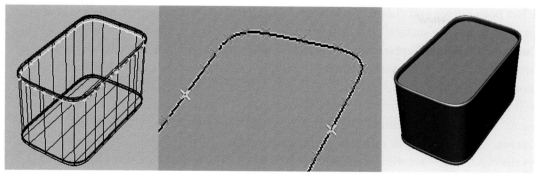

(Left) Curve duplicated off top lip. (Middle) Close-up of edit points used to detach curve. (Right) Final loft.

Filling In a Trimmed Hole A generic trimmed object is included as `trimmed.mb` in the Chapter 2 scene file on the CD. Open the file and select the edge isoparm of the trimmed opening of the object. Choose **Edit Curves → Duplicate Surface Curves**. The resulting curve contains a high number of vertices. Nevertheless, the curve follows the surface fairly tightly. With the curve selected, choose **Edit → Duplicate**. While the second duplicated curve remains selected, choose **Modify → Center Pivot**. Transform the second duplicated curve deeper into the object. This will form an inset lip for the new surface (as if it's a window, screen, or hatch).

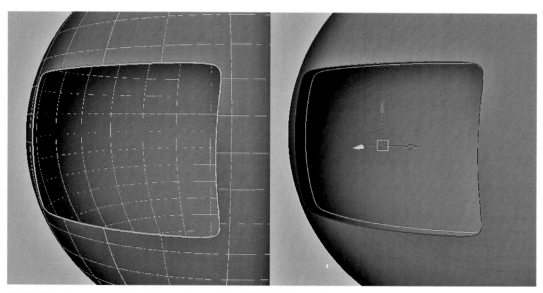

(Left) Edge isoparm of the trimmed opening. (Right) Second duplicate curve transformed deeper into the sphere.

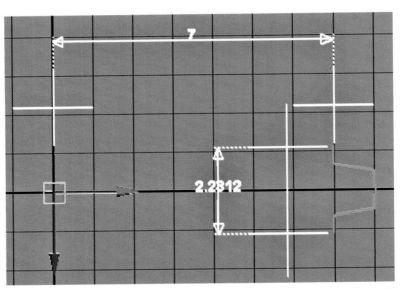

A single tooth is drawn with the CV Curve tool. The Distance tool is applied twice to ensure that measurements are correct.

4. With the curve selected, choose **Edit → Duplicate Special → ◻**. In the Duplicate Special Options window, change Rotate Y to the number of degrees determined in step 1. Change the **Number Of Copies** value to 1 less than the number of teeth determined in step 1 (for example, if there are 20 teeth, enter 19). Click the Duplicate Special button. The curve is duplicated with the duplicates arranged in a circle. No more than a tiny gap should exist between the teeth.

5. Select the two side-by-side teeth curves. Choose **Edit Curves → Attach Curves → ◻**, uncheck **Keep Originals**, and click the Apply button. The result is a single curve. Select this curve and a neighboring tooth curve and apply the Attach Curves tool again. Continue this process until all the individual teeth curves are attached into a single large curve. Should any curve become twisted during the attaching process, undo the attach, select the curve that is causing the twist, choose **Edit Curves → Reverse Curve Direction**, and apply the Attach Curves tool a second time.

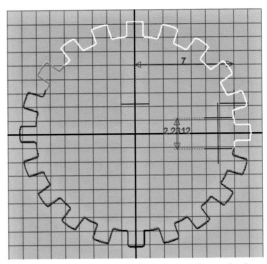

Attaching all the teeth curves to make a single curve

6. With the final curve selected, choose **Edit Curves → Open/Close Curves**. The curve is closed and the remaining gap disappears. **Choose Surfaces → Planar**. A surface is created across the curve. (A planar surface is a type of trimmed surface.) Select the curve and choose **Edit → Duplicate**. Move the duplicated curve below the original curve. With both curves selected, choose **Surfaces → Loft**. This creates the gear's side. Select the newest curve and choose **Surfaces → Planar**. This creates the gear's back side. To increase the accuracy of the gear's front and back, select both planar surfaces and choose **Edit NURBS → Rebuild Surfaces** with the default settings.

7. Delete the curves, name the parts, and group the three surfaces together. The gear is complete. The gear illustrated in this section is included as gear_final.mb in the Chapter 2 scene folder on the CD. This technique works for a gear with any number of teeth and with any radius.

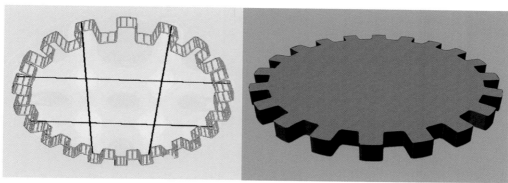

(Left) Lofting the gear's side. (Right) The final gear.

Building a NURBS Eye

NURBS surfaces are ideal for character eyeballs since they are extremely smooth and are extremely light when it comes to geometry. You can quickly adapt a primitive sphere so that it renders correctly when it comes to texturing and lighting. You can follow these steps:

1. Choose **Create → NURBS Primitives → Sphere → ☐**, change **Axis** to Z, **Number Of Sections** to 12, and **Number Of Spans** to 12. Click the Create button. A NURBS sphere is created with its two poles aligned to the Z axis. Rotate the sphere by −90 degrees in the Z axis. The rotation orients the NURBS seam so that it points downward.

2. Select a isoparm position halfway between the second and third isoparms from one of the poles. Choose **Edit NURBS → Detach Surfaces**. The detached portion becomes the eye's cornea. Move it aside for now.

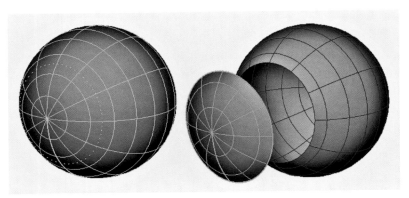

Detaching the cornea

3. Choose the edge isoparm of the new hole. Choose **Edit Curves → Duplicate Surface Curves**. A new curve is created along the edge. While the new curve remains selected, choose **Modify → Center Pivot**, and then choose **Edit → Duplicate**. Scale the newest curve down slightly. Choose **Edit → Duplicate** again. Scale the third curve down even further. This will become the edge of the pupil. Move the second and third curves back into the eyeball so that they form a dish-like shape.

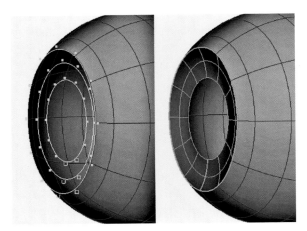

Constructing the iris

4. Select the three curves in order and choose **Surfaces → Loft**. The new surface forms the iris. The concave shape of the iris copies the optical properties of the human cornea fairly well. This effect is the most noticeable when the side of the iris opposite the light source is appropriately bright. If the iris surface isn't smooth enough or concave enough, adjust the positions of the curves.

5. Choose **Create → NURBS Primitives → Sphere**. Scale and move the new sphere so that it sits inside the eyeball without intersecting any of the surfaces. Assign this surface to a Lambert material with the **Diffuse** attribute set to 0 percent black. This sphere blacks out the interior of the eye and prevents the white of the eyeball from being seen through the pupil.

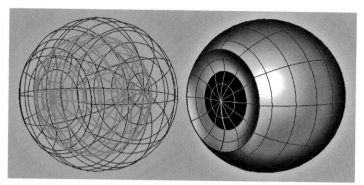

Blocking out the inside of the eye

6. Move the cornea surface back to the proper position. Delete unneeded curves and name the surfaces appropriately. Group the surfaces together. At this point, you should shape the eye to fit a particular head. If the eye is destined for a stylized or cartoonish character, you can leave the iris oversized. If the eye is intended for a more realistic character, scale and shape the surfaces. You can do this by either transforming vertices or applying a lattice deformer to the entire eye group and manipulating the lattice points (from the Animation menu set, choose **Deform → Create Lattice** with the group selected).

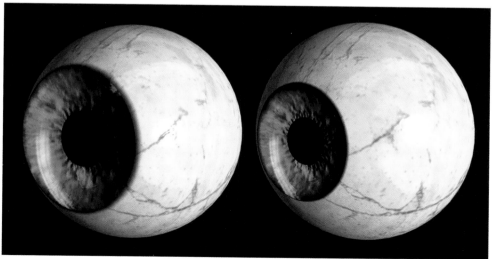

Two versions of the lit, textured eye. A lattice deformer is used to change the scale of the eyeball.

7. Assign the cornea surface to a Blinn material with 100 percent white **Transparency**, a low **Eccentricity** value, a high **Specular Roll Off** value, and a high **Specular Color** value. Assign the eyeball surface to a Blinn with an appropriate eyeball color bitmap mapped to **Color**. An eyeball bitmap is included as eyewhite.jpg in the Chapter 2 textures folder on the CD.

Mapping the Iris

The trickiest part of modeling a NURBS eye is the mapping of the iris. The easiest solution requires the application of a bitmap to the **Color** attribute through a planar projection. You can follow these separate steps:

1. Assign the iris surface to a new Blinn material. Open the Blinn's Attribute Editor tab. Click the Map button for the **Color** attribute. In the Create Render Node window, check **As Projection** in the 2D Textures section and click the File button.

2. While the Projection utility remains loaded in the Attribute Editor, click the Fit To BBox button. This snaps the projection icon to the iris surface bounding box. Click the arrow beside the **Image** attribute to switch to the new file node's Attribute Editor tab. Browse for an appropriate iris bitmap. An iris bitmap is included as iris.jpg in the Chapter 2 textures folder on the CD. Render a test. If you choose iris.jpg, interactively scale up the projection icon until the iris fits the surface. Checking on **Shading → Smooth Shade All** and **Shading → Hardware Texturing** in a workspace view makes this task easier.

3. Select the projection icon and parent it to one of the eye surfaces, such as the eyeball. This guarantees that the projection won't be left behind when the eye is animated. You can also convert the projected texture into a permanent bitmap by using the Convert To File Texture tool — in the Hypershade, choose **Edit → Convert To File Texture** (Maya Software).

A finished version of the eye illustrated in this section is included as eye_final.mb in the Chapter 2 scene folder on the CD.

Cleaning Up Imported Polygons

Thanks to the Internet, it's easy to purchase, or even download for free, a 3D model. Rarely, however, is the model ready for texturing, lighting, rigging, or animation as is.

OBJ is the most common format used for import, followed by the DXF, DWG, and IGES formats. Although OBJ support is integrated into Maya, DXF, DWG, and IGES support is provided by plug-ins. DXF is supported by the fbxmaya.mll plug-in, which is auto-loaded by default. DWG is supported by the DirectConnect.mll plug-in, which is also auto-loaded by default. IGES, on the other hand, is supported by the Iges.mll plug-in, which must be loaded. To load a plug-in, choose **Window → Settings/Preferences → Plug-in Manager**, and check the Loaded check box for the plug-in in question. To import an OBJ, DXF, DWG, or IGES file, choose **File → Import → ❏**, set **File Type** to the appropriate file format, click the Import button, and browse for the file. Unfortunately, the imported models often suffer from an incorrect up axis, disproportionately large scale, faceting, bad normal smoothing, missing UV texture information, and grouping errors.

Z-Up Although Maya's up axis is the Y axis by default, many programs operate with the Z axis as the up axis. Hence, many imported models come into Maya on their side. A quick way to rotate an imported model back onto the Maya "ground plane" is to set the model's **Rotate X** to 270.

Monster Scale Depending on the scale and linear units used by the program that created the model, imported models often appear monstrously large in Maya. Sometimes, in fact, the model cannot be seen in the workspace views. If this happens, select the model node in the Hypergraph Scene Hierarchy window and set its **Scale** to 0.1, 0.01, or 0.001 in the Channel Box.

Faceting Imported polygon models often arrive with no normal smoothing. In this situation, every single face is rendered with a hard edge. To soften the entire model, select the model as an object, switch to the Polygons menu set, and choose **Normals → Soften Edge**. To soften specific parts, such as the hood, select the faces that make up that part, and apply the Soften Edge tool. For greater control, choose **Normals → Set Normal Angle**, and set the **Angle** attribute to a value from 0 to 180. For example, when Angle is set to 90, only vertex normals of adjacent polygon faces that form an angle from 0 to 89 degrees are smoothed. Vertex normals of adjacent polygon faces that form an angle from 90 to 180 degrees are not smoothed and receive a hard edge.

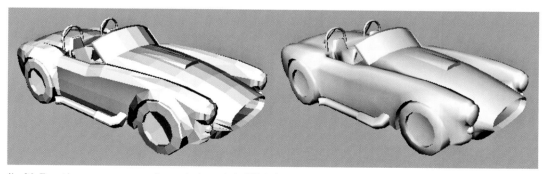

(Left) Faceting occurs on an imported model. (Right) The same model cleaned up with the Set Normal Angle tool. *Low-poly model created by Gamester Art.*

Bad Normals Black streaks often appear on imported models. The streaking is a result of poor normal averaging that fails at an abrupt corner or transition. In this situation, it is often best to re-facet the entire model and apply normal softening techniques to only the parts of the model that need it. To re-facet, select the model, switch to the Polygons menu set, and choose **Normals → Harden Edge**. To smooth out various parts, use the Soften Edge or Set Normal Angle tool as described in the previous paragraph. Keep in mind that the black streaking is not limited to imported models but can be induced by an improperly applied Soften Edge or Harden Edge tool or poor modeling techniques. In addition, normal errors that occur during the Maya import do not necessarily exist in the program that originally created the model, such as 3ds Max or SoftImage|XSI.

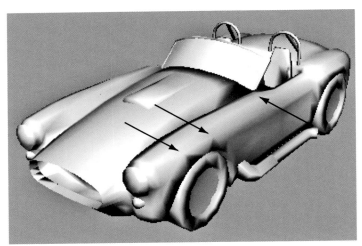

Bad normals waiting to be fixed on an imported polygon model

UVs Imported DWG, DXF, and IGES polygons lack UV information. UV mapping and UV tools must be used for the surface to render with a texture. The OBJ format, on the other hand, is able to carry its UV texture space into Maya.

Grouping Maya is unable to import group information from IGES and OBJ files. However, if you check the **Group** attribute in the Import Options window, all the imported nodes are parented to a single group node. DWG and DXF formats, on the other hand, successfully transfer group information and therefore automatically provide appropriate group nodes during the import regardless of the number of groups that might exist.

The DWG format is a native CAD format of Autodesk AutoCAD. DXF (Drawing Exchange Format) is a second AutoCAD file type that supports drawn lines and polygons. The OBJ format is a native Wavefront format that supports both polygons and NURBS surfaces. IGES (Initial Graphics Exchange Specification) is a neutral file format that is not pinned to a specific translator.

Industry Tip: Building a Polygon Head by Extruding Edges

The human head is one of the most difficult subjects to model. When employing polygons, many animators use box modeling techniques. The advantage of box modeling is the ability to start with a primitive that possesses dimension as soon as it's created. However, the primitives often lead novice modelers astray and the final results appear much like the original primitive (for example, a head appears more spherical than it should). Another technique, involving the incremental extrusion of edges, offers an alternative approach. Modelers who find themselves frustrated by box modeling often find success with this technique.

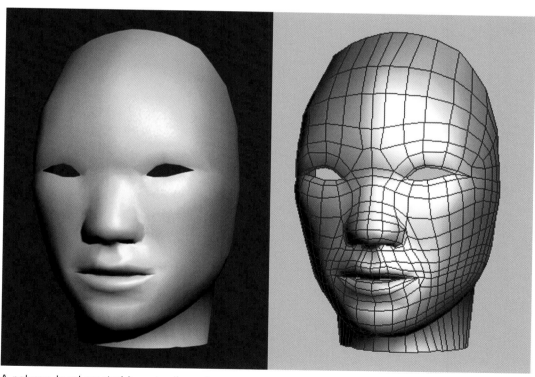

A polygon head created by extruding edges

Matt Orlich, training director at Vykarian Studios in Shanghai, China, demonstrates this approach. You can follow these steps to produce similar results:

1. Import front and side character reference bitmaps into Maya, either as image planes or as File texture images mapped to primitive plane geometry. If you use geometry, check on **Smooth Shade All** and **Hardware Texturing** in the workspace views. Align the reference

images so that key features line up. For example, the tip of the nose or the center of the eye should be the same height in Y for all images.

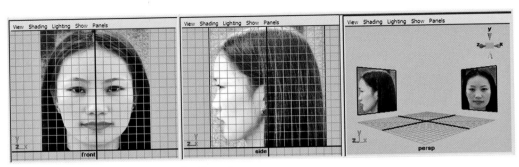

Reference bitmaps mapped to primitive planes

2. Switch to the Polygons menu set, choose **Mesh → Create Polygon Tool**, and draw an outline of the character profile in the side workspace view. When you're finished with the shape, press Enter. A single, multi-edged polygon is created. At this step, you should add enough detail to include critical components, such as the turn of the nose, without creating an excessive number of vertices. To see through the polygon to the bitmap, check on **Shading → X-Ray** in the workspace view.

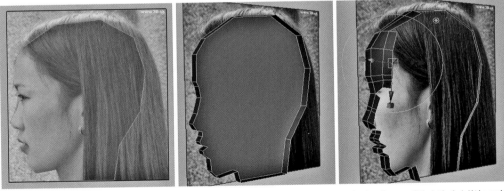

(Left) Profile outlined with the Create Polygon tool. (Middle) Extruded edges. (Right) Additional extrusions to shape various sections of the head.

3. Choose, and thereby check on, **Edit Mesh → Keep Faces Together**. This option ensures that edges do not separate as they are extruded. Select all of the edges of the drawn polygon, choose **Edit Mesh → Extrude**, and interactively drag the extrude manipulator until the new faces reach the edge of the nose. Delete the large, drawn polygon face.

4. Select smaller sets of edges, such as those that form the bridge of the nose, and apply the Extrude tool once again. Continue this process, focusing on specific areas of the head (for example, the side of the nose, the upper lip, the forehead, and so on). At each step, transform vertices to follow the shape of the face. Check the side, front, top, and perspective views as you go. If two extrusions meet, feel free to merge overlapping vertices (choose **Edit Mesh → Merge**).

5. As you build up additional extrusions, check to see if any area needs additional detail. For example, you may need to split polygons around the lips, nose, and eye (choose **Edit Mesh → Split Polygon Tool**). Conversely, some area may acquire too many polygons. You can remove an unneeded polygon face by selecting all its vertices and merging them together. If you delete a face or faces, you can append new faces to the model, and thus seal up any holes, by choosing **Edit Mesh → Append To Polygon Tool**.

6. If possible, follow the tenets of edge loop modeling as you go. The term *edge loop* refers to the natural loops that the musculature of the human body forms. For instance, the muscles surrounding the mouth form a natural circle, as well as those around the eye. Although edge looping is by no means mandatory, it can improve the quality of facial animation through more accurate deformation of the geometry. Along those lines, quadrilateral polygon faces are generally more desirable. Triangular faces, if they do exist, will work for most animations but are somewhat inferior to quads during deformation.

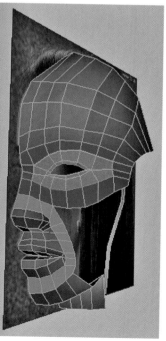

(Left) Additional extrusions form the eye, nose, and mouth. (Right) Low-resolution edge loops are modeled into the areas around the eye and mouth.

MATT ORLICH

Matt began his game career at Virgin Interactive Entertainment in Irvine, California. He went on to serve as marketing manager, as well as a concept artist and modeler, for Electronic Arts in Austin, Texas, and Las Vegas, Nevada. Matt recently relocated to Shanghai, China, to help run Vykarian Studios (www.vykarian.com), which specializes in video game production. During his career, he has worked on such games as *James Bond Goldeneye: Rogue Agent*, *Ultima Online*, and *Wing Commander Prophecy*.

7. Continue to apply all the techniques listed in steps 4 through 6 until the head is complete. Duplicate and mirror the head by choosing **Mesh → Mirror Geometry → ❑**, switching **Mirror Direction** to –X, and clicking the Mirror button. To see a smooth version of the model, choose **Normals → Soften Edge**.

The model illustrated in this exercise is included as head.mb in the Chapter 2 scene folder on the CD. At this point in the modeling process, the head possesses 1,082 triangles. Although it's possible to get by with significantly fewer faces, the model is not intended for any polygon smoothing operation (for example, **Mesh → Smooth**) and thus needs extra cuts to make the lips, nose, and eyes satisfactorily detailed. The two reference bitmaps, along with numerous other 3D reference materials, are available at www.3d.sk.

▮ Industry Tip: Adjusting the Maya Grid for Linear Units

When working in standard units within Maya, it's generally best to set the **Linear** attribute to Inch. (The Linear attribute is found in the Settings section of the **Window → Settings/ Preferences → Preferences** window). This prevents clipping plane errors that tend to occur in Maya when the **Linear** attribute is set to Foot or Yard. Unfortunately, the Inch setting makes it difficult to measure models that represent large, real-world objects, such as architectural elements. Michael Stolworthy, an exhibit designer at GES, suggests creating shelf buttons that allow you to toggle between grid settings. (To read Michael's biography, see Chapter 1.)

For example, the following shelf button script changes the grid so that each visible grid line is an inch (assuming **Linear** is set to Inch):

```
grid -spacing 12 -divisions 12;
```

In this case, the foot lines are not visible. However, you can choose **Display → Grid → ☐** and change the **Grid Lines & Numbers** color swatch to a color other than the default, which makes the foot lines stand out. The -spacing flag is equivalent to the **Grid Lines Every** attribute and the -divisions flag is equivalent to the **Subdivisions** attribute.

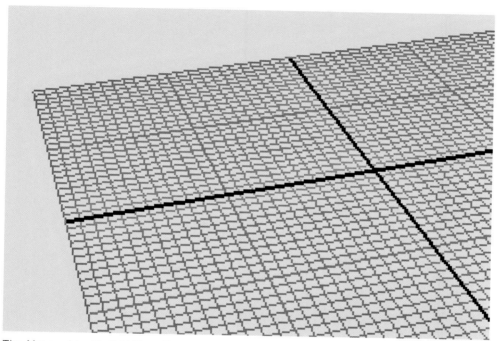

The Maya grid with **Grid Lines Every** set to 12, **Subdivisions** set to 12, and **Grid Lines & Numbers** set to red

The following shelf button script changes the grid so that no subdivision lines exist and each visible grid line is a foot:

```
grid -spacing 12 -divisions 1;
```

With these two shelf buttons, you can toggle back and forth between inch and foot grid views while leaving the **Linear** attribute permanently set to Inch.

History, Scripting, and Animation

3

TIME TAKES SEVERAL forms in Maya. The history function stores innumerable steps an animator takes as nodes and hence provides a malleable record of the past. The Graph Editor threads curves through keys at specific points along the Timeline. Expressions and MEL scripts, on the other hand, are able to sidestep history, the Graph Editor, and the Timeline by permanently linking the attribute of one object to another and thus create automation. Of course, it is the animator who must break down time and determine when and where objects and characters should be for a believable keyframe animation.

This chapter's topics are organized into the following techniques:

- Deleting Select History in the Hypergraph
- Using Variables within Expressions or MEL Scripts
- Choosing between Local and Global Variables
- Driving Vehicle Wheels and Bike Pedals
- Massaging Curves in the Graph Editor
- Wilting a Paint Effects Flower
- Creating Realistic Eye Movement
- Animating Realistic Camera Moves

Deleting Select History in the Hypergraph

By default, every time you apply a tool in Maya, the tool's application is stored as construction history. In many cases, a history node for the tool is created and linked to the affected object. Although you can view history nodes in the Hypershade window, it is far easier to examine them in the Hypergraph Input And Output Connections window. As such, you can selectively delete history nodes.

A node is simply a construct designed to hold particular information and any action associated with that information. In Maya, every single box that appears in the Hypershade and Hypergraph is a node. Two major forms of nodes exist: transform and shape. All surfaces, lights, and cameras are represented by these two nodes. Transform nodes hold all the transform information (**Translate**, **Rotate**, **Scale**, and **Visibility**) and are present in the Hypergraph Scene Hierarchy window view. Shape nodes hold all the non-transform attributes, such as **Spans UV**, **Intensity**, **Focal Length**, and so on. History nodes, on the other hand, hold all the settings of the tool when it was applied. If a history node is deleted, the tool application is removed. If you choose **Edit → Delete By Type → History**, all the history nodes connected to the selected object are deleted. If the Construction History On/Off button is toggled off in the Status line, history nodes are not created and tool applications are immediate and permanent.

> With Maya 8.5, the Hypergraph Input And Output Connections window is renamed the Hypergraph Connections window. The Hypergraph Scene Hierarchy window is renamed the Hypergraph Hierarchy window.

To view shape and history nodes, select an object and choose **Window → Hypergraph Input And Output Connections**. For example, if a CV curve has the Revolve tool applied to it, the hierarchy appears similar to what you see here.

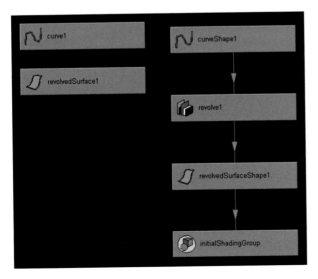

The Hypergraph Input And Output Connections view of a curve with the Revolve tool applied to it

The history node, revolve1, is connected to the curve and revolved surface shape nodes. The node furthest downstream is the initialShadingGroup, which automatically assigns new surfaces to the default Lambert material. The curve and revolved surface's transform nodes, named curve1 and revolvedSurface1, sit to the left side with no visible connection to any other node. (To stack nodes vertically in the Hypergraph Input And Output Connections window, choose **Options → Orientation → Vertical** from the Hypergraph menu.)

At this point, if the curve is transformed or is reshaped, the revolved surface automatically updates. If the revolve1 history node is deleted, the relationship between the curve and revolved surface is broken and the effect of the Revolve tool becomes permanent. This result is identical to the application of **Edit → Delete By Type → History**.

The manipulation of history nodes becomes more useful when a hierarchy contains a whole series of them. In this situation, you are free to delete any history node that you don't need. Depending on the position of the node and the nature of the history, exact results vary. For example, if two NURBS surfaces are attached with the Attach Surfaces tool and the resulting surface (attachSurface1) has the Insert Isoparms and Reverse Surface Direction tools applied, the hierarchy appears similar to the following. Note how the original NURBS shape nodes are ghosted; although the original surfaces are not visible in the workspace view, they are kept as history.

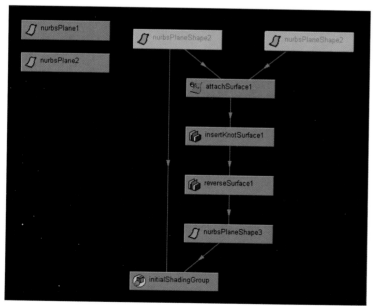

The Hypergraph Input And Output Connections view of two NURBS surfaces with the Attach Surfaces, Insert Isoparms, and Reverse Surface Direction tools applied in order.

In this situation, you can delete either the insertKnotSurface1 or reverseSurface1 history node to respectively remove the effect of the Insert Isoparms or the Reverse Surface Direction tool. If you delete the attachSurface1 node, however, the original surfaces are permanently attached; interestingly enough, this also makes the effect of the Insert Isoparms and Reverse Surface Direction tools permanent while deleting their history nodes.

The deletion of selective history nodes is also valid for polygon objects. For example, a primitive cube has the Insert Edge Loop tool applied once and the Extrude tool applied three times to form the letter *M*.

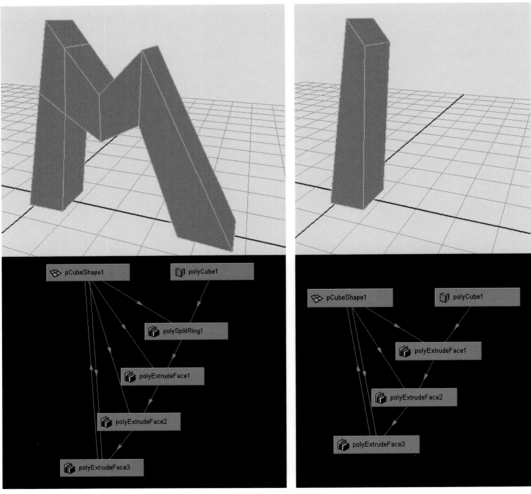

(Left) The letter *M* is created with the Insert Edge Loop and Extrude tools. (Right) The polySplitRing1 node is deleted, removing the extrusions.

The first history node, named polyCube1, holds the construction history of the primitive; if it is deleted, the cube is destroyed. Removing any of the remaining history nodes can lead to more unusual results. Ultimately, downstream nodes are impacted by the disappearance of upstream nodes. This is due to the downstream node's intrinsic dependence on the output of what's upstream. In the Hypergraph and Hypershade windows, the arrows point from the upstream (output) nodes to downstream (input) nodes. For example, if polySplitRing1 is deleted, the impact of polyExtrudeFace1, polyExtrudeFace2, and polyExtrudeFace3 becomes nonexistent since the face the extrusions are based upon no longer exists (see the preceding Hypergraph screen shot).

However, if polyExtrudeFace2 is deleted, the extrusion created by polyExtrudeFace3 is joined to the extrusion created by polyExtrudeFace1. If you delete polyExtrudeFace3, the last extrusion is cleanly deleted without affecting the rest of the model. (This scene is included as polyM.mb in the Chapter 3 scene folder on the CD.)

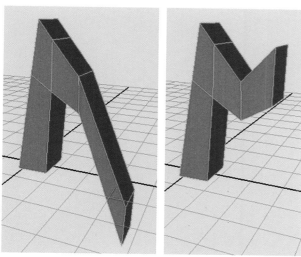

(Left) The polyExtrudeFace2 node is deleted. (Right) The polyExtrudeFace3 node is deleted.

Not all tools produce history nodes. Transform tools, for instance, are stored as history and are undoable with Crtl+Z but do not create visible history nodes. This is true for the transformation of object types (surface, curve, and so on) as well as component types (unless vertices are transformed on a skinned character). On the other hand, some tools produce history nodes only when particular options are activated in their options window. The Cleanup tool follows this pattern (switch to the Polygons menu set and choose **Mesh → Cleanup**).

Using Variables within Expressions or MEL Scripts

Variables are virtual buckets that hold information that can be read at any time and updated repeatedly. Two types of variables are available to expressions and MEL scripts within Maya: custom and predefined. For custom variables, six subtypes exist: integer, float, string, vector, array, and matrix.

Custom variables are any variable that you define. You can define a variable by *declaring* it. For example, declaring a variable named test in an expression or script looks like this:

```
int $test;
```

In this example, the variable $test is defined as an integer variable with the inclusion of int. An integer variable stores any whole number (one without decimal places). Once a variable is declared as a specific type, such as int, you cannot re-declare it as a different type (unless you restart Maya). To make a new variable a float, which can store decimal places, you can use this:

```
float $test2;
```

When a variable is declared in such a fashion, its default value is 0. To give the variable a definitive value, you can use a line similar to this at a different point in the expression or script:

```
$test2 = 10.5;
```

If $test2 was declared as an integer, 10.5 would be stored as 10. The third type of variable, string, holds letters, words or phrases. Here's an example:

```
string $testString = "Howdy Pardner";
```

The fourth type of variable, vector, holds three floating-point numbers. To declare a vector variable and fill it with three numbers, use this line:

```
vector $testVector = <<1, 3.3, 5>>;
```

To access the declared vector variable's individual components, add .x, .y, or .z to the variable name. For example, to read and print the first component of $testVector, try this:

```
string $temp = $testVector.x; print $temp;
```

An array is an ordered list of values. The array variable can store a long list of values under a single variable name. For example, you can declare an array like so:

```
string $testColors[3] = {"red", "green", "blue"};
```

The [3] defines the number of value positions available to the array. You can retrieve a single value by designating its position within the array. The first position is 0, the second is 1, and so on. For example, to print the word *green*, you can use this line:

```
print ($testColors[1]);
```

A matrix is an ordered list of values arranged into rows and columns. You can declare a matrix variable with the following line:

```
matrix $test[3][2];
```

In this example, the matrix has three rows and two columns. You can declare a matrix and fill it with values using a single line. The values are written across rows from left to right, starting with the top row:

```
matrix $test[3][2] = <<5, 10; 15, 6; 12.2, 4.7>>;
```

Note that an extra semicolon must be inserted at the end of each row. You can also write values to specific locations or retrieve values from specific locations in a previously declared matrix:

```
$test[0][1] = 52;

print ($test[2][1]);
```

As with arrays, the first row or first column of a matrix is numbered 0. You can use variables at almost any point in an expression or script. The value that the variable holds is swapped for the variable name. For example, you can use variables as part of an If statement or a button command:

```
int $testNumber = 5;

string $testCommand = "SaveScene";

if ($testNumber < 10) {

    button -label "Save" -command $testCommand;

}
```

You can update variables by using math operators and specific values or other variables:

```
$test = ($test + 100) / $test3;
```

Common operators include * (multiply), / (divide), + (add), and - (subtract). A long list of math functions are also available, such as rand() (random) and sqrt() (square root). The list of functions is accessible by browsing through the **Insert Functions** menu in the Expression Editor (choose **Window → Animation Editors → Expression Editor**). You can find descriptions of the functions by choosing **Help → MEL Command Reference** in the Script Editor.

You can give a variable any name so long as that name doesn't exist as a predefined variable. (Keep in mind that Maya is case sensitive to variable names.) A predefined variable is one that is supplied by Maya and is globally available to all expressions, scripts, and procedures therein. Predefined variables include time and frame. (Procedures may be thought of as isolated subroutines that are activated only when the procedure name is called.)

◼ Choosing between Local and Global Variables

In Maya, custom variables are either local or global. If they're local, they can be "seen" only by the expression, script, or procedure in which they are declared. (All the variables declared in the previous section are local.) In contrast, a properly applied global variable can be seen everywhere. To declare a global variable, the word *global* must be added:

```
global int $test;
```

If global, the variable is potentially accessible by all expressions, scripts, and procedures therein. Even though the variable is declared as global, however, it must be re-declared in each procedure that needs to employ it:

```
proc routineA () {

    global int $test = 10;

    routineB;

}

proc routineB () {

    global int $test;

    int $test2 = $test;

    print $test2;

}
```

In this example, two procedures exist. $test is declared within the body of procedure routineA. For procedure routineB to successfully utilize $test, $test must be re-declared within the body of routineB.

Global variables, although easy to include, are potentially dangerous. A global variable, once declared, outlives the expression or script in which it's declared. If more than one expression or script uses the same global variable name, results can become confusing or undesirable. (To print a list of all global variables declared by MEL scripts, execute `env` in the Script Editor; custom variables are at the end of the list.)

As an alternative to global variables, you can *pass* local variables from one procedure to the next:

```
int $varA;

stepA($varA);

proc stepA(int $varA) {

    $varA = 10;

    stepB($varA);

}

proc stepB(int $varA) {

    int $varB = $varA;

    print $varB;

}
```

In this example, $varA is declared on the first line as a local variable. On the second line, procedure stepA is called with $varA listed in the parentheses. $varA is thereby passed to stepA. In order for $varA to be utilized by stepA, the procedure parentheses must include int $varA. The second procedure, stepB, must also include int $varA in its procedure parentheses if it is to use the variable.

Additionally, you can pass more than one variable to a procedure. An economical method with which to achieve this involves the use of an array:

```
float $testArray[5] = {5.4, 7, 12, 2.1, 4};

stepA($testArray);

proc stepA(float $testArray[]) {

    $testArray[2] = $testArray[2] + 3;

    stepB($testArray);

}

proc stepB(float $testArray[]) {

    print ($testArray[2]);

}
```

Procedures have the ability to become global and thus become executable from the work area of the Script Editor and accessible to expressions, scripts, and procedures therein, as with this example:

```
global proc testProcedure () {

}
```

For a description of array variables, see the previous section. For other examples of advanced variable construction, browse through your Maya scripts folder (for example, C:\Program Files\Alias\Maya8.0\scripts\). Dozens of MEL scripts are provided with the program. Last, when testing any of the examples in this section, I recommend that you substitute your own variable and procedure names. If, by accident, you attempt to declare a variable whose name has already been utilized, you will receive an "invalid redeclaration of variable" error.

Driving Vehicle Wheels and Bike Pedals

When animating a wheeled vehicle, applying the proper amount of rotation to the tires can be difficult. Although hit-or-miss keyframing may provide a decent solution, an expression is able to provide a precise solution. The solution boils down to a single formula:

```
rot = dis * 2 * pi * r
```

rot is the rotation of the tire. dis is the distance the vehicle travels. pi is the mathematical constant that rounds off to 3.14. r is the radius of the tire. You can write this formula into an expression like so:

```
frontTire.rz = bike.tx * 2 * 3.14 * 3;
```

In this example, the front tire radius is 3, the rotation of the front tire is on the Z axis, and the forward/back axis of the parent bike is X. To test whether the rotation is actually correct, you can temporarily assign a Checker texture via a material to the tires and check on Smooth Shade All and Hardware Texturing in a workspace view. As the vehicle moves forward or backward, any sliding of the tires is instantly recognizable. A second trick requires the temporary parenting of a locator to the tire; if the locator doesn't "stick" to the ground for an appropriate period of time, the rotation is incorrect. An example scene, using a similar expression and shading, is included as tire.mb in the Chapter 3 scene folder.

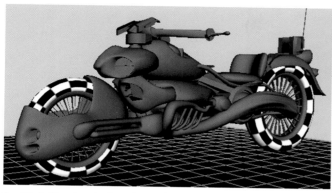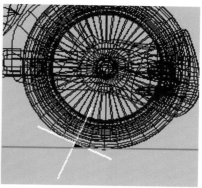

(Left) A Checker texture is assigned to tires to check their automated rotation. (Right) A locator is temporarily parented to the tire to check the same. *Futuristic motorbike modeled by Pinarci Sender.*

Bicycle pedals, on the other hand, present a different problem. Through the use of gears, the pedal gear turns at a different rate than the wheels themselves. You can represent bicycle gears with the ratio x:y. *x* is the number of teeth on the pedal gear, or driver gear, and *y* is the number of teeth on the sprocket gear, or driven gear. Thus, if a bicycle has a gear ratio of 2:1, a single rotation of the pedal gear leads to two rotations of the sprocket gear and rear tire. That is, the driver gear has twice as many teeth as the driven gear. If gear teeth are present in the 3D model, then the expression becomes fairly simple:

```
sprocket.rz = pedal.rz * (pedal_teeth / sprocket_teeth);
```

For example, if the pedal gear has 60 teeth, the sprocket gear has 40 teeth, and the pedal gear is rotated 90 degrees on the Z axis, the solution looks like this:

```
135 = 90 * (60 / 40);
```

In this case, the gear ratio would be 1.5:1. If the model is not detailed enough to possess teeth, you can compare the circumferences of the gear discs to determine a virtual gear ratio. An equivalent expression looks like this:

```
sprocket.rz = pedal.rz * ((2 * pi * p_radius) / (2 * pi * s_radius));
```

pi is the mathematical constant, p_radius is the pedal disc radius, and s_radius is the sprocket disc radius. (This expression assumes that the virtual "teeth" on each gear disc have the same width, which is identical to a real-world bicycle.) Thus, if the pedal disc has a radius of 2, the sprocket disc has a radius of 1.5, and the pedal is rotated 90 degrees on the Z axis, the solution looks like this:

```
120 = 90 * ((2 * 3.14 * 2) / (2 * 3.14 * 1.5));
```

In this example, the bicycle has a virtual gear ratio of 1.33:1 (the pedal circumference is 1.33 time larger than the sprocket circumference). A sample scene with this gear ratio is included as bike_pedal.mb in the Chapter 3 scene folder on the CD.

A simplified bicycle setup with a gear ratio of 1.33:1. The circle on the ground constrains the orientation of the pedals.

Once the pedal gear drives the sprocket gear, you can also force the rotation of the pedal gear to drive the translation of the entire bicycle. The sample scene includes this line:

```
bicycle.tx = (sprocket.rz / (2 * 3.14 * 2)) * -1;
```

The * -1 is added to convert a pedal push down (a negative rotation) into forward motion.

Another issue that arises with bike pedals is their orientation. As they are pedaled, pedals have a tendency to stay parallel to the ground. You can automate this by applying an orient constraint to the pedal geometry (as opposed to the pedal crank or pedal gear). To achieve this, follow these steps:

1. Choose **Create → NURBS Primitives → Circle**. Select the new NURBS circle and Shift+select the first pedal. Switch to the Animation menu set and choose **Constrain → Orient**.

2. Select the circle and the second pedal and choose **Constrain → Orient** once again. Since the circle will not render, it can be left at 0, 0, 0. If pedal rotation variation is desirable during an animation, you can rotate the circle and key it.

Massaging Curves in the Graph Editor

Maya's Graph Editor offers a powerful way to fine-tune animation. With the window, you can fix errors and refine animation by quickly manipulating the curves via their tangents and keys. (*Key* is simply short for *keyframe*.)

Removing Pops

Animation *pops* and *glitches* are often a result of keys placed too closely together. In this situation, a joint or similar object moves to a new position in an unrealistically short amount of time. Pops and glitches are inadvertently created when an animation has been worked on for a significant number of hours and has gained a large number of keys. In addition, such problems occur as the unintended result of key transformation operations undertaken on the Timeline itself.

To remove a pop or glitch, identify the approximate frame where it occurs by scrubbing the Timeline or creating a Playblast. Select the part that suffers, open the Graph Editor, and use the camera controls to zoom into the problem area. On closer inspection, misplaced keys or tangent handles generally becomes visible. For example, a set of generic curves contains pops and glitches in the form of dense, sometimes overlapping, keys. In this situation, you can move keys, delete extra keys, and adjust the tangent handles to create a smooth flow for the curves.

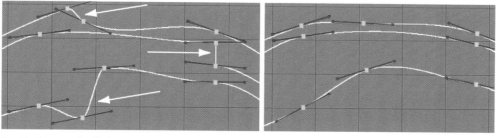

(Left) Pops and glitches on a set of curves. (Right) Same curves smoothed out.

Introducing Float

Few living things in the universe are truly static. This is particularly true when it comes to character animation. Even if a character stands quietly listening, many body parts are in motion. The hips sway. The fingers twitch occasionally. The arms swing a bit. The head rocks itself subtlety back and forth. Should the character begin speaking and gesturing, the fluidity of all the body parts becomes even more evident.

For example, if a character suddenly lifts an arm, points, then drops the arm back down to their side, at no stage does the arm become completely static. Before the arm is lifted, there may be a bit of swaying motion. As the finger is pointing to the interesting object, there is movement back and forth. When the arm returns to it original position, it continues to move a little. This subtle motion, which even the laziest body part is guilty of, is sometimes called *float*.

You can quickly introduce float to an animation by setting multiple, identical keys and moving them within the Graph Editor. For example, a sample scene, arm_drop.mb, features an arm dropping down and becoming static. Using this scene, which is saved in the Chapter 3 scene folder, you can improve the animation with the following steps:

1. Move the Timeline to the end of the animation (frame 12). Select the upper arm joint. Choose **Animate → Set Key → ❑**, switch Set Keys At to Prompt, and click the Set Key button. Enter 22 into the Set Key window field. Click OK to close the window. This sets the current position of the joint as the position for frame 22. In essence, it duplicates the key.

2. With the upper arm selected, open the Graph Editor (choose **Window → Animation Editors → Graph Editor**). Click Rotate Y in the left column. This isolates the corresponding curve. Frame the curve in the window by pressing the F key.

3. Click the Insert Keys Tool button (the second button from the left at the top left of the window). LMB click the curve to select it. MMB click the curve roughly halfway between frame 12 and 22. A new key is inserted. MMB move this new key slightly below its current position. Adjust the positions of the original keys so that the curve eases out and becomes flat by frame 22.

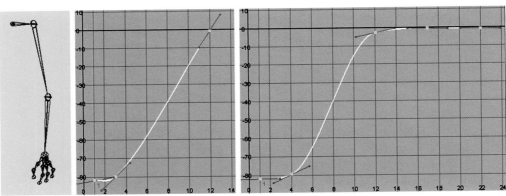

(Left) A character arm. (Middle) Original **Rotate Y** curve. (Right) **Rotate Y** curve with new keys added and old keys and tangents transformed.

If necessary, adjust the tangent handles. To adjust a handle, click on one end and MMB move it. If the tangent handles are not visible, choose **View → Tangent → Always** from the Graph Editor menu. To achieve a desirable curve shape, try different tangent types (select a key and choose **Tangents → Tangent Type**). Insert similar keys on the **Rotate X** and **Rotate Z** curves. Play the Timeline. Instead of abruptly stopping, the arm now drops to the side, moves slightly forward, and gradually stops moving. A finished scene is included as arm_fixed.mb in the Chapter 3 scene folder on the CD.

4. Repeat the process listed in steps 1 through 3 for other joints. Experiment with the placement of inserted keys for different animation styles. Insert multiple keys on some curves for a maximum amount of variation. Delay the motion of select joints, such as the wrist; not all human body parts come to a rest at the same time (this is known as secondary action in traditional animation).

Mimicking Motion with Curves

Occasionally, the path an object takes in 3D space is mimicked by the curves it creates in the Graph Editor. In these cases, you can quickly move keys around to create the exact animation you desire.

For example, a classic ball bounce is edited easily. The **Translate Y** curve, when viewed in the Graph Editor, looks exactly like a bouncing ball path. With such an animation, you can create "rubbery," "sticky," or "dead weight" bounces by moving or scaling keys.

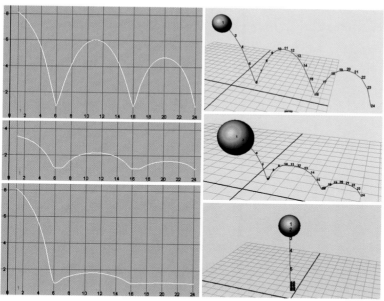

(Top row) **Translate Y** curve and 3d view of "rubbery" ball. (Middle row) **Translate Y** curve and 3d view of "sticky" ball. (Bottom row) **Translate Y** curve and 3d view of "dead weight" ball.

If you'd like to see the path an object is traveling over in a workspace view, switch to the Animation menu set, choose **Animate → Create Motion Trail → □**, switch **Draw Style** to Line, and click Create Motion Trail. Frame numbers and a line are laid across the motion path.

When working in the Graph Editor, you can move or scale selected keys only if the Move tool or Scale tool has been selected in Maya's Toolbox. If the tools remain unselected, the arrow will become a circle and no key will budge. In addition, the Move Nearest Picked Key Tool button must be clicked in the Graph Editor. If you'd like to move keys left or right along the Timeline without changing their values, MMB drag while holding down the Shift key in the Graph Editor. If you'd like to move a single key to a specific frame number or a specific value, enter the number or value into the Stats fields at the top left of the Graph Editor. (The left field is the frame number and right field is the key value.)

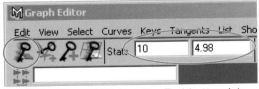

The Move Nearest Picked Key Tool button (circled in red) and Stats fields (circled in green) in the Graph Editor

Wilting a Paint Effects Flower

As detailed in Chapter 1, Paint Effects offer an easy way to create complex geometry with the stroke of a brush. Better yet, you can easily animate Paint Effects strokes for unusual results. For example, you can wilt a flower, in the style of time-lapse cinematography, with a few extra steps:

1. Select a flower Paint Effects brush, such as daisySmall.mel. Paint a stroke. Select the stroke in a workspace view and open its Attribute Editor tab. Switch to the Paint Effects tab to the immediate right of the stroke tab. The Paint Effects tab is named after the brush type (for example, daisySmall1) and is distinguished in the Hypergraph Scene Hierarchy window by a small paint brush symbol.

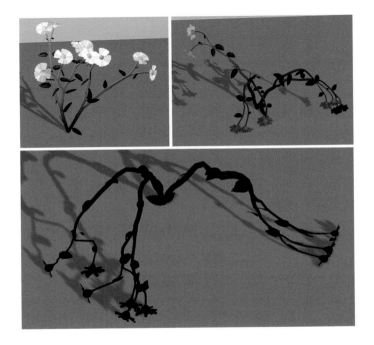

A Paint Effects daisy is wilted over time.

2. Set the **Global Scale** attribute, found at the top of the Attribute Editor tab, to 2. While the Timeline remains on frame 1, key the **Color1** attribute, found in the Shading section. To set a key, RMB click the color swatch and choose Set Key from the shortcut menu. In the Tube Shading subsection, key the **Color2** attribute.

3. Expand the Tubes section. Expand the Growth subsection. Expand the Leaves subsection. Key the **Leaf Color1** and **Leaf Color2** attributes, which are just below the Leaf Curl subsection. In the Leaf Width Scale subsection, key **Leaf Angle1** and **Leaf Angle2**. Collapse the Leaves subsection. Expand the Flowers subsection. Key the **Petal Color1** and **Petal Color2** attributes, which are found just below the Petal Curl subsection. In the Petal Curl subsection, key **Flower Size Decay**. In the Buds subsection, key the **Bud Color** attribute.

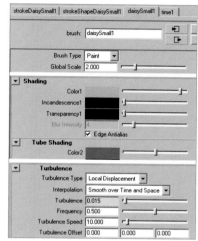

4. Collapse the Growth subsection. Expand the Behavior subsection, which is found below the Growth subsection. In the Forces subsection, key the **Gravity** attribute. In the Turbulence subsection, switch **Turbulence Type** to Local Displacement. Set **Frequency** to 0.5. Set **Turbulence Speed** to 10. Set the **Turbulence** attribute to 0.015 and set a key. (Different Paint Effects brushes and different **Global Scale** values may require different **Turbulence** settings for the proper look.)

(Top) Paint Effects tab with Global Scale attribute. (Middle) Shading section. (Bottom) Turbulence subsection.

5. Move the Timeline to the last frame of the desired animation, such as frame 100. Set **Color1**, **Color2**, **Leaf Color1**, **Leaf Color2**, **Petal Color1**, **Petal Color2**, and **Bud Color** to various shades of dark green, brown, and black to emulate a dead or dying plant. Key these attributes. Change **Leaf Angle1** and **Leaf Angle2** to 180 and set a key; this causes the petals to droop over time. Change **Flower Size Decay** to 0 and set a key; this causes the petals to randomly shrink. Change **Gravity** to 1 and set a key; high **Gravity** values force the Paint Effects tubes to drop downward. Change **Turbulence** to 0.1 and set a key; the higher the **Turbulence** value, the more severe the noisy displacement of the Paint Effects geometry.

Render a test animation. The flower will wilt and die over time. The high degree of jitter is intended to replicate the jitter found on plants photographed through time lapse. If the jitter is too intense for your taste, either reduce the intensity of the various turbulence attributes or remove the turbulence animation altogether. For alternative detail, try animating various Creation, Growth, and Behavior subsection attributes for the leaves, flowers, and buds. There are hundreds of attributes to choose from, which provides almost infinite flexibility. You can also increase the smoothness of the flower stalks and branches by increasing the **Segments** attribute (found in the Creation subsection). A final version of the daisy is included as flower_wilt.mb in the Chapter 3 scene folder on the CD. A QuickTime movie is included as flower_wilt.mov in the Chapter 3 movies folder.

Creating Realistic Eye Movement

Although the motion of a character's eye is fairly limited (left, right, up, down), believable eye motion is sometimes difficult to achieve. Here are a few tips for animating eyes (and eyelids):

- Eyes tend to dart back and forth. That is, they move rapidly from one position to the next. For example, for a 30 fps animation, realistic eyes may take 4 to 6 frames to move from a straight ahead look to a look to one side. If the eye pauses, the length of the pause is determined by what the character is watching and how long the character has been watching it. When a character is engaged in the subject and the subject is new, the eyes tend to dart rapidly to different points with little or no pause. When the subject has become familiar and the character remains interested, the eyes tend to stay put.

- More often than not, an eye dart occurs at a diagonal and not along a strict left/right or up/down axis. Many of these darts cover a short distance and may need only 2 to 4 frames. At the same time, the majority of eye movement is extremely subtle. Rotations as little as 2 or 3 degrees may be necessary to replicate the numerous fluctuations of the eye. These fluctuations are the result of the eye staying focused on a subject even when the head moves slightly. That is, the eye is able to remain aligned to a fixed point despite minor head turns and tilts.

- Although eye movement appears to be the most linear part of the body, you do not have to stick to linear curve. For example, the eye can move the greatest distance in the first 2 frames, then ease into a stop over the next 4 frames. The eye can also takes dips and other circular paths. In a generic example, the Graph Editor displays the **Rotate X**, **Rotate Y**, and **Rotate Z** curves of an eye.

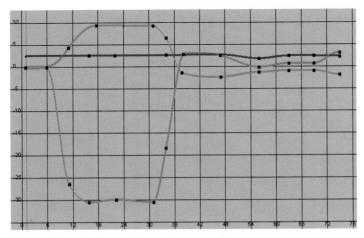

Rotate X, **Rotate Y**, and **Rotate Z** curves of an eye

In this example, the eye undertakes two major "looks": a look from center to the left (between frames 6 and 16) and a look from left back to center (between frames 31 to 38). All the remaining keys create minor fluctuations. Plateaus are formed as the eye pauses. In addition, subtle ease-ins and ease-outs exist at most of the key positions. Such curves must be fine-tuned in the Graph Editor. This scene is included as eye_anim.mb in the Chapter 3 scene folder. (For examples of excellent eye animation, refer to *Monsters, Inc.* (2001) or *The Incredibles* (2004).)

■ When a character focuses on a significantly new subject and the subject requires a head turn or major movement of the eye, the character usually blinks. The blink occurs at the mid-point of the eye motion. In addition, the turn of the head and the movement of the eye are often separated by several frames.

■ Generally, during a blink, the lids move more slowly when closing than they do when opening. For a 30 fps animation, closing the lids in 3 frames, keeping the lids closed for 2 frames, and opening the lids in 2 frames works fairly well. Slowing the rate of the lid closing and opening makes the character appear sluggish, bored, or daft. Speeding it up makes the character appear surprised, excited, or wired. Extending the duration of the close makes the character appear to be in disbelief of what they are seeing.

■ Eyelid animation should not be limited to blinking. Humans constantly squint and widen their eyes to underscore their emotional state. The motion is often independent of the eyebrows (which, of course, convey a huge amount of emotional information). For example, a character with an insincere smile tends to squint slightly, while a sincere character unconsciously widens the eyes.

Animating Realistic Camera Moves

The strength — and simultaneous weakness — of 3D animation is its lack of boundaries. That is, if you have the time and enough available CPU cycles, you can create *anything*. Although this freedom is a huge boon to creativity, it generates an equal number of pitfalls.

One significant pitfall is the creation of unrealistic or unbelievable camera moves. Animators new to 3D, in fact, are liable to create flying, spinning, twirling, or zooming movements for the most mundane subjects simply because they can. Although such motion is acceptable for surreal or abstract projects, it doesn't bode well for most animation. This is because the majority of people on the planet are accustomed to seeing motion pictures and television shows shot in a very specific way — a way that is determined by common camera equipment and the simple laws of physics. Although it might be nice to create a flying, spinning, twirling, or zooming camera move for a feature film, odds are that you'll opt to skip such moves because of the limitations of the equipment, the production schedule, or the budget. Even a film filled with outlandish digital effects shots is generally carried along by the more mundane. Hence, for each superhuman flyby in *Superman Returns* (2006) or swooping battle flyover in *The Lord of the Rings: The Return of the King* (2003), there are several wide shots, two shots, or close-ups identical to an average drama that hasn't a single effect.

When creating a camera move in Maya, it helps to be familiar with camera equipment and cinematography/videography styles. For example, if a reality television show follows characters around a room or down the street, the footsteps of the videographer visibly affect the camera movement with a side-to-side sway. If the footsteps are negated by a Steadicam rig or similar vibration-dampening device, the camera moves take on a unique glide that is nonetheless limited by the walking/crouching ability of the videographer.

Motion pictures are even more limited by their camera equipment. A 35 mm Panavision Panaflex camera or a Sony 24P HDW-F900 High Def camera almost always sits on a *head* attached to tripod legs, a dolly, or a crane. Movement of the head is controlled by the cinematographer or camera operator. Top-end motion picture heads are operated by a pair of reduction gear handwheels that must be manually spun to tilt up/down or pan left/right. Other heads possess *pan drag* and *tilt drag* handles. Low-end heads or tripods usually have a single pan/tilt handle. In any case, the human manipulation of the camera cannot be disguised. Oddly enough, contemporary motion control heads, which are run by computers, are able to repeat human-driven camera moves and thus appear more spontaneous.

Once you are aware of traditional camera movement, you should pick a method of working within Maya that is comfortable to you. Some animators prefer standard 1-node (**Create → Cameras → Camera**) or 3-node cameras (**Create → Cameras → Camera, Aim, And Up**), while others prefer customized cameras with unique hierarchies and extra group nodes. The type of camera you use doesn't really matter so long as you're able to produce satisfactory motion. In the following sections are a few tips for moving the camera.

Limiting Camera Motion

Real-world cameras, as discussed earlier, have physical limitations. They can pan (left/right pivot), tilt (up/down pivot), cant (side-to-side pivot that creates a tilted **Dutch Angle**), crane (vertical up/down), or truck (horizontal left/right) a specific distance. The following ideas are suggested for controlling the camera in an appropriate way:

■ Rotate or translate the camera by entering values into the Channel Box or by interactively transforming the camera icon in an orthographic view. This allows for more precise control than is available by interactively moving the camera through its perspective view with the Alt keys. Entering specific values in the Channel Box also helps to prevent sudden camera "flips," where the keyed rotation inadvertently changes from 360 degrees to 0 degrees.

- Check on translation and rotation limits for the camera. You can find these in the Limit Information section of the camera transform node's Attribute Editor tab. You can pick and choose which axis to limit and whether or not there is a low and/or high limit. For example, in the following screen shot, the values approximate the practical range of motion for a motion picture camera mounted on a reduction gear head. The head is assumed to be mounted on a dolly; thus, there are no limits for **Translate X** or **Translate Z**. The scene is set to inches. A 1-node camera is used in this example.

Limit Information						
Translate						
		Min		Current		Max
Trans Limit X ☐	0.00		<	0.00	>	0.00 ☐
Trans Limit Y ☑	0.00		<	0.00	>	70.00 ☑
Trans Limit Z ☐	0.00		<	0.00	>	0.00 ☐
Rotate						
		Min		Current		Max
Rot Limit X ☑	-60.00		<	0.00	>	60.00 ☑
Rot Limit Y ☑	-90.00		<	0.00	>	90.00 ☑
Rot Limit Z ☑	-30.00		<	0.00	>	30.00 ☑

The Limit Information section of a camera transform node's Attribute Editor tab

Fine-Tuning Camera Stops

A real-world camera rarely comes to an abrupt stop. A camera operator often overshoots a designated end frame and must subtly move the camera into the correct position. If there is continuous action in a shot, such as actors milling about, the operator will continually adjust the frame to ensure the best composition. This holds equally true for individual close-ups. (The one shot that is traditionally static is the establishing wide shot that doesn't include actors or any significant movement within the frame.) The best way to prevent abrupt stops in Maya is to introduce float. For float strategies, see the section "Massaging Curves in the Graph Editor" earlier in this chapter. For additional reference, two scene files are included in the Chapter 3 scene folder: `no_float_cam.mb` features a camera move with an abrupt stop, and `float_cam.mb` features an improved version of the same move.

Matching the Camera to the Subject Matter

Over its 100-year history, the motion picture industry has developed a set a specific rules that determine how each shot is best framed and how actors and props are allowed to move in or through the frame. The framing is commonly known as shot composition. Although you may be familiar with common shot names, such as wide shot, over-the-shoulder, or close-up, it pays to be aware with their exact construction. For instance, close-ups traditionally stop below the top of the shoulder. Choker close-ups crop the neck. Extreme close-ups show only elements of the face (for example, the eyes). On the other hand, the placement and motion of actors and props in a shot is commonly known as screen direction. Specific rules determine where subjects look (screen left or screen right) and how subjects enter or exit the frame. More detailed information on shot composition and screen direction is readily available in myriad books on the subject of cinematography, editing, and storyboarding. Television borrows the majority of its shot composition and screen direction techniques from motion pictures.

With these techniques firmly in mind, you can choose shots and moves that are appropriate to their subject matter. For instance, if a piece of animation features two characters talking, you may choose a static two shot that fully frames both characters, then judiciously switch to individual medium shots or close-ups at the critical points in the dialogue (common to most dramas before the 1960s). On the other hand, if you're animating a car chase, you may choose strategically placed, low-angle, panning wide shots patterned after *Bullitt* (1968). If you're animating an action sequence where characters battle it out, you may choose old-fashioned, long-duration wide shots a la *The Adventures of Robin Hood* (1938) or frenetically cut, swooshing extreme close-ups a la *Gladiator* (2000).

Dynamics, Particles, and the Ocean System

THE MAYA DYNAMICS menu set includes an amazing range of effects. Although dynamic simulations, particle simulations, and the Ocean System are fairly easy to create, their refinement is often esoteric and unintuitive. In particular, rendering problems often plague ocean wakes, for which a Fluid Texture 3D volume is used. The dynamic simulation of a linked chain can create problems when combined with a character. The Instancer tool, with its default settings, can suffer from an uninteresting sameness. Nevertheless, once a few basic tricks are mastered, powerful effects become available to you.

This chapter's topics are organized into the following techniques:

- Driving a Boat through an Ocean
- Creating an Ocean Wake
- Building a Dynamic Chain
- Filling a Water Glass with Particles
- Animating Gelatin with a Soft Body
- Generating Swarms with Goals
- Industry Tip: Scattering Geometry with Instanced Particles and Expressions
- Adding Additional Variation to Instanced Geometry
- Offsetting Animation within an Instancer

Driving a Boat through an Ocean

One of the more astounding menu items in Maya is **Fluid Effects → Ocean → Create Ocean**. With a single click, you can create an entire Ocean System, complete with animated waves. Once an ocean exists, you can automatically float geometry of your choice by choosing **Fluid Effects → Ocean → Float Selected Objects**. Better yet, you can float a boat and add realistic roll and pitch by utilizing the Make Motor Boats tool. To apply this tool, follow these steps:

1. With an Ocean System in place, position a boat model at 0, 0, 0. Move the boat down in Y so that the hull is half above and half below the XZ axis plane. With the boat hierarchy selected, choose **Modify → Freeze Transformations**.

2. With the boat hierarchy selected, switch to the Dynamics menu set and choose **Fluid Effects → Ocean → Make Motor Boats**. Play the Timeline. The boat drifts up and down. The boat hierarchy is automatically parented to a locator, which in turn receives translation and rotation information from an expression node connected to the oceanShader node. The expression is given a generic name, such as expression1, and is editable in the Expression Editor.

If you'd like to animate the boat moving under its own power, specialized attributes are available in the Extra Attributes section of the locator shape node's Attribute Editor tab.

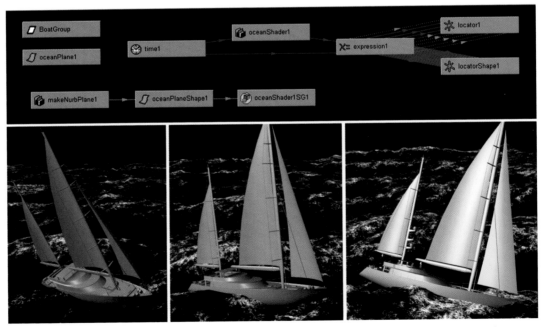

(Top) The Make Motor Boats hierarchy as seen in the Hypergraph Input And Output Connections window. (Bottom) The resulting sailboat struggles through a stormy sea. *Sailboat modeled by Singing Bridge.*

Descriptions of the most useful attributes follow:

Buoyancy, Object Height, and Scene Scale Scientifically speaking, buoyancy is the upward force exerted by a fluid onto an object less dense than itself. For this tool, **Buoyancy** determines what percentage of the boat is below water. A value of 0.5 sets the boat so that it is half in the water and half out. Values close to 1 float the boat on top of or above the water. For **Buoyancy** to work correctly, the locator must be placed at the volumetric center of the boat's hull and the **Object Height** attribute must be set to the hull's actual height in world units. In addition, for an accurate result, **Scene Scale** should match the **Scale** attribute of the Ocean Shader material. An Ocean Shader material is automatically assigned to a new Ocean System. The **Scale** attribute is found in the Ocean Attributes section of the material's Attribute Editor tab.

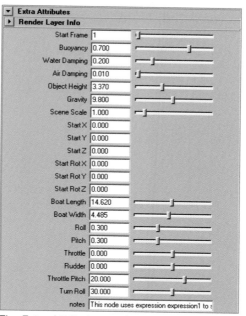

The Extra Attributes section of a locator shape node's Attribute Editor tab. The attributes are added automatically by the Make Motor Boats tool.

Boat Length and Boat Width The boat size in world units. Correct values are automatically inserted into these fields when the Make Motor Boats tool is applied. However, you can change the values for stylized results.

Roll and Pitch **Roll** controls the amount of port-to-starboard (left-to-right) rotation. **Pitch** controls the amount of bow-to-stern (front-to-back) rotation.

Throttle and Throttle Pitch **Throttle** serves as a virtual accelerator pedal. Negative values send the boat into reverse. **Throttle Pitch** controls the amount of "bow up" the boat achieves when accelerating forward. A value of 0 makes the boat bow hug the water. The default value of 20 lifts the bow approximately 20 degrees on a hard acceleration.

Rudder Turns the boat by *n* number of degrees. Positive values turn the boat to the port side. Negative values turn the boat to the starboard side.

Turn Roll Sets the amount of additional port-to-starboard rotation the boat undertakes on a turn. For instance, if the boat turns to port (left), the port side drops lower and the starboard side rises higher. A **Turn Roll** value of 0 removes the roll completely.

With the Make Motor Boats tool, there is no need to animate the boat directly. The specialized attributes serve as a "remote control" for the boat and may be keyed. No matter how the attributes are set, Maya takes into account the current size, orientation, and strength of the wave or waves on which the boat sits or pushes through.

Creating an Ocean Wake

Once you've applied the Make Boats or Make Motor Boats tool, you're free to generate a foam wake. To do this, select the locator to which the boat model is parented and choose **Fluid Effects → Ocean → Create Wake**. A Fluid Texture 3D volume and an ocean wake emitter are created and the virtual foam is added to the boat's path.

A sailboat creates a foamy wake. The wake dissipates behind the boat as the boat moves forward.

The ocean wake emitter, which is parented automatically to the locator, defines the area in which the wake foam appears. By default, it's created as a spherical volume that is 2×2×2 world units in size. However, you can change the volume shape by selecting the OceanWakeEmitter node in the Hypergraph Scene Hierarchy window, opening its Attribute Editor tab, expanding the Volume Emitter Attributes section, and switching the **Volume Shape** attribute to Cube, Cylinder, Cone, or Torus. You're also free to scale, rotate, and translate the volume icon to a point on the ship where the wake should originate. The

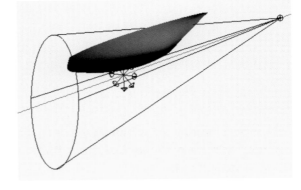

An ocean wake emitter, set to a cone volume shape, is scaled and positioned around the sailboat's hull.

shape should match the type of boat. For example, a narrow cone shape works best for a sail-boat, while a rectangular cube might be best suited for a large tanker.

The Fluid Texture 3D volume, on the other hand, affects the render of the ocean plane. In this case, the fluidTexture3D node produces the fluid volume shape and stores the shape's transforms. If the boat leaves the volume shape, the foam is no longer generated; you are free to scale and position the shape to avoid this. The OceanWakeFoamTexture node, whose tab appears to the right of fluidTexture3D, carries all the fluid texture attributes. For example, the **Temperature Scale** attribute, found in the Temperature subsection within the Contents Details section, controls the amount of rendered foam in the wake. In the previous illustration, **Temperature Scale** is set to 0.1. Higher values create a greater amount of foam. Although the fluid texture is a 3D texture, the fluid foam is converted to 2D and placed on top of the ocean surface. Maya accomplishes this by connecting the **outAlpha** of the OceanWakeFoam-Texture node to the **foamOffset** of the oceanShader node.

Adjusting the wake is often difficult. Here are a few additional tips for fine-tuning the look:

- To preview an ocean's waves and wakes in a workspace view, select the ocean plane and choose **Fluid Effects → Ocean → Add Preview Plane**. You can scale and reposition the preview plane, usually named transform1, to view different areas of the ocean. By default, the plane's displacement accurately matches the corresponding render. If you check on **Shading → Smooth Shade All** in a workspace view, the wake's foam is rendered as white splotches.

- The **Temperature Scale** attribute of the OceanWakeFoamTexture node works hand-in-hand with the **Heat/Voxel/Sec** attribute of the OceanWakeEmitter node. **Heat/Voxel/Sec**, found in the Fluid Attributes section, controls the wake intensity. Higher values increase the foam width and make the foam more opaque. When adjusting the **Heat/Voxel/Sec** attribute, you will have to replay the Timeline to see an accurate result.

- If the foam survives for too many frames and you'd like it to fade away more quickly, raise the **Dissipation** attribute, which is found in the Temperature subsection of the OceanWakeFoamTexture Attribute Editor tab. Conversely, if the foam disappears too rapidly behind the boat, lower the value. When the **Dissipation** value is changed, you will have to replay the Timeline to see an accurate result.

- You can add additional fading to the foam by increasing the **Edge Dropoff** attribute, which is found in the Shading section of the OceanWakeFoamTexture Attribute Editor tab. Higher values cause the bulk of the foam within the volume shape to fade more quickly from the edges of the volume shape. You can enter values higher than the slider's maximum default of 1.

- You can change the noise pattern contained within the foam by switching **Texture Type** (found in the Textures section of the OceanWakeFoamTexture Attribute Editor tab) to any of the standard Maya noise types. You will have to replay the Timeline to see an accurate result.

■ The various attributes belonging to the OceanWakeFoamTexture node's built-in noise should not be overlooked. For example, if the foam is rendering as a solid sheet of white, you can introduce grainy noise by raising the **Opacity Tex Gain** or the **Threshold** attribute. If you'd like to change the size of the noise pattern contained within the foam, adjust the **Frequency** attribute. Higher values scale the pattern down, and lower values scale the pattern up. To randomize the noise pattern of a Billow style noise, increase the **Spottyness**, **Size Rand**, and **Randomness** attributes. You can find these attributes in the Textures section below the **Texture Type** attribute.

■ The color of the wake's foam is not affected by the Color, Incandescence, and Opacity gradients found in the OceanWakeFoamTexture Attribute Editor tab. Instead, the foam color is based on the **Foam Color** attribute of the Ocean Shader material assigned to the ocean plane. The **Foam Color** attribute is found in the Common Material Attributes section of the material's Attribute Editor tab.

■ To create the look of water spray, you can parent particle emitters to the bow of the boat. Small Cloud particles generated by cone-shaped volume emitters can do the trick. (A photorealistic ocean simulation, as demonstrated by *The Perfect Storm* (2000), requires the combination advanced particle simulations, expressions, custom fields, renders split into multiple passes, and numerous compositing filters.)

   A simplified version of the scene illustrated in this section is included as boat_wake.mb in the Chapter 4 scene folder on the CD. For additional information on various Fluid Texture 3D attributes, see the "fluidShape" Maya help file.

■ Building a Dynamic Chain

A chain may seem like a difficult object for Maya to dynamically simulate. In reality, such a simulation requires only a few steps:

1. Create a new scene. Model a chain with five links. To quickly model a chain link, choose **Create → NURBS Primitives → Torus → □**, set **Minor Radius** to 0.2, and click in a workspace view. You can position the links loosely at this point. The dynamic simulation will move them into their rest position.

2. Switch to the Dynamics menu set, select all the links, and choose **Soft/Rigid Bodies → Create Active Rigid Body**. Select all the links and choose **Fields → Gravity**. Play the Timeline. All the links fall as a monolithic unit.

3. To pin the top link to a point in space, select the link and choose **Soft/Rigid Bodies →
    Create Nail Constraint**. A constraint is created and is represented by a small green box
    at the link's pivot point. You can move this box by selecting the constraint node in the
    Hypergraph Scene Hierarchy window. The link then swings as if attached to a string.
    Once the constraint exists, the remaining links relax as a real chain would.

    If you'd like the chain to be carried by a character, you can, in turn, parent the constraint
node to a joint in a character's hand. An example scene is included as `chain_hand.mb` in the
Chapter 4 scene folder on the CD. Keep in mind that a parented dynamic constraint slows
the dynamic calculation significantly. In addition, the parenting raises the likelihood that
calculation errors will separate the links. To prevent the errors, you can lower the **Step Size**
and **Collision Tolerance** attributes, which are found in the rigidSolver's Attribute Editor tab
(to the right of the rigidBody tab and to the left of the time1 tab). Although you may find it
tempting to parent the top link directly to a joint, such a parent will not work.

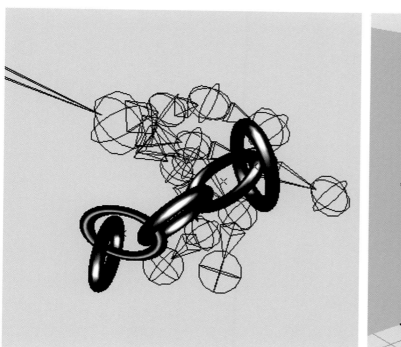
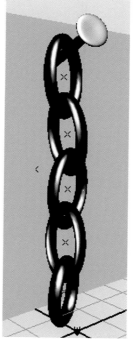

(Left) A chain's nail constraint parented to a hand joint. (Right) A chain bound by a passive rigid
body nail and passive rigid body wall plane.

    To hang the chain off another object, you can convert additional geometry into passive
rigid bodies (select the geometry and choose **Soft/Rigid Bodies → Create Passive Rigid Body**).
For example, you can have the chain interact with a NURBS nail and wall. An example scene
is included as `chain_nail.mb` in the Chapter 4 scene folder on the CD.

As a final touch, you can adjust the dynamic quality of each active and passive rigid body in the scene. A long list of dynamic attributes is accessible in the Channel Box under the corresponding rigidBody entry. For example, to make the a chain link more slippery, reduce the **Static Friction** and **Dynamic Friction** attributes. Additionally, you can "pull" the end of the chain by selecting the bottom link and choosing, once again, **Soft/Rigid Bodies → Create Nail Constraint**. You can animate the resulting constraint moving around the scene, thereby pulling the chain about.

Filling a Water Glass with Particles

Particles, once in a scene, are not likely to become static unless special measures are taken. This creates a problem when a solid body of water is needed, such as the water in a standing glass. One trick for filling a glass involves capping the glass with an invisible surface. For example, a NURBS glass is set at a slant, anticipating a tip-over. A NURBS plane is assigned to a 100 percent transparent Lambert material, making it invisible during the render. An emitter, in the glass center, spits out Blobby Surface particles until they fill the volume. The particles are forced to collide with the glass and plane with the Make Collide tool (see the next section for more information). The geoConnectors, connected to the glass and plane, are given high Friction values and low Resilience values. The net result is a fairly solid mass of particles within 60 frames.

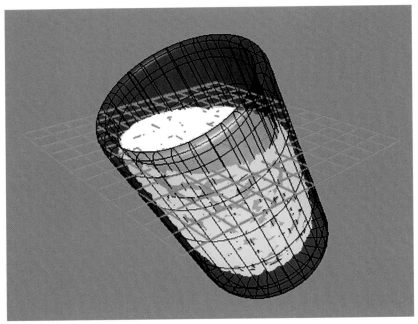

A NURBS plane keeps Blobby Surface particles contained within a glass.

After frame 60, the glass is animated tipping over. The plane is quickly withdrawn, allowing the particles to spill forth. The **Friction** values are reduced and the **Resilience** values are raised, thus giving more spring to the particles. A Gravity field is assigned to particles; its Magnitude value is keyed to change from 0 to 50 between frames 60 and 65. Delaying the pull of gravity allows the particles to fill the glass more quickly and thoroughly at the beginning. The **Rate (Particles/Sec)** attribute of the emitter is also keyed changing from 1000 to 0 between frames 60 and 61, thus instantly stopping the birth of new particles. It's assumed that the first 60 frames will not be used for the final animation but are only provided to transport the particles into a useful position. An example scene using this technique is saved as glass_cap.mb in the Chapter 4 scene folder on the CD. A QuickTime is included as glass_cap.mov in movies folder.

Swapping Solid Geometry for Particles

Although the use of the plane prevents the particles from escaping the glass, it does not completely calm the particles. If an absolutely static body of water is needed, you can add a piece of geometry with the same material. For example, you can model a "chunk" of water with NURBS surfaces. On frame 60, when the glass begins to tip over, key the chunk's **Visibility** off. On frame 61, key the **Visibility** on. Over the same two frames, key the **Transparency** attribute of the material assigned to the particle node so that its value changes from 100 percent white to 0 percent black. Although the render of the chunk and the render of the particles is not an exact match, the 1-frame swap is hard to detect in a busy scene. If the 1-frame swap is too abrupt, you can make the chunk become invisible and the particles become visible over multiple frames, forming a gradual cross-fade. An example scene using this technique is included as glass_chunk.mb in the Chapter 4 scene folder on the CD. A QuickTime is included as glass_chunk.mov in the Chapter 4 movies folder.

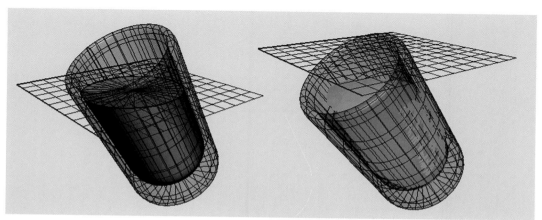

(Left) A modeled "chunk" of water sits in the glass. Particles discretely fill the glass while the particle material is 100 percent transparent. (Right) One frame later, the chunk is made invisible and the particles are made visible.

The most efficient method of rendering water requires the use of multiple render passes. For example, you can render the particles in one pass, the shadows in a second pass, the glass in a third pass, and the set in a fourth pass, thus creating a four sets of images. Breaking up the render allows for the maximum amount of flexibility in the resulting composite. For more information on render management, see Chapter 8.

Animating Gelatin with a Soft Body

Soft-body dynamics create interesting deformations on otherwise solid objects. The difficultly lies, however, with the degree to which the object deforms and the methods by which the deformations are controlled. Suggested steps follow for creating a block of gelatin hitting a wall and sliding down. The steps include the use of a particle goal, per-particle goal weights, and springs:

1. Create a simple set that includes a wall and ground plane. The geometry should be relatively dense so that the dynamic calculations are accurate. Switch to the Dynamics menu set. Select the wall and ground plane and choose **Soft/Rigid Bodies → Create Passive Rigid Body**.

2. Create a polygon primitive cube. Switch to the Polygons menu set, select all the faces of the cube, choose **Edit Mesh → Add Divisions → ❏**, set **Division Levels** to 2, and click Add Divisions. Delete the history of the cube and place it above the ground and away from the wall. With the cube selected as an object, switch back to the Dynamics menu set, choose **Soft/Rigid Bodies → Create Soft Body → ❏**, set **Creation Options** to Duplicate Make Copy Soft, check **Make Non-Soft A Goal**, and click the Create button. With these options, the cube is duplicated and a particle node is parented to the duplicate.

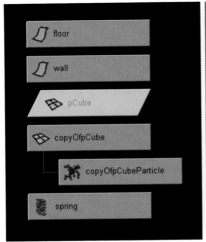 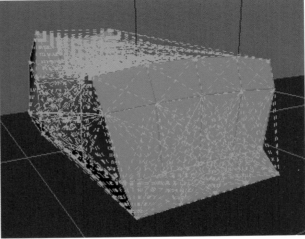

(Left) The hierarchy of a soft body with a goal and springs. (Right) A soft body cube with springs.

For each vertex on the duplicate cube, there is a single particle. Ultimately, the particles drive the deformation of the cube. The goal, in this case, is the original cube. The particles have a "desire" to match the corresponding vertices on the goal and will move to do so. The strength of this desire is determined by the **Weight** attribute (which is 0.5 by default).

3. Key the original cube flying through the air, bouncing off the wall, and landing on the floor. Play the Timeline from frame 1. The soft-body cube follows the original cube automatically. However, the soft body intersects the floor and ground. Since the soft body is controlled by particles, the particles must be told to collide with the geometry. Select the particle node in the Hypergraph Scene Hierarchy window, Shift+select the floor and wall, and choose **Particles → Make Collide**.

4. Hide the original cube. (You may have to delete the **Visibility** attribute keys.) Play the Timeline from frame 1. The soft body should no longer intersect the floor or ground. If some intersection remains, you can increase the **Tessellation Factor** attribute of each geoConnector Attribute Editor tab. geoConnectors serve as a go-between for particle and passive rigid bodies nodes. By default, one geoConnector is created each time the Make Collide tool is applied. You'll find the geoConnector tabs to the right of the rigidSolver and time1 tabs in the Attribute Editor. The **Tessellation Factor** attribute controls the accuracy of the calculation involving collisions. geoConnectors also provide **Resilience** and **Friction**, which control the namesake qualities of the connected surface during a dynamic simulation. (**Resilience** is equivalent to bounciness.)

At this point, the soft body deforms to a great degree—much greater than a chunk of gelatin would in the real world. One way to stem the deformation is to adjust the particle's **goalPP** values, which were remotely set by the **Weight** attribute of the Create Soft Body tool. To do this, select the particle node in the Hypergraph Scene Hierarchy window, switch back to a workspace view, RMB click over the cube, choose Particle from the marking menu, and select individual particles. With the particles selected, open the Component Editor (choose **Window → General Editors → Component Editor**). In the Particles tab, each selected particle is listed. You can change the **goalPP** value of each particle individually or all the particles at once. A value of 0 indicates that the particle has "no interest" in the goal and will only react to dynamic forces. If there are no dynamic forces, such as a gravity field, the particles and the soft body will not budge. A value of 1 indicates that the only "desire" of the particle is to match the corresponding vertex on the goal. A value above 1 will exaggerate the particle's quest. When the value is 1 or greater, the particle is able to overcome the power of the dynamic forces to some degree. In fact, if all the **goalPP** values are 1 or greater and the goal comes to a quick stop, the soft body quickly catches up and attempts to assume the exact shape of the goal.

If higher **goalPP** values are unable to control the deformation of the soft body, springs are also available. To apply springs, select the particle node and choose **Soft/Rigid Bodies → Create Springs**. Thin spring lines are drawn from each particle to every other particle. If the springs allow too much wiggle in the soft body, you can adjust the **Stiffness** and **Damping** attributes found in the springShape Attribute Editor tab. When raising these value, use caution. Springs have a tendency to "blow up" and destroy the soft body when **Stiffness** and/or **Damping** become too high.

A sample scene, which utilizes both custom **goalPP** weights and springs, is included as gelatin.mb in the Chapter 4 scene folder on the CD. A QuickTime movie is included as gelatin.mov in the Chapter 4 movies folder.

Generating Swarms with Goals

In addition to soft bodies, you can apply goals to regular particle simulations. In particular, goals come in handy for the simulation of insect swarms. In order to create such a swarm, follow these steps:

1. Create a new scene. Switch to the Dynamics menu set. Choose **Particles → Particle Tool**. Click a dozen times in a top workspace view to create 12 particles. Press Enter to fix the number of particles.

2. Select the particle1 node. Switch to the particleShape1 tab in the Attribute Editor. In the Render Attributes section, switch the **Particle Render Type** attribute to Spheres. Click the Current Render Type button. The **Radius** attribute is revealed. Adjust the **Radius** value until the particle spheres are the size of insects.

3. Select the particle1 node. Choose **Fields → Turbulence**. The turbulence field imparts random motion to the particles. Open the field's Attribute Editor tab. Raise **Magnitude** to 100. Lower **Attenuation** to 0.1. **Attenuation** controls the falloff of the field. High values cause the field influence to fall off more rapidly. Low values increase the influence and speed up the particle's movement. Play the Timeline. Adjust the **Frequency** attribute until the particle motion is insect-like. High values, such a 100, generally work by introducing a finer "jitter" into the particle motion.

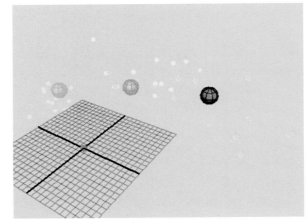

Particles swarm around a goal.

4. Create a primitive sphere. Animate the sphere moving rapidly around the scene (pretend it's a person running and ducking from the swarm). Select the particle node, Shift+select the sphere, and choose **Particles → Goal** with the default settings. Play the Timeline from frame 1. The particles will now follow the general path of the sphere.

The Goal tool tends to produce particle movement that is elliptical. That is, the particles tend to orbit the goal as they would a planetary body or as if they're stuck onto an elastic string. You can combine various methods to defeat this trait:

- In the particleShape1 tab of the Attribute Editor, adjust the **Goal Smoothness** value (found in the Goal Weights And Objects section). Lower values make the particles more aggressive and more likely to "land" on the goal. Higher values make the particles more lazy and more likely to make wide orbits around the goal. If the **Goal Smoothness** value is too high, the particles ignore the goal completely.

- Change the individual **goalPP** values of the particles in the Component Editor (see the previous section). Each particle can carry a unique value to maximize the amount of randomness.

- Randomly generate **goalPP** values as the Timeline progresses. You can add the following line to an expression to achieve this:

```
particleShape1.goalPP=rand(.4, 1);
```

With this line, goal values from 0.4 to 1 are randomly assigned to each particle. Since particles are involved, you must create such an expression by adding a custom **goalPP** attribute to the Per Particle (Array) Attributes section of the particle shape node's Attribute Editor tab. Once the **goalPP** attribute is added, you can RMB click the attribute field and choose the Creation Expression option from the shortcut menu, which brings up the Expression Editor in a special mode. For more information on the custom per-particle attributes, see the next section, as well as Chapter 6.

- Change the **Mass** attribute of each particle in the Component Editor. You can find **Mass** to the left of **lifespanPP** and to the right of **Position Z**. The default value is 1, but you can enter any value. A **Mass** set to 0 causes the particle to react very weakly to fields. A low **Mass** value also counteracts a high **goalPP** value. A **Mass** value above 1 is the same as 1.

- Animate field attributes, such as **Magnitude** or **Direction**, changing over time. This makes the particle paths even more unpredictable.

An example scene, which employs all the methods listed in this section, is included as angry_swarm.mb in the Chapter 4 scene folder. A QuickTime movie is included as angry_swarm.mov in the Chapter 4 movies folder.

▪ Industry Tip: Scattering Geometry with Instanced Particles and Expressions

Maya particles are extremely flexible and can emulate a wide range of objects. One key to their flexibility is their ability to instance geometry and derive transformation information from expressions. James Chandler, a Maya instructor for Westwood Online College, offers a method for "planting" rocks across a surface with instanced particles.

Rocks are planted on a ground plane by instancing them to particles. The scale and rotation is randomized by an expression.

To plant rocks, follow these steps:

1. Create a new scene. Create a NURBS or polygon surface that will serve as a ground plane. Switch to the Dynamics menu set. With the surface selected, choose **Particles → Emit From Object → ▢**, switch **Emitter Type** to Surface, set **Rate (Particle/Sec)** to 10, set Normal Speed to 0, and click the Create button. An emitter is created and particles are randomly generated across the surface when you play the Timeline. Since **Normal Speed** is 0, however, the particles appear on the surface but do not move. (If **Emitter Type** is left on Omni, each vertex becomes its own omni emitter, and the particles clump together.)

2. Select the particle1 node and open the Attribute Editor. Switch to the particleShape1 tab. Click the General button in the Add Dynamic Attributes section. The Add Attribute window opens. Switch to the Particle tab. Scroll to the bottom of the list and highlight

userVector1PP. This is a generic per-particle attribute that you can repurpose. Click the Add button at the bottom of the window. Highlight **userVector2PP**. Click the Add button again and close the window.

3. In the Per Particle (Array) Attributes section, **userVector1PP** and **userVector2PP** are listed as new per-particles attributes. RMB click the field to the right of either attribute and choose Creation Expression from the shortcut menu. The Expression Editor opens in the particle creation expression mode. In the work area, enter this code:

```
float $sX = rand(.5,2);

float $sY = rand(1,2);

float $sZ = rand(.5,2);

particleShape1.userVector1PP = <<$sX,$sY,$sZ>>;

float $rX = rand(1,359);

float $rY = rand(1,359);

float $rZ = rand(1,359);

particle1Shape1.userVector2PP = <<$rX,$rY,$rZ>>;
```

Click the Create button at the bottom of the window. If the expression is successful, the word *Expression* appears in the **userVector1PP** and **userVector2PP** fields in the Per Particle (Array) Attributes section. Close the Expression Editor.

4. Model a simple rock. Select the rock, Shift+select the particle node, and choose **Particles →
    Instancer (Replacement)**. Play the Timeline from frame 1. An instanced rock appears at
    each particle position. At this point, all the instanced rocks are the same size and have the same rotation.

5. Select the particle1 node and open the Attribute Editor. Switch to the particleShape1 tab. In the Instancer (Geometry Replacement) section, switch **Scale** to userVector1PP and **Rotation** to userVector2PP. Play the Timeline from frame 1. The rocks take on different scales and rotations.

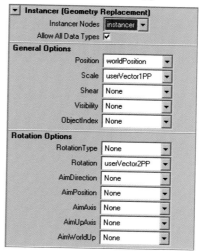

The Instancer (Geometry Replacement) section of a particle shape node's Attribute Editor tab

You can create variations in the rock pattern by choosing different values for the emitter's **Min Distance**, **Max Distance**, and **Speed Random**. (Keep **Min Distance** and **Max Distance** values equal or the rocks might disappear.) You can also assign the original rock to a material with a texture, thus allowing the texture to appear on all the instanced rocks.

 Once the rocks are satisfactorily spread out on the ground plane, you can make their positions permanent by selecting the particle1 node and choosing **Solvers → Initial State → Set For Selected**. (Use caution, as this step cannot be undone.) From that point forward, the rocks appear in place from the very first frame. To avoid creating new rocks at that point, set the emitter's **Rate (Particle/Sec)** to 0. An example scene is included as rocks.mb in the Chapter 4 scene folder on the CD.

Adding Additional Variation to Instanced Geometry

One disadvantage of the Instancer tool is its desire to orient all the instanced geometry in the same direction. As demonstrated in the previous section, you can create an expression to help randomize rotation. You can also choose Instancer attribute options that relate rotation, position, and scale to standard particle traits. These attributes and options are found in the Instancer (Geometry Replacement) section of the particle shape node's Attribute Editor tab.

For example, you can vary the rotation of individual particles by switching the **Rotation** attribute to worldPosition. In this situation, the particles take on unique rotations as they travel through the scene. The following list includes some other unique attributes:

Shear Creates a horizontal distortion in the instanced geometry. For example, a cube becomes a trapezoid.

RotationType Determines whether the instanced objects are rotated according to the **Rotation**, **AimDirection**, or **AimPosition** attribute values. If **RotationType** is set to None, **Rotation** is the chosen attribute value. If **RotationType** is set to 1, the value is taken from **AimDirection**. If **RotationType** is set to 2, the value is taken from **AimPosition**. To feed a value of 1 or 2 to **RotationType**, you can create a custom per-particle attribute, set it to a 1 or 2 in an expression, and choose the new attribute in the drop-down option list available to **RotationType**.

AimDirection Orients the instanced object by pointing it along a particular axis. For example, if **RotationType** is given a value of 1 and **AimDirection** is set to velocity, the object points in the direction it is traveling.

AimPosition Orients the instanced object to a particular point in space. For example, if **RotationType** is given a value of 2 and AimPosition is set to None, the object points toward 0, 0 ,0. For all the attributes in the Instancer (Geometry Replacement) section, the None option is interpreted as 0 or 0, 0, 0.

AimAxis Determines the axis used by **AimDirection** and **AimPosition** to point the object.

For each of the attributes in the Instancer (Geometry Replacement) section to access the full list of particle traits, the **Allow All Data Types** attribute must be checked. Aside from worldPosition and those per-particle attributes added by the user, available particle traits include acceleration, position, age, mass, lifespan, and radius.

```
acceleration
force
position
rampAcceleration
rampPosition
rampVelocity
velocity
worldPosition
worldVelocity
age
birthTime
mass
particleId
lifespanPP
lifespan
radius
```

Particle traits available to attributes in the Instancer (Geometry Replacement) section

Offsetting Animation within an Instancer

The Instancer (Replacement) tool is able to transfer animation from the source object to the instances. Unfortunately, the animation on every single instance is in perfect sync. In order to offset the animation on a particular instance, additional preparation is needed.

As an example, a small flock of primitive birds is created. In this case, three source birds are constructed. Although each of the source birds has an identical skeleton and body surface, their animation curves are unique. One flaps faster, one flaps slower, and so on. This scene is included as birds.mb in the Chapter 4 scene folder on the CD. A QuickTime is included as birds.mov in the Chapter 4 movies folder.

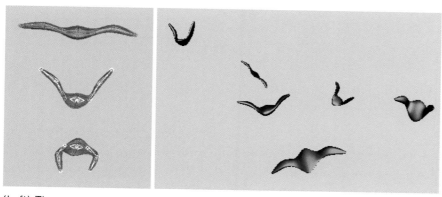

(Left) Three source birds with unique animation curves. (Right) The resulting flock of instanced birds created with a single particle node.

To create a single Instancer node that uses multiple sources, such as the three birds, you can follow these steps:

1. Select the source surfaces or surface hierarchies (do not select the skeletons). Shift+select the particle node of choice and choose **Particles → Instancer (Replacement) → ▢**. The Particle Instancer Options window opens. Note that each source is listed in the Instanced Objects area with a number to its left . The number determines where the source is used. (If the particle node is listed, you can remove it by highlighting it and clicking the Remove Items button.) Set any of attributes in the General Options and **Rotation** Options section that make sense. In the previous graphic, Rotation was set to worldPosition. Click the Create button to close the window.

   The Instanced Objects area of the Particle Instancer Options window

2. The first source object is instanced onto the particles. To utilize all the source objects, you must add a per-particle attribute. Open the particle shape node's Attribute Editor tab. In the Add Dynamic Attributes section, click the General button. The Add Attribute window opens. Switch to the Particle tab. Scroll down and select **userScalar1PP**. (If **userScalar1PP** is already employed, choose one of the remaining scalarPP attributes.) Click the OK button. **userScalar1PP** appears in the Per Particle (Array) Attributes section in the Attribute Editor.

3. RMB click the field beside **userScalar1PP** and select Creation Expression from the shortcut menu. The Expression Editor opens. In the work area, add the following code:

```
int $temp = rand(0, 3);

particleShape1.userScalar1PP = $temp;
```

   Click Create and exit the window. The word *Expression* appears beside the **userScalar1PP** field if the expression is successful.

4. In the Instancer (Geometry Replacement) section of the particle shape node's Attribute Editor tab, change **ObjectIndex** to userScalar1PP. **ObjectIndex** determines which source object a particle receives, as defined by the numbers assigned in the Instanced Objects area the Particle Instancer Options window. For variations in the distribution of sources, try different expressions. For example, use the seed command to force the rand function to choose a different string of values.

Character Rigging

CHARACTER RIGGING IS like fine wine—it is an acquired taste. For many animators, it presents a considerable headache. The steps are often long and convoluted. If you skip a step or apply a step in the wrong order, you must sometimes re-do your work. Nevertheless, once you master the basics, many powerful approaches become available to you. This chapter touches on a few unique tips and techniques for dealing with various aspects of the rigging process. While it won't cover everything there is to know about rigging, it will hopefully give you some clever workarounds should you ever get stuck.

This chapter's topics are organized into the following techniques:

- Resetting Bind Poses with *dagPose*
- Creating a Poor Man's Foot and Leg Rig
- Setting Up an Easy Spine Controller
- Picking Up a Prop with a Constraint
- Using Blended Wire Deformers for Facial Rigging
- Weighting a Head with the Component Editor
- Preventing Cluster Drift
- Industry Tip: Creating an Advanced Arm Rig

◼ Resetting Bind Poses with *dagPose*

When binding one surface of a multi-surface character with the Smooth Bind tool, it's not unusual to come across the following error:

```
Skin on joint_name was bound at a different pose.

Go to the bindPose to attach new skins.
```

The error occurs when a joint in the hierarchy has at least one surface bound to it, but is not in its bind pose position. For instance, if you try to rebind a character's face while the torso and legs remain bound, problems may arise. Generally, the error message names the joint that sits at the top of the hierarchy, such as the pelvis. Nevertheless, multiple joints may have failed to reach their bind pose. (A bind pose is simply the rotation a joint possessed at the point that it was bound to a surface.)

To prevent this error, you can select the joint hierarchy, switch to the Animation menu set, and choose **Skin → Go To Bind Pose**. Maya will attempt to rotate all the joints in the selected hierarchy to the appropriate bind pose. Although this is often successful, occasionally the Go To Bind Pose tool returns the following error:

```
Error: Pose not achieved. See diagnostics in Script Editor.
```

Additional lines in the Script Editor list the joints that failed to reach their bind pose. This failure often stems from subtle, inadvertent transformations of joints and custom controls after the original binding. At other times, the problem occurs when IK handles introduce unwanted rotation of joints when they are created. Constraints and expressions can also prevent the Go To Bind Pose tool from reaching its goal. You can temporarily disable IK handles, constraints, and expressions by choosing **Modify → Evaluate Nodes → Ignore All**. Once the Go To Bind Pose and Smooth Bind tools are successfully applied, you can restore the node functions by choosing **Modify → Evaluate Nodes → Evaluate All**.

Despite these various efforts, the Go To Bind Pose tool can fail to find the proper bind pose. Luckily, you can force joints to derive a new bind pose from their current transformations regardless of what they might be. To do this, select the joints and execute the following line in the Script Editor:

```
dagPose -reset -name dagPosex
```

x represents the bind pose number. This is generally 1. If you're not sure, select a joint and open the Channel Box. In the OUTPUTS section, the bind pose number is displayed as *bind-Posex*. This assumes that at least one other surface remains bound to the skeleton. (If all the surfaces have been detached, no bind pose exists and a new application of the Smooth Bind tool should work fine.) If dagPose is successful, the bind pose name is returned on the Command line. You can reapply the Smooth Bind tool at that point. Keep in mind that dagPose only works on joints that are selected. If you would like to reset the bind pose for all the joints in a skeleton, select all the joint nodes in the Hypergraph Scene Hierarchy or Outliner window.

On a more technical level, a dagPose node stores and can restore the matrix information of a dag hierarchy. Hence, when the Smooth Bind tool is applied, a dagPose node named bindPose*x* is created and is used to store the translate, rotate, and scale information of the joints at the point that they are bound without regard to subsequent transformations.

The use of `dagPose` is not limited to problem solving. For instance, you can use the command to create custom dagPose poses for a character. To create a start position, for instance, select all the joints in the skeleton and execute the following line in the Script Editor:

```
dagPose -save -selection -name startPose;
```

To force the character to return to your custom start pose once you've begun to animate, select the skeleton hierarchy and execute the following line:

```
dagPose -restore startPose;
```

Creating a Poor Man's Foot and Leg Rig

Various character rigs dictate different leg and feet mechanisms. Many of these mechanisms, such as the notorious reverse foot, are complex and can thus be frustrating to master. One rig, however, remains basic and fairly easy to apply. To create this "poor man's" setup, follow these steps:

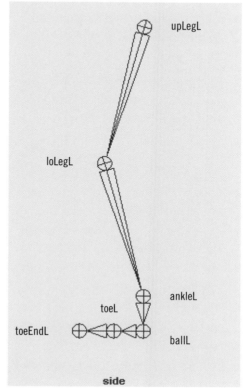

Six joints form a leg.

1. With the Joint tool (switch to the Animation menu set and choose **Skeleton → Joint Tool**), draw a leg in the side workspace view. Generally, it's best to draw the character so that the feet rest on the XZ virtual "ground plane." The leg should have six joints and five bones. Name the joints accordingly, starting from the top: upLegL, loLegL, ankleL, ballL, toeL, toeEndL.

    Feel free to choose your own naming convention so long as the names are easy to understand. Placing the *L* at end of each name will allow you to use the Mirror Joint tool in step 4.

2. In the front workspace view, select the top joint and move the entire hierarchy to screen right. The distance should be appropriate for half the hip width of the resulting character.

Choose **Skeleton → Joint Tool** and draw two joints that represent the hips. The first joint should be lower and the second joint should be higher. Name the first joint Tail and the second joint Pelvis. Select the upLegL joint and parent it to the Pelvis joint. Parenting one joint to another automatically draws a bone between the two joints. The Tail joint will give the character an extra degree of hip rotation, which is demonstrated at the end of this section. With this setup, spine joints are parented to the Tail joint and not the Pelvis joint.

3. At this point, it's a good habit to double-check the local rotation axis of each joint. In the Hypergraph Scene Hierarchy window, select all the joints. On the Status line, toggle on Select Miscellaneous Components (represented by the question mark icon in the component section). By default, the local rotation X axis points down the center of each bone.

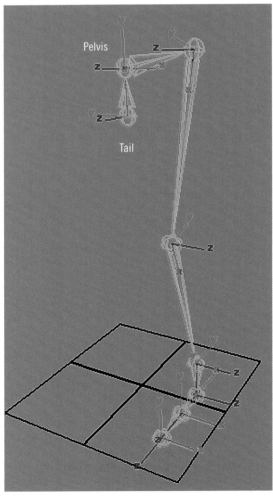

If you'd like to change the local axis of one joint, click the local axis handle and rotate it. If need be, you can display the local axis of a single joint by checking **Display Local Axis** in the Display section of the joint's Attribute Editor tab. (Although this step is not as critical for leg and feet joints, it is doubly important for spine, hand, and finger joints.)

4. Choose **Skeleton → IK Handle Tool**. Click the upLegL joint first and the ankleL joint second. An IK chain is drawn from the top of the upper leg to the ankle. Select the IK handle and rename it kneeIKL. (You can select IK handles by clicking the Select Handle Objects button on the Status line; the icon is a plus sign.) Choose **Skeleton → IK Handle Tool** again and click the ankleL joint first and the toeL joint second. An IK chain is drawn from the ankle to the toe, which is necessary for the custom handles created in step 6. Select the new IK handle and rename it ballIKL.

Tail and Pelvis joints are drawn and the rotation axis for each joint is checked.

5. Select the upLegL joint, and choose **Skeleton → Mirror Joint → ❑**, switch **Mirror Across** to YZ, set Mirror Function to Orientation, enter L into the **Search For** field, enter R into the **Replace With** field, and click the Mirror button. The entire left leg, including its IK handles, is duplicated and mirrored, creating the right leg. The news joints are properly labeled with an *R*. The Orientation option attempts to match the local rotation axis of each joint on both legs. (Although Orientation works in the majority of cases, a few joints may be given an incorrect axis orientation; in this situation, you must manually rotate the local axis handle.)

6. Create a primitive circle and delete its history. In the top workspace view, scale and move the circle until it surrounds the left foot. The circle should be large enough to be easily selected but small enough to avoid overlapping other parts of the character. With the circle selected, choose **Modify → Freeze Transformations**. This resets the circle's **Translate** and **Rotate** values to zero, making its start position easy to return to during the animation process. Select the circle and rename it footControlL. Select the kneeIKL and ballIKL IK handles and parent them to footControlL. Duplicate footControlL. Move the duplicate into position around the right foot, freeze its transformations, and rename it footControlR. (In this example, the *L* and *R* naming convention is based on the character's view of him/herself and not the animator's screen view.) Select kneeIKR and ballIKR and parent them to footControlR.

7. Choose **Create → CV Curve Tool → ❑**, set **Curve Degree** to 1 Linear, and draw a curve that represents the global transform handle for the character. Select the curve and freeze its transformations. Rename the curve appropriately (for example, heroTransform). Select footControlL and footControlR and parent them to the new global transform handle. Select the Tail joint and parent it to the new global transform handle.

8. Create two primitive circles and delete their history. Place one in front of each foot at the ground level and freeze their transformations. Rename them toeOrientL and toeOrientR. Shift+select toeOrientL first and the toeL joint second. Choose **Constrain → Orient**. Thereafter, toeOrientL controls the rotation of the left toe. Following the same steps, make toeOrientR a constraint for the toeR joint. Parent toeOrientL and toeOrientR to the global transform handle.

9. Create two primitive circles and delete their history. Rotate each circle 90 degrees in the Z axis. Place one circle in front of each knee of the character. Freeze their transformations. Name the circles kneeOrientL and kneeOrientR. Shift+select kneeOrientL first and the kneeIKL IK handle second. Choose **Constrain → Pole Vector**. Repeat the process for kneeOrientR and kneeIKR. Select kneeOrientL and kneeOrientR and parent them to the Tail joint. (Do not attempt to parent the circles to the upLeg or loLeg joints or the leg

hierarchy will become nonfunctional.) These circles now control the orientation of each knee. The leg and foot rig is complete. A finished version is included as `leg_rig.mb` in the Chapter 5 scene folder on the CD.

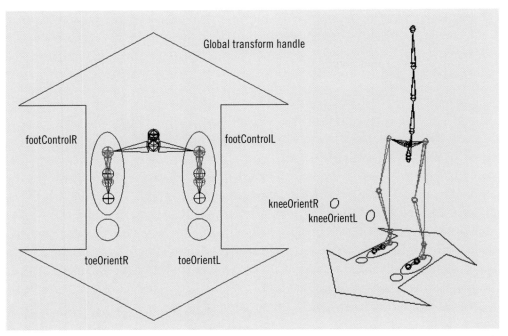

The finished foot and leg rig. To demonstrate hip wiggle, three spine joints are parented to the Tail joint.

Controlling the Leg and Foot Rig

Here are a few tips for controlling the resulting rig:

- By rotating the Pelvis joint, you can wiggle the hips without rotating the upper body. You can rotate the upper body by rotating the Tail joint.

- To move the entire character, you have two choices. You can select the global transform handle and translate and rotate it. This drags the character along without affecting the pose of the feet or legs. You can also select the Tail joint, footControlL, and footControlR and translate them together. This will leave behind the global transform handle, which is not necessarily a bad thing. In fact, ignoring the global transform handle can make the animation of walk cycles easier. Use whichever method you find more comfortable.

- To pose a leg, select a footControl circle and translate and rotate it. When you do this, the toe remains parallel to the ground. If you'd like to reorient the toe, select the corresponding toeOrient circle and rotate it. Note that the toeOrient circles stay with the global transform handle, wherever it may be.

- To orient a knee, select and move the corresponding kneeOrient circle. Be careful to keep the kneeOrient circles in front of the character or the knees may suddenly "pop" into a new position during an animation.

- As you animate, you need only set keys on the various custom handles. The advantage of using primitive circles and CV curves as handles is the curves' ability to be exclusively selected. That is, if Select Curve Objects is the only button toggled on the Status line, the joints and IK handles are ignored during the selection process.

Setting Up an Easy Spine Controller

As with legs and feet, many rigs exist for character spines. Spline IK handles are popular but are odd in their need to employ curves, vertices, clusters, and the occasional "dummy" box. Another approach, which involves a single custom handle and an expression, is much cleaner. To create this spine controller, follow these steps:

1. Make sure your character spine is ready to go. The joints should be intuitively named (for example, spine1, spine2, and so on). Double-check the local rotation axis of each spine joint. You will need to know which axis runs up and down, left and right, and front and back. To change the axis orientation of a joint, see step 3 of the section "Creating a Poor Man's Foot and Leg Rig."

2. Create a custom handle and place it in front of the character about chest high. You can either use a primitive circle or draw a CV curve with the 1 Degree option. Rename the handle spineControl and freeze its transformations (again, see "Creating a Poor Man's Foot and Leg Rig" for more information).

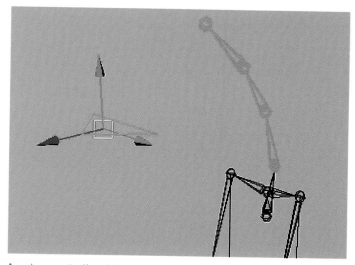

A spine controller driven by an expression

3. Choose **Window → Animation Editors → Expression Editor**. Enter a name into the **Expression Name** field. In the work area, enter an expression similar to this:

```
spine1.rx=spineControl.ty*2;

spine1.ry=spineControl.tx*2*-1;

spine1.rz=spineControl.tz*2;

spine2.rx=spine1.rx*.75;

spine2.ry=spine1.ry*.75;

spine2.rz=spine1.rz*.75;

spine3.rx=spine2.rx*.75;

spine3.ry=spine2.ry*.75;

spine3.rz=spine2.rz*.75;
```

In this example, spine3's rotation is based on a percentage of spine2's rotation, and spine2's rotation is a percentage of spine1's rotation. (In terms of the hierarchy, spine3 is parented to spine2 and spine2 is parented to spine1.) This creates a more realistic style of spine rotation. Feel free to vary the values in the expression to produce different results. The expression assumes that the joints' X axis runs down to up, the Y axis runs back to front, and the Z axis runs left to right (when viewed from the front workspace view). The *2 (at the end of the first three expression lines) increases a potentially small translation value. The *-1 (at the end of the second line) ensures that the spine bend matches the translation of the handle in X as opposed to a bend that runs the opposite direction.

If your joints possess different names or axis orientations, update the expression to reflect this. Once the expression is written, click the Create button. If the expression is successful and returns no errors, close the Expression Editor.

4. Test the spineControl handle by moving it about. Moving the handle up or down should cause the spine to twist. Moving the handle left or right should cause the spine to bend side to side. Moving the handle forward or backward should cause the spine to bend in the same direction.

5. Select the spineControl handle and parent it to the character's global transform handle. If no handle exists, parent the spineControl to the joint or other node that sits at the top of the hierarchy.

The spine controller is complete. A spine controller example is included as `spine_rig.mb` in the Chapter 5 scene folder on the CD. For a demonstration of a more traditional spline IK spine, see the section "Preventing Cluster Drift" at the end of this chapter.

Picking Up a Prop with a Constraint

You can force an object to follow the joint of a character by applying a point constraint. To do this, select a joint, such as a hand joint, and Shift+select the object. Switch to the Animation menu set and choose **Constrain → Point**. The object automatically snaps to the joint. That is, the pivot point of the object is snapped to the pivot point of the joint, bringing the object along for a ride.

The constraint lasts indefinitely unless it is turned off. To turn off the constraint, select the constraint node (parented to the constrained object), and set the ***constrainer_name* W0** attribute to 0 in the Channel Box. You can animate ***constrainer_name* W0** changing from 0 to 1 and back, thus allowing the character to grab and release the object. One problem with this scenario, however, is the object's habit of returning to its rest position (the position at which it rested when the constraint was applied) or hopping off to one side.

To avoid this sudden movement, you can place overriding animation on a separate node. If the object possesses only one node, group the object to itself before creating the constraint. For example, if a primitive sphere is grouped to itself, it winds up with two nodes. To group an object to itself, simply select the object and choose **Edit → Group**. In this situation, the constraint is applied to the original object node and overriding animation is applied to the group node. As an example, the following steps are necessary for a character to pick up a cylinder and then toss it aside:

1. Create a primitive NURBS cylinder. Select the cylinder and choose **Edit → Delete By Type → History**. Group the cylinder to itself by choosing **Edit → Group**. Select the nurbsCylinder1 node. Press the Insert key and move the pivot to a position that makes

   sense for a constraint. Placing the pivot to one side of the cylinder works fairly well. If the pivot is in its default position, the cylinder will intersect the hand when it's constrained. Select the group1 node and move its pivot to the same position.

2. Move the group to a place where it can be picked up. (The animation will be easier to achieve if the group is snapped to a grid line with the Snap To Grids button.) Select the group1 node and the nurbsCylinder1 node and choose **Modify → Freeze Transformations**.

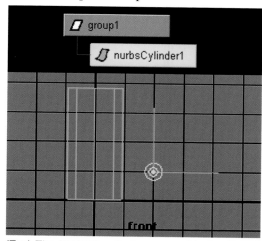

(Top) The NURBS cylinder grouped to itself. (Bottom) Offsetting the cylinder's pivot to one side.

3.   Build a simple arm or import a rigged character. A sample scene, named arm_grab.mb, is included in the Chapter 5 scene folder in the CD.

4.   Move the Timeline to frame 1. Choose a start position for the arm joints and key them. Determine the frame at which the hand should grab the cylinder (for example, frame 20). Move the Timeline to that frame. Rotate the arm joints so that the wrist joint is in the same position as the cylinder's pivot. Select the wrist joint and Shift+select the nurbsCylinder1 node. Choose **Constrain → Point**. If the center of the wrist joint is aligned with the pivot point, the cylinder will not move, which is preferable. If the wrist joint is positioned away from the pivot, the cylinder will suddenly jump to the joint.

5.   Select the nurbsCylinder1_pointConstraint1 node, set *joint_name* **W0** to 1, and key the attribute. (You can highlight the attribute name in the Channel Box, RMB click, and choose Key Selected from the shortcut menu.) Move the Timeline back one frame (frame 19). The cylinder is lifted by the arm. Select the nurbsCylinder1_pointConstraint1 node, set *joint_name* **W0** to 0, and key the attribute. The cylinder hops back to its start position. (If the cylinder does not return to it start position, it may be suffering from undeleted history.)

6.   Move forward on the Timeline. Animate the joints lifting the cylinder up into the air. Determine the frame at which the hand should let go (for example, frame 30). Move the Timeline back one frame (frame 29), select the nurbsCylinder1_pointConstraint1 node, and key the *joint_name* **W0** attribute while it remains set to 1.

7.   Select the group1 node and key it. Since the group1 node has not been interactively transformed, its **Translate** and **Rotate** attributes remain 0, 0, 0. If the point constraint is on, group1's pivot is "left behind" and sits at the cylinder's rest position. Although odd, this does not affect the animation.

8.   Move one frame ahead (frame 30), set *joint_name* **W0** to 0, and key the attribute. The cylinder suddenly jumps back to its start position. Select the group1 node and move the cylinder back up to the point where it was released by the hand. Set a key. Move the Timeline ahead and position and key the group1 node so that the cylinder tumbles through the air. Rotate and key the arm joints so that the character finishes the motion of tossing the cylinder.

9.   As a final step, check the animation curves of the constraint node to make sure the constraint is neatly turning on and off. To do this, select the nurbsCylinder1_point-Constraint1 node, choose **Window → Animation Editors → Graph Editor**, select all the keys of the *joint_name* **W0** curve, and choose **Tangents → Stepped** in the Graph Editor menu. Also, check the **Translate** curves of the group1 node to make sure the cylinder does not move before it is released by the hand.

Scrub the Timeline. The arm swoops down, takes hold of the cylinder, lifts it up, and tosses it away. If this process is carefully undertaken, no "pops" in the animation are visible.

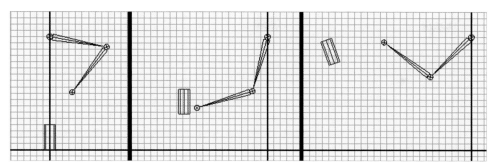

An arm grabs a cylinder and tosses it away with the help of an animated constraint node.

Using Blended Wire Deformers for Facial Rigging

Although blend shapes create a flexible and convincing facial rig, they are often tedious to set up and prone to errors. If you apply the Create Blend Shape tool to curves, however, you can avoid some of these problems. With such a setup, various parts of the face are driven by blended wire deformers. To create a blended wire system for a character's mouth, follow these steps:

1. Create a default primitive NURBS circle. Rotate the circle 90 degrees in the X axis. Move the circle so that it sits in front of the character's mouth. Display the circle's vertices. Move and scale vertices so that the circle mimics the contour of the mouth in the front and side workspace views. The curve should not touch the face geometry but should "float" off of it slightly. As with all facial rigging, the best results are achieved if the character's mouth is modeled slightly open.

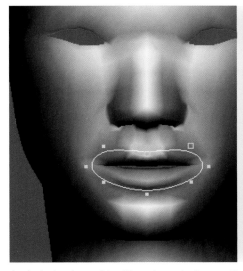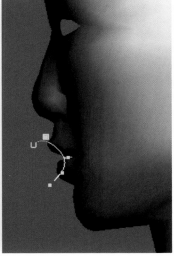

A circle is shaped to fit a character's mouth.

Once the circle is shaped, choose **Modify → Freeze Transformations** and **Edit → Delete By Type → History**. Rename the circle mouthNeutral.

2. Duplicate mouthNeutral. Make one duplicate for each desired target phoneme or mouth blend shape. Move the duplicated target circles to the left or right so that they can be easily seen and edited. Do not, under any circumstance, freeze the transformations of the target circles or adjust their pivots. Rename the target circles to match their intended shapes (for example, mouthSmile, mouthFrown, mouthO, and so on).

3. Open the Hypergraph Scene Hierarchy window. Parent the mouthNeutral node to the character's neck joint. Switch to the Animation menu set, and choose **Deform → Wire Tool**. The Wire tool steps you through the tool's application by printing messages on the Help line at the bottom of the Maya window. First, select the head geometry and press Enter. Second, select the mouthNeutral circle and press Enter. The tool automatically creates a mouthNeutralBaseWire node, which is parented to the neck joint. As a transform node, mouthNeutralBaseWire must travel with the mouthNeutral circle for the deformation to function. The Wire tool also creates a mouthNeutralBaseWireShape node and a wire1 node, which control the deformation in tandem.

4. As a test, move mouthNeutral forward. The lips should be pulled along with the curve. If not, adjust the strength of the wire deformer by selecting the head, expanding the wire1 section in the INPUTS area of the Channel Box, and raising the **Envelope** attribute value. If the wire deformer's influence is traveling too far and is affecting too much of the nose or chin, reduce the **Dropoff Distance[0]** attribute, which is found in the same section. **Envelope** is a scaling factor, which increases or decreases the overall strength of the deformation. **Dropoff Distance[0]** represents the world distance the wire deformer's influence travels.

5. Return the mouthNeutral to its start position by zeroing out its **Translate** values. Select all the target circles, Shift+select mouthNeutral, choose **Deform → Create Blend Shape → ▢**, enter a blend shape name into the **BlendShape Node** field, and click the Create button.

6. Open the Blend Shape window by choosing **Window → Animation Editors → Blend Shape**. A blend slider is created for each target circle. Select the first blend shape slider and move it up to 1. In a workspace view, select the corresponding target circle and display its vertices. Move the vertices into the appropriate target shape (smile, frown, and so on). Since the blend slider is at 1, the face deforms as you massage the vertices. Once the target circle makes a satisfactory deformation, return the slider to 0. Select the next blend slider, push it up to 1, and tweak its corresponding target circle. Repeat this process for each of the blend sliders and target circles.

Although this section uses primitive circles to create wire deformers, you are free to use curves created by the CV Curve and EP Curve tools. As such, the curves do not need to be closed. At the same time, the curves do not need to have an excessive number of vertices. If you'd like to add similar wire deformers to other parts of the face, such as the eyes or eyebrows, repeat the steps with new sets or neutral and target circles or curves. A sample scene is included as mouth_wire.mb in the Chapter 5 scene folder on the CD.

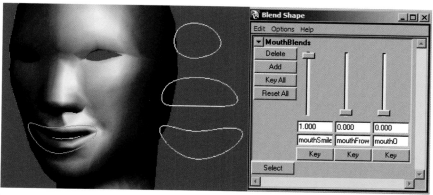

(Left) A completed blended wire deformer system. Target circles sit to the right of the face and form an O shape, a frown, and a smile . (Right) The corresponding blend shape sliders.

Weighting a Head with the Component Editor

The Paint Skin Weights tool provides an intuitive and interactive method by which to weight the vertices of a bound surface. Unfortunately, the tool can be slow and tedious when adjusting the weights for a skin that is newly bound. In particular, a character's head and neck often need a great deal of adjustment. In this case, you can use the Component Editor to save time.

For example, a polygon head is smooth bound to the spine, neck, jaw, and head joints of a skeleton. The Smooth Bind tool (**Skin → Bind Skin → Smooth Bind**) is used with the default settings. Initially, the binding causes the face to grotesquely twist if the neck joint is rotated.

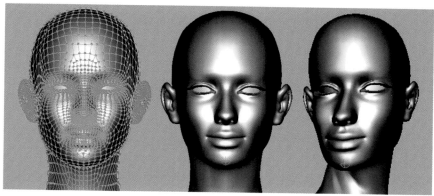

(Left) Vertices colored by the Smooth Bind tool. (Middle) Default bind with no rotation. (Right) Distortion created by default bind when the neck joint is rotated.

To solve this problem, choose **Window → General Editors → Component Editor** and switch to the Smooth Skins tab. Display the vertices of the head. By default, the vertices are color-coded to indicate which joint they are most influenced by. In a side workspace view, use the Lasso selection tool to pick all the vertices that surround the skull (from the neck up, including the lower jaw). If there are a great number of vertices, Maya may take 5 or 10 seconds to select them. The selected vertices are listed vertically in the Component Editor. The joints within the skeleton are listed horizontally.

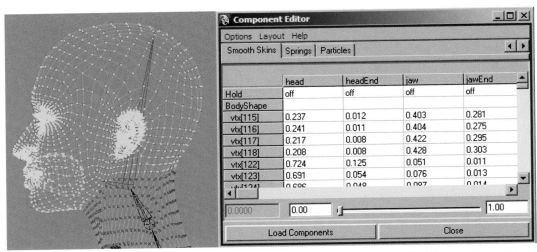

(Left) The vertices that surround the skull are selected with the Lasso tool. (Right) A portion of the selected vertices are displayed in the Component Editor.

If every joint of the skeleton is listed, even if they have no influence over the head, choose **Options → Hide Zero Columns** from the Component Editor menu; this restricts the view to only those joints that affect the selected vertices. It is important to properly name all the joints before working in the Component Editor or the joint list becomes confusing.

The right-most column contains the total joint weight received by any given vertex. By default, the joint weights must add up to 1.0 (in other words, 100 percent). To properly adjust the weighting of the selected vertices, locate the head joint column. Highlight the first cell in the column. Shift+select the last cell in the column. The entire column of cells is highlighted. One cell is given a blinking cursor. While the cursor is visible, press the Backspace key, press the 1 key, and press Enter. All the cell values are changed to 1.

	head	headEr
Hold	off	off
BodyShape		
vtx[2244]	0.542	0.301
vtx[2246]	0.572	0.279
vtx[2247]	0.507	0.257
vtx[5047]	0.542	0.301
vtx[5049]	0.506	0.257
vtx[5050]	0.572	0.279

A highlighted column. In this image, only six vertices are selected.

When any cell in changed, the corresponding cells in the other columns are updated. In this example, all the other cells in all the other columns are set to 0, ensuring that the joint weight total for each vertex is no greater than 1.0. You are free to enter any weight value into any cell. For instance, if you enter 0.5 into the cells belonging to the head joint, the weights are readjusted for the neck and jaw joints. Joints closest to the head joint receive the highest weight value. Joints farther from the head joint receive lower weight values. The number of joints across which weights are readjusted is determined by the **Max Influences** attribute of the Smooth Bind tool. In addition, the Smooth Bind tool's **Dropoff Rate** sets the rapidity with which the influence of a joint fades; the lower the value, the greater the distance the joint's influence travels and the more likely it is favored in the re-weighting process.

Once the vertices around the skull are properly weighted, select the vertices that cover the lower jaw. The selection does not need to be perfect at this point. Locate the jaw joint column in the Component Editor and change all its cells to 1.0. In this fashion, the weights are "stolen back" from the head joint. Select the vertices that make up the neck and change the neck joint column to 1.0. If the neck is composed of two joints, weight the columns accordingly.

At this point, you can rotate the neck. The face does not distort. However, the transition between the neck and head is harsh. Also, the jaw cannot be opened without creating an ugly result. Ultimately, the Component Editor provides an efficient way to "rough in" the weighting. The Paint Skin Weights tool can easily refine the result from that point forward.

Using the Paint Skin Weights Tool

Here are a few tips for painting skin weights:

- You can select multiple surfaces before choosing **Skin → Edit Smooth Skin → Paint Skin Weights Tool → □**. You can paint across multiple surfaces without any significant problems.

- If **Paint Operation** is set to Replace or Add, you can set the **Value** attribute to any number from 0 to 1. Although you can go below 0 and above 1 if the **Min/Max Value** attribute is changed, it is not recommended. Such values will interfere with the weighting process and can cause vertices to either lag behind the character or shoot off in an unexpected direction.

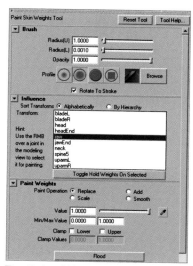

- You can quickly smooth out rough transitions created by adjustments within the Component Editor by switching the tool's **Paint Operation** to Smooth.

- The black and white shading displayed by the tool is only a rough approximation (**Shading → Smooth Shade All** must be checked on in the workspace view). For instance, if a section of the surface appears

The Paint Skin Weights Tool options box

100 percent white, vertices with lower weights might exist in the middle of that section. To make sure the weighting is absolutely correct, select the vertices in question and check the Component Editor.

- You can paint weights while a character is in a nonneutral pose. In fact, this is the best way to determine if weight problems exist. For example, when refining the neck weights, rotate the head to its maximum extension in one direction. When weighting the upper arm and shoulder, rotate the arm into various positions that are required by upcoming animation.

- Surfaces bound with the Rigid Bind tool cannot be reweighted with the Paint Skin Weights tool. Any given rigid bound vertex is influenced by a single joint. That said, you can reweight a rigid bound surface by selecting the surface and choosing **Deform → Paint Cluster Weights Tool → ❑**. With this tool, you can remove the influence of a joint by painting with Value set to 0.

Preventing Cluster Drift

Clusters serve as convenient handles for groups of vertices. When clusters are used as part of a character setup, however, problems can occur if their creation is not carefully undertaken.

You can create two styles of clusters: absolute and relative. To create an absolute cluster, select a vertex or vertices on a curve or surface, switch to the Animation menu set, and choose **Deform → Create Cluster** with the default settings. An absolute cluster receives transformation information from the hierarchy above and below. This trait is not noticeable unless the cluster is parented to the hierarchy of a character. For example, if a spline IK chain is applied to the spine of a character and each vertex of the spline IK curve is converted into an absolute cluster, the motion of the clusters becomes an issue.

If the clusters are left unparented, and the character moves forward, the clusters are left behind. Although the clusters function properly (their transformation bends the spine), the location of the clusters is inconvenient for animation. If the clusters are

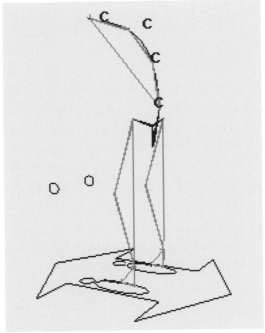

A spline IK chain on a spine. The vertices of the spline curve are converted to clusters.

parented to the global transform handle of the character, the clusters follow the character. However, other issues arise. First, Maya often inserts a group node above each cluster node as they are parented. This is necessary, as the Command line message states, to "preserve position." Second, as the character is moved, the clusters drift, which causes the spine to bend unintentionally.

To avoid the cluster drift, you can create relative clusters. To do so, select the vertex or vertices and choose **Deform → Create Cluster → ❒**, check **Relative**, and click the Create button. When a relative cluster is parented to the global transform handle, an extra group node is inserted. However, when the character is moved about, the clusters do not drift. On a more technical level, the **Relative** attribute prevents the use of any pre-matrix or post-matrix for its transformation calculation. That is, only the transformation of the cluster node—and no other node—can affect the deformation of the cluster.

You can also tackle the problem of cluster drift by dictating a different deformation order on the absolute cluster. You can achieve this by selecting the vertex or vertices, choosing **Deform → Create Cluster → ❒**, switching to the Advanced tab, changing **Deformation Order** to After, and clicking the Create button. **Deformation Order** is an important attribute of all Maya deformers (clusters, nonlinear deformers, lattice deformers, jiggle deformers, and so on). When multiple deformers are "stacked" on a character or object, the order in which they are applied can adversely affect the end result. Therefore, it often pays to experiment with different **Deformation Order** options when creating deformers.

Creating a Spline IK Spine

If you'd like to create your own spline IK spine, follow these steps:

1. Switch to the Animation menu set and choose **Skeleton → IK Spline Handle Tool**. Click the lowest spine joint. Click the highest spine joint. A spline IK chain is created and is indicated by a line drawn from the lower joint to the higher joint. Although an IK handle is created at the higher joint, it cannot be moved. A special spline IK curve is drawn down the center of the spine joints. Parent this curve to the character's global transform handle or any other node that sits at the top of the character hierarchy. To bend the spine, select any of the vertices of the curve and move them. To bend the spine in a more traditional, less snakelike manner, select the top vertex and move it.

2. To make the movement and animation of the curve vertices easier, you can convert them into clusters. Select the first vertex, choose **Deform → Create Cluster → ❒**, check **Relative**, and click the Create button. Select the resulting cluster and parent it to the character's global transform handle or any other node that sits at the top of the character hierarchy. Some animators prefer to parent the clusters to a custom handle, such as a curve or primitive "dummy box"; this makes the selection of the cluster a little easier. In any case, repeat this process for each of the remaining vertices. A sample scene is included as spline_spine.mb in the Chapter 5 scene folder on the CD.

Industry Tip: Creating an Advanced Arm Rig

Numerous methods of rigging hands and arms exist. Simple setups leave the joints in a forward kinematics state. Some setups create custom handles with remote controls built from expressions or set driven keys. Other variations combine forward and inverse kinematics into a single rig.

Kirk Buckendorf, from the Global Gaming Group, offers his own take on the problem. His rig utilizes inverse kinematics and a custom hand, wrist, and forearm controller. A working example is included as `arm_rig.mb` in the Chapter 5 scene folder on the CD.

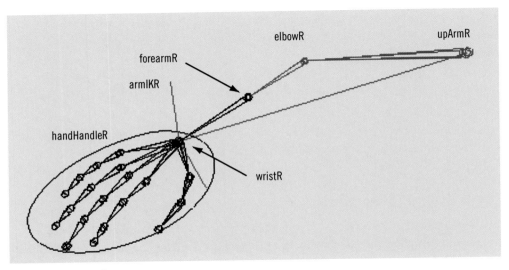

The custom arm rig

To manipulate the sample arm, follow these guidelines:

- To position the arm, select armIKR IK handle and move it.

- To rotate the wrist and hand, select the handHandleR circle and rotate it in any direction. The forearm joint twists when the handHandleR circle twists in the appropriate direction.

- To reorient the elbow, select the elbowOrientR control and move it.

To create a similar rig, you can follow these steps:

1. In the top workspace view, draw four joints with the Joint tool to create a right arm. One bone serves as the upper arm. Two bones make up the lower arm. The lower arm

bones should form a straight line; if necessary, magnet snap the joints to the grid lines to ensure this. Name the joints upArmR, elbowR, forearmR, and wristR. Move the upArmR joint, and thus the whole hierarchy, to the correct height in Y. Double-check the local rotation axis of each joint. The X axis should run down the center of each bone. You can display a joint's local rotation axis by checking **Display Local Axis** in the Display section of the joint's Attribute Editor tab. To adjust an incorrect axis, click the axis handle, and rotate it with the Rotate tool.

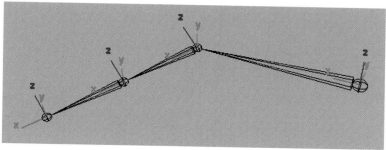

The four joints of the right arm and the ideal orientation of each local rotation axis

2. Draw finger bones and parent them to the wristR joint. Double-check the local rotation axis of each finger joint; adjust any axis that is aligned with the world axis and not its own bone. Name the finger bones appropriately.

3. Create a primitive circle. Move it to the center of the hand. Choose **Modify → Freeze Transformations** and **Edit → Delete By Type → History**. Rename the circle handHandleR. If you'd like to reshape the handle for aesthetic reasons, do so by moving and scaling the circle's vertices. Press the Insert key. Move the handHandleR's pivot to the center of the wristR joint. Toggle on the Select Miscellaneous Components button on the Status line (the question mark icon in the component section). This displays the local rotation axis. Click the axis handle and rotate it so that the X axis runs in the same direction as the local rotation axis of the forearmR joint (in the top workspace view, the X axis points toward screen left and the Z axis points toward the top of the screen).

4. Parent handHandleR to the elbowR joint. Once again, choose **Modify → Freeze Transformations**. Since handHandleR is parented to elbowR, the rotation is set to 0, 0, 0 without the reorientation of the local rotation axis. (If the rotation axis does move, the lower arm bones do not run in a straight line, or their own local rotation axis is slightly off.)

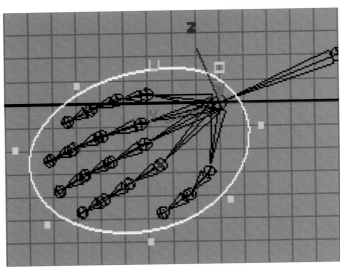

The reshaped handHandleR circle and the ideal orientation of its local rotation axis (as seen from the top workspace view)

5. Select the wristR joint and display its local rotation axis. Click the axis handle and rotate it so that matches the handHandleR axis. Choose **Window → General Editors → Connection Editor**. Select the wristR joint and click the Reload Right button in the Connection Editor. Select the handHandleR and click the Reload Left button. Click the **Rotate X** attribute in both the left and right columns. The attribute names become italicized, indicating that a connection has been made. Repeat the process for the **Rotate Y** and **Rotate Z** attributes. The rotation of the handHandleR circle now drives the rotation of the wristR joint.

6. Choose **Skeleton → IK Handle Tool**, and click the upArmR joint first and the forearmR joint second. An IK chain is drawn between the joints. When you stop short of the wrist joint, the forearm is freed up for rotation. Select the IK handle. Rename it armIKR, and choose **Modify → Freeze Transformations**.

7. Open the Hypergraph Scene Hierarchy window. Select the effector1 node, which is parented to the elbowR joint. Unhide it by choosing **Display → Show → Show Selection**. The effector is drawn as a small X in the workspace view. Press the Insert key. The pivot point for the effector becomes visible. Move the pivot so that it sits in the center of the wrist joint. The IK handle is automatically moved to the new position. Even though the IK chain ends at the forearm joint, the IK handle is now at the wrist. This allows you to keep the IK handle in a traditional position while freeing up the forearm joint for

rotation. If there was no forearm joint, and if the IK ran from the upArmR joint to the wristR joint, no independent forearm rotation would be possible.

8. Hide the effector after it is positioned. Test the IK by selecting armIKR and moving it. The hand should stay aligned with the arm. Return the IK handle to it start position by zeroing out its **Translate** attributes. If the IK handle is too small to make its manipulation easy, choose **Display → Animation → IK Handle Size** and enter a value larger than 1.0 in the size field of the IK Handle Display Scale window.

9. Choose **Window → General Editors → Connection Editor**. Select the forearmR joint and click the Reload Right button in the Connection Editor. Select the handHandleR circle and click the Reload Left button. Click the **Rotate X** attribute in both the left and right columns. The attribute names become italicized, indicating that a connection has been made. handHandleR now rotates the wristR and forearmR joints in X, which matches a human arm.

10. Create a primitive circle and position it behind the elbow at the same height as the elbow. Delete its history and freeze its transformations. Rename it elbowOrientR. Select elbowOrientR, Shift+select armIKR, and choose **Constrain → Pole Vector**. If you are building a complete character, parent elbowOrientR to the global transform handle or top of the skeleton hierarchy. To change the orientation of the elbow, simply move this circle.

The arm rig is complete. To animate the arm and hand, keys need only be set on the handHandleR, armIKR, and elbowOrientR handles. To create a similar rig for the left arm, it is recommended that you do so manually. The Mirror Joint tool will be unable to properly duplicate the custom IK and handHandleR controller.

KIRK BUCKENDORF

Kirk started his career as a professional illustrator and airbrush artist, spending time in Colorado and Arizona. Kirk recently made the transition to 3D at the Media Arts and Animation program at the Art Institute of Las Vegas, where he specialized in character rigging. He currently works as a production artist at Global Gaming Group, where he is able to combine 2D digital artwork with 3D animation for the next generation of casino games. To see more of Kirk's work, visit www.myspace.com/kirkwb.

Texturing

TEXTURING TRANSFORMS THE dull-gray denizens of the modeling world into lifelike objects. Although texturing is nothing without good lighting, good lighting is nothing without good texturing. In fact, good texturing can disguise limitations within the model itself. This is most true with displacement mapping. In any case, Maya does not limit itself to the texturing of NURBS surfaces and polygons. You can texture Particles and Paint Effects brushes with a wide range of techniques. Whichever element you choose to texture in Maya, certain basic steps will help you achieve great results. These steps include the creation of a diverse, high-resolution texture library and the ability to slap generic bitmaps together in the Hypershade.

This chapter's topics are organized into the following techniques:

- Building a Texture Library
- Fractals and Noise in Math, Nature, and Maya
- Combining Generic Bitmaps in Maya
- Coloring Particles Individually
- Texturing Paint Effects Tubes
- Industry Tip: Rendering ZBrush Displacement Maps in Maya

Building a Texture Library

An important task for successful texturing is the creation of a texture library. This holds true for a professional as well as an independent or student animator. A thoroughly stocked texture library can save you a tremendous amount of time and supply a great deal of diversity for any texturing project.

A texture library is generally stocked with three types of bitmaps: photos, scans, and hand-painted maps. With current technology, high-resolution digital cameras and flatbed scanners are relatively cheap and should be a part of any animator's arsenal. Hand-painted bitmaps, due to their labor intensiveness, represent the pinnacle of texturing. Feature, visual effects, and game studios regularly employ full-time texture painters. Regardless, the best hand-painted textures usually start with photos and scans.

As an animator, you can either create your own bitmaps, purchase them, or download them for free. You can buy texture-library CDs, such as Total Textures (www.3dtotal.com), that are stocked with hundreds of images at a reasonable price. Due to the low resolutions and a lack of useful diversity, however, such library bitmaps are generally inferior to those you might make yourself. Online texture archives, such those available at 3D Cafe (www.3dcafe.com), suffer from the same issues, although you can often find a limited number of high-quality maps for free. If you do choose to use a premade library or download bitmaps, be aware of any copyright issues. In today's litigious society, it's best to play it safe.

If you choose to photograph your own textures, it's best to avoid strong lighting situations. That is, you want to avoid heavy shadows or intense light colors that betray the time of day. In other words, a bright, noonday sun is not necessarily the best light source for photographing a chunk of rusty metal or brick wall. Rather, a bright but overcast day, where the light and shadows are diffuse, gives you the best results. Ideally, you want to use the textures in your library for a wide range of 3D lighting situations. Thus, their integral lighting should be neutral. Along those lines, avoid wide-angle lenses, such as 24mm or 28mm; they will insert a great deal of perspective distortion into the photo and make the resulting texture difficult to apply in Maya

In terms of texture resolutions, bigger is better. Although it's easy enough to scale down an image, a scaled-up image is fraught with quality-destroying artifacts. If possible, keep all your bitmaps somewhere between 512 and 2048 (2K) lines of resolution. The resolutions should be large enough to stand up to a full-screen render. If the texture is applied to a model that fills the screen, the texture quality should not break down. Thus, if you're rendering for video, a 1024 texture resolution, which is twice the resolution of the 480 lines dedicated to standard television, is a safe bet. In comparison, textures created for 35mm feature film are sometimes as large as 4096 (4K) lines of resolution. That said, if a texture is destined for a small item that will never get close to the screen, such a button, pencil, or sticker, you can reduce the resolution to twice the number of vertical lines the texture might take up. For example, the button on a character's shirt may never take up more the 10 vertical lines of the render, thus a 20×20 pixel size will suffice.

Choosing Texture Bitmaps

Some texture bitmaps are more useful than others. In fact, once you create a texture library, you may discover your own favorites that have a wide range of applications. The following are suggestions for stocking a library:

Rusty metal Rusty metal bitmaps are extremely flexible. Although their origin is obviously metallic, they are excellent for creating any material that is noisy, depredated, or dilapidated. Even if the existing colors are not perfect, rusty metal can make aesthetic bump maps. If the bitmap color is tweaked in a digital paint program, the flexibility becomes even greater.

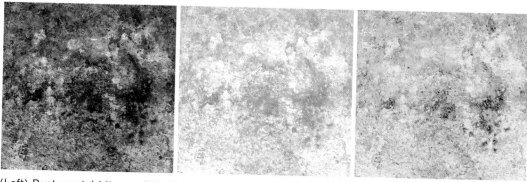

(Left) Rusty metal bitmap. (Middle) Bitmap converted to grayscale, which is ideal for bump mapping. (Right) Bitmap color adjusted in Photoshop to create a brand-new material.

Ground Various ground textures are important to any modeled set piece. This includes dirt, concrete, asphalt, and tile.

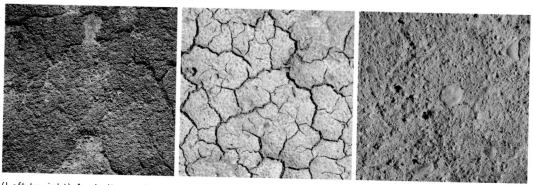

(Left to right) Asphalt, parched earth, and dirt bitmaps

Wall Wall textures go hand in hand with ground textures. Photos of plaster and painted drywall are needed for interiors. Stucco, metal siding, cinderblock, and bricks are needed for exteriors.

The use of bricks brings up the issue of tiling. Many 3D textures made available through texture library CDs and online archives feature a small section of brick that is intended to be repeated over and over. In reality, photos of brick walls at different scales provide the greatest flexibility. For example, if you need to texture the exterior of a 3D building, applying a bitmap that features a 10×10-foot section of brick wall is far more convincing than a 1×1-foot section that has been tiled repeatedly. If the model features a smaller section of brick, a bitmap that features a 5×5- or 1×1-foot section may be fine.

Three brick bitmaps with different scales

Brick is not the only benefactor of multiple scales. Any texture, whether it be metal, ground, wall, fabric, or wood, is best represented in the library by the equivalent of close-up, medium, and wide shots. That said, the two wall textures that are best suited for tiling are wallpaper and tile. Assuming that the wallpaper or tiles are in good condition, only the key pattern need be captured by the bitmap.

Wallpaper and ceramic tile bitmaps ready to tile in 3D

Fabric Although you can apply the Cloth texture in Maya in a convincing manner, it cannot duplicate specific woven or printed patterns. In addition, the Cloth texture does not address any kind of fabric wear and tear. Scans of various cloths, such a denim, silk, and lace, prove to be handy. Scans of patterned or embroidered clothing are equally useful. For example, when replicating a pair of jeans, scans of various jean parts can be combined into a texture bitmap. Thus, detail such as stitching, buttons, and frayed holes are captured easily.

A texture constructed from multiple scans of a pair of blue jeans

Wood Wood is difficult to replicate with procedural textures alone. Photos of actual wood provide the best solution. Photos featuring uncut wood panels, such a plywood or veneer, give you the most flexibility when positioning the texture on model furniture or other man-made objects. Photos featuring interlocking wood slats are ideal for floors or the walls of rustic buildings. Close-ups of various tree barks are also useful for re-creating outdoor foliage.

(Left to right) Particle board, wood siding, and tree bark bitmaps

Grayscale Grayscale textures are ideally suited for many Maya attributes, such as **Diffuse**, **Transparency**, and **Bump Mapping**. Maintaining a unique set of grayscale bitmaps gives you more flexibility when texturing. For example, a unique map that represents smudges or condensation is useful for anything made out of glass. On the other hand, it is beneficial to keep grayscale variations of color bitmaps. For example, you can adjust a grayscale version of a skin texture and map it to the **Specular Roll Off** attribute.

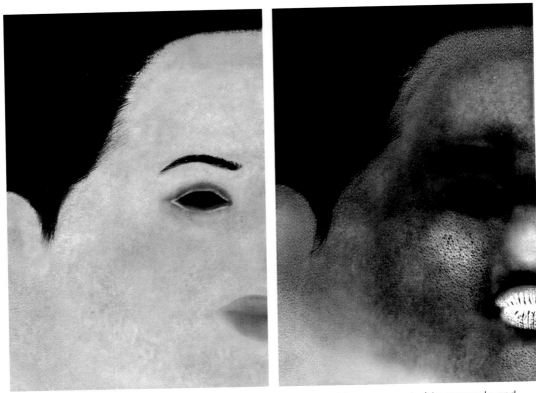

(Left) A color bitmap for a character's face. (Right) The same bitmap converted to grayscale and adapted for the **Specular Roll Off** attribute. *Original bitmap painted by Andrey Kravchenko.*

Although you can apply color bitmaps to single-channel attributes, Maya must discreetly convert their color values to scalar values. In this situation, contrast is usually lost and the resulting texture is not as ideal.

Project photos and scans Specific projects usually require specific textures. As such, photos and scans must be taken. This texture category would include printed materials (magazine covers, book pages, written notes, labels, posters, and so on) and architectural details (wall plates, molding, warning signs, and so on). Once a project has ended, it pays to keep the project-specific textures in the texture library. Although it's difficult to predict what the texture requirements of future projects will be, a large texture library can ultimately save texturing time. Even if a particular texture proves to be unusable as is, you may be able to quickly adapt it in a paint program.

Exporting Maya Shaders

A texture library need not be limited to bitmaps. You can export Maya shading networks at any point. Exporting the shading network allows you to maintain all the attribute settings of the material plus maintain connections to various maps and utilities. To export a shading network, highlight the material icon in the Hypershade window and choose **File → Export Selected Network**. Exported shading networks are saved, by themselves, in the .mb or .ma format. To import a saved shading network, choose **File → Import**.

Fractals and Noise in Math, Nature, and Maya

Mathematically, fractals are geometric objects that feature self-similar patterns at every scale. That is, when a fractal is viewed graphically, the patterns seen at every level of magnification are similar (although not strictly identical). Although fractals appear chaotic at a distance, they are each based on a simple, reiterative mathematical equation. The equation is solved over and over with each output serving as an input for the next step. The most famous fractal, the Mandlebrot set, is based on the equation $z(n + 1) = zn^2 + c$.

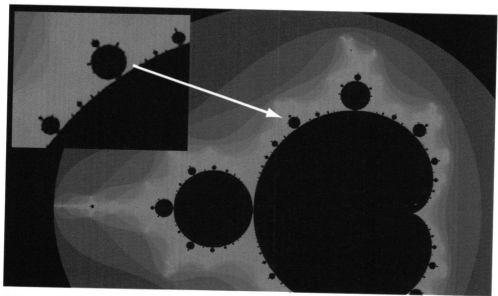

A Mandlebrot set. The circular "buds" appear on all edges at all levels of magnification.

Fractals are common in nature. Fractal patterns are found in mountain ranges, cloud formations, ice crystals, lightning bolts, seed pods, plant leaves, and seashells. For a mathematician studying fractal math, the cracks and crevices of a rock are similar to those of an entire mountain range.

Naturally occurring fractal patterns

Fractals in the natural world differ from mathematical fractals in two major ways:

- Self-similarity encompasses a limited range of scale. That is, the recursion is finite. In other words, a tree branch does not split indefinitely into smaller and smaller branches.

- The self-similarity is less exact.

In contrast, Maya provides two fractal textures: Fractal and Solid Fractal. However, these textures do not replicate any specific fractal in nature or popular fractal studied in fractal mathematics. In fact, they are based on the Perlin noise. Perlin noise was developed by Ken Perlin in the early 1980s as a means to develop procedural textures. Perlin noise is able to create patterns by averaging multiple noise functions generated from a series of random numbers. In other words, multiple noise patterns, each at a different scale or frequency, are combined for complex results.

(Left) Three Perlin noise functions, each at a different scale. (Right) The averaged result.

Since the various scales are similar in appearance (interlocking blobby tubes), Perlin noise qualifies as a unique style of fractal. The purest Perlin noise in Maya is produced by the Fractal texture with its **Level Max** attribute set to 1. The Noise texture, when its **Noise Type** attribute is set to Perlin Noise, is almost identical. In fact, the **Level Max** attribute of the Fractal texture is similar to the **Depth Max** attribute of the Noise texture. Both attributes allow for additional scales of noise to be added.

All Maya procedural textures utilize variations of classic Perlin noise. For example, the Mountain texture generates Perlin noise but skips a smoothing function, which leaves hard-edged grains. The Marble and Wood textures apply Perlin noise to separate trigonomic functions, which in turn create looping or snaking veins.

The one tool in Maya that mimics natural fractals is Paint Effects. Any of the plant or tree brushes follow simple rules to determine where branches, leaves, and flowers are produced. For example, when comparing the treeBare brush to a real tree, the way in which branches split is surprisingly similar. You can change the rules governing Paint Effects brushes by adjusting various attributes within the Tubes section of the Paint Effects Attribute Editor tab.

(Left) treeBare Paint Effects brush. (Right) Real tree.

Ultimately, it pays to think of Maya fractal textures as a means to "dirty up" or "randomize" a surface. Even the cleanest, most finely manufactured surfaces in the world are not immune to patterns. For example, plastic products often carry an extremely fine grain, which you can replicate by applying a Noise texture as a low-intensity bump map. A water glass picks up smudges, which you can replicate by applying a low-contrast Fractal texture as a transparency map. Of course, texturing is not limited to man-made items. If you'd like to convert a smooth hill into a 3D mountain range, apply a Noise texture as a displacement map. If you'd like to convert a primitive sphere into a slightly lumpy ball of clay, apply a Volume Noise texture as a bump map.

Combining Generic Bitmaps in Maya

Tight production deadlines often necessitate quick texturing jobs. One trick is to combine generic textures within Maya. The **Color Gain** and **Color Offset** attributes, common to every texture, provides an efficient means of achieving this. For example, when a bitmap featuring a clean brick wall is combined with rusty metal and asphalt bitmaps, the end result is more complex and interesting.

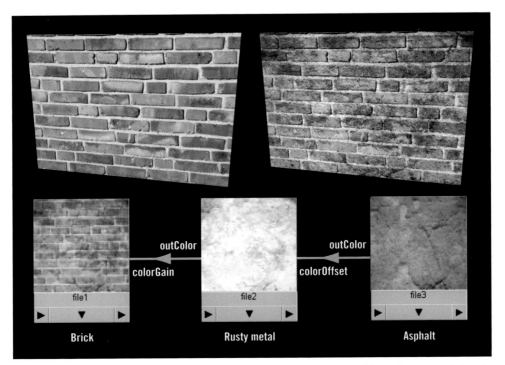

(Top left) Clean wall bitmap. (Top right) Same bitmap with the addition of rusty metal and asphalt bitmaps connected through its **Color Gain** attribute. (Bottom) The corresponding shading network.

To achieve a similar result, open the Attribute Editor tab of the file texture in which the wall bitmap is loaded. In the Color Balance section, click the Map button beside the **Color Gain** attribute. In the Create Render Node window, click the File button. Load the rusty metal bitmap into the new file node. In the new file node's Color Balance section, click the Map button beside the **Color Offset** attribute. In the Create Render Node window, click the File button. Load the asphalt bitmap into the new file node. Continue the process of nesting file textures within file textures by mapping the Color Gain or Color Offset attributes. Theoretically, no limit exists for the number of textures that are strung together in a single shading network.

Technically speaking, **Color Gain** works as a multiplier. Whatever is mapped to **Color Gain** is *multiplied* by the original map. In contrast, **Color Offset** works as an offset factor. Whatever is mapped to **Color Offset** is *added* to the original map. Hence, **Color Gain** maps tend to make the end result darker and **Color Offset** maps tend to make the end result whiter and more washed out.

Coloring Particles Individually

You can divide particle texturing into two main categories: hardware rendered and software rendered.

You can assign hardware-rendered particles, which include MuliPoint, MultiStreak, Points, Spheres, and Streak, to any material. However, only the color information is used. In addition, you must render the particles with the Hardware Render Buffer window or the Hardware renderer, or else the particles disappear. Although texturing capability of hardware-rendered particles is limited, you are free impart unique colors to individual particles. To do so, create a per-particle attribute with the following steps:

1. Create a new scene. Create a particle emitter by switching to the Dynamics menu set and choosing **Particles → Create Emitter**. Open the Hypergraph Scene Hierarchy window, select the particle1 node, and open its Attribute Editor tab. Switch to the particleShape1 tab. In the Lifespan Attributes section, switch **Lifespan Mode** to Constant. Change **Lifespan** to the number of seconds you would like the particles to live. In the Render Attributes section, switch the **Particle Render Type** attribute to the hardware-rendered particle type of your choice.

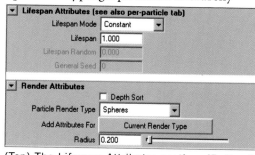

(Top) The Lifespan Attributes section. (Bottom) The Render Attributes section.

2. In the Add Dynamic Attributes section, click the Color button. The Particle Color window opens. Check the **Add Per Particle Attribute** check box and click the Add Attribute button. The window closes and the **rgbPP** attribute is added to the Per Particle (Array) Attributes section.

3. RMB click the field to the right of **rgbPP** and choose Create Ramp from the shortcut menu. A Ramp texture and an Array Mapper utility are added to the particleShape1 shading network. This is represented by the following text, which appears in the field to the right of **rgbPP**:

```
<- arrayMapper1.outColorPP
```

The Per Particle (Array) Attributes and Add Dynamic Attributes sections

4. Open the Hypershade window. Switch to the Textures tab. MMB drag the ramp1 texture icon into the work area. Click the Input And Output Connections button (the icon has two arrows surrounded by a box). The arrayMapper1 and particleShape1 nodes are revealed. The Array Mapper utility is designed to relate the age of each particle to a position on the ramp texture. A young particle receives its color from the bottom of the ramp. An old particle receives its color from the top of the ramp. At this stage, the particles simply change from red to green to blue.

5. To make the particle colors more interesting, open the ramp1's Attribute Editor tab. Insert additional color handles into the ramp field. The more color handles you create, the greater the particle diversity. Change the **Noise** attribute to 1 and the **Noise Freq** attribute to 5. The ramp is thereby scrambled.

6. In a workspace view, check on Smooth Shade All. Play the Timeline. The particles take on unique colors based on the ramp1 texture.

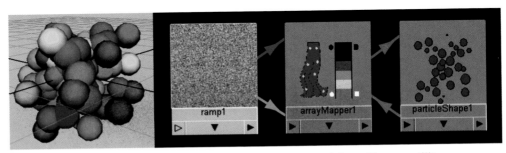

Hardware-rendered particles colored with a Ramp texture and Array Mapper utility

An example scene, which uses Sphere hardware-rendered particles, is included as hard_color.mb in the Chapter 6 scene folder on the CD. With this example, the particles move through various colors. To assign a specific color to a particle and have the particle keep that color throughout its life, you must apply an expression. To adapt the particle emitter that was created at the start of this section, continue with these additional steps:

7. In the Per Particle (Array) Attributes section, RMB click the field to the right of **rgbPP**. Highlight the <-arrayMapper1.outColorPP menu item, which reveals a secondary shortcut menu. Choose Break Connection. The connections to the arrayMapper1 node are destroyed.

8. RMB click the field to the right of **rgbPP** and choose Creation Expression from the shortcut menu. The Expression Editor opens. Type the following code into the work area and click the Create button:

```
float $r = rand(1) + .25;
float $g = rand(1) + .25;
float $b = rand(1) + .25;
vector $pColor = <<$r, $g, $b>>;
particleShape1.rgbPP = $pColor;
```

9. Play the Timeline. Each particle receives a randomly chosen **Red**, **Green**, and **Blue** channel value, which is stored by the $r, $g, and $b variables. The rand(1) function generates random values from 0 to 1. An additional 0.25 is added to each channel, thereby biasing brighter colors. The three channels are stored in the vector $pColor so that they may be passed to the **rgbPP** attribute. A sample scene is included as hard_color_2.mb in the Chapter 6 scene folder on the CD.

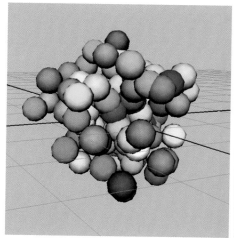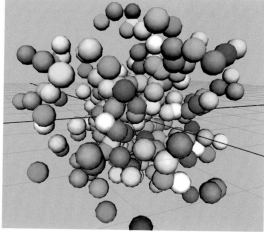

Hardware-rendered particles assigned random, life-long colors

If you're curious as to which colors are assigned to an individual particle, RMB click over the particle in a workspace view, select Particle from the marking menu, and select the particle. Choose **Window → General Editors → Component Editor** and switch to the Particles tab. **rgbPP R**, **rgbPP G**, and **rgbPP B** values are listed in their own columns.

Coloring Software-Rendered Particles

Cloud and Tube particles must be assigned to a Particle Cloud material. You can base the Cloud and Tube particles' color, transparency, and incandescence on their lifespan by mapping a Ramp texture to the **Life Color, Life Transparency**, and **Life Incandescence** attributes of the assigned Particle Cloud material. Maya automatically provides an Array Mapper utility and all the appropriate connections.

In contrast, you can assign Blobby Surface particles to Lambert, Blinn, Phong, Phong E, and Anisotropic materials. Blobby Surface particles have the advantage of supporting all the standard attributes of these materials, including specularity, transparency, and the application of color maps. However, to color Blobby Surface particles individually, you must connect a Particle Sampler utility to the particle network. To do this, follow these steps:

1. The initial steps are identical to those used for hardware-rendered particles. In fact, you can begin by following steps 1 through 4 at the start of the preceding section. The end result should be a particleShape1 node connected to arrayMapper1 and ramp1 nodes via the added **rgbPP** attribute.

2. Open the Attribute Editor tab for the particleShape1 node. Switch **Particle Render Type** to Blobby Surface. In the Hypershade, create a new Blinn material and MMB drag it into the work area. Assign the blinn1 node to the particleShape1 node. Play the Timeline. At this point, the particles remain the same color as the blinn1 node's **Color** attribute.

3. MMB drag a Particle Sampler utility (found in the Particle Utilities section of the Create Maya Nodes menu) into the work area and drop it on top of the blinn1 node. The Connect Input Of menu appears. Choose Other. The Connection Editor opens. In the left column, highlight **rgbPP**. In the right column, highlight **Color**. Close the Connection Editor.

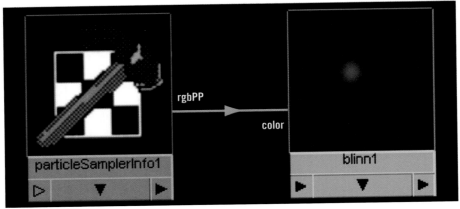

A Particle Sampler utility connected to a Blinn material. No connection line exists between the Particle Sampler and the Array Mapper, which is connected to the particle node.

4. Play the Timeline and randomly choose frames to test-render. The appropriate ramp colors appear. (The particles must be rendered; the workspace view is not accurate in this situation.)

The Particle Sampler utility serves as a go-between, retrieving information from the Array Mapper utility and passing in on to the assigned material. For the Particle Sampler utility to function, it must be connected to a material that is assigned to a particle node that is connected directly to an Array Mapper utility. Since **Particle Type** is set to Blobby Surface, the particles have a desire to stick together. As such, the colors of the particles bleed onto neighboring particles. This effect is even more extreme if the **Threshold** attribute is raised above 0. A sample scene is included as `soft_color.mb` in the Chapter 6 scene folder on the CD.

Although the Particle Sampler utility is needed to individually color software-rendered particles, you are free to adjust the ramp texture or apply expressions as described in steps 5 through 9 of the preceding section.

Texturing Paint Effects Tubes

Many Paint Effects brushes utilize Maya IFF bitmaps as textures. You can replace these with your own bitmaps for a customized result. The way in which the bitmaps wrap around the Paint Effects tubes, however, does not match standard geometry. Regardless, you can replace the texture following these steps:

1. Switch to the Rendering menu set. Choose **Paint Effects → Get Brush**. The Visor opens. Pick a brush by highlighting a brush icon. Brushes such as birchLimb (in the trees folder) or hotel (in the cityMesh folder) make obvious use of texture bitmaps. Paint a test stroke.

2. Select the resulting stroke and open its Attribute Editor tab. Switch to the Paint Effects tab to the immediate right. Expand the Shading section. In the Texturing subsection, change the **Image Name** attribute by browsing for the bitmap of your choice. Paint Effects brushes support any of the standard Maya image formats. Render a test. Your bitmap appears on the tubes generated by the stroke.

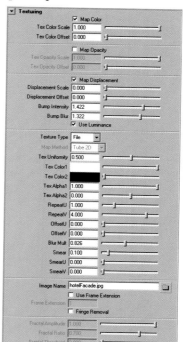

The Texturing subsection of a Paint Effects Attribute Editor tab

Controlling the Paint Effects Texture

To control the way in which your bitmap repeats across each tube and how it is rendered, you an adjust the various attributes found above **Image Name** in the Texturing subsection.

Descriptions of these attributes follow:

Texture Type Determines what type of texture is applied to the tube. Checker, U Ramp, V Ramp, and Fractal options provide built-in procedural textures. The File option allows for a bitmap to be named by the **Image Name** attribute.

Map Method Determines the method by which the chosen texture is applied to the tube. The Full View option projects the texture from the camera view. The Brush Start option also projects the texture from the camera view, but the scale of the texture is determined by the distance the stroke is from the camera. The Tube 2D option maps the texture in world space and always centers the texture on the tube so that it faces the camera. The Tube 3D option maps the texture directly onto the tube so that it wraps around the circumference. If the camera is animated and the view shifts, Tube 3D is the best option. All the **Map Method** options are grayed out and inaccessible to any of the "mesh" brushes (for example, those in the plantsMesh, objectsMesh, and flowersMesh folders). Generally, mesh brushes map the texture in a fashion similar to 3D Tube.

RepeatU, RepeatV, OffsetU, OffsetV, and Tex Uniformity **RepeatU** and **RepeatV** determine how many times the texture is repeated in the U and V directions. On a tube, U runs the length and V runs around the circumference. **OffsetU** and **OffsetV** offset the texture in the U and V directions. Keep in mind that the **RepeatU** and **RepeatV** values do not always correspond directly to the render. For example, If both **RepeatU** and **RepeatV** are set to 1, a texture may appear multiple times along the tube of a long stroke. To control this, you can adjust the **Tex Uniformity** attribute. Low **Tex Uniformity** values force the renders to correspond more closely to the actual **RepeatU** and **RepeatV** values. High **Tex Uniformity** values increase the number of times the texture is tiled. **Tex Uniformity** works in a similar fashion for both the Tube 2D and Tube 3D mapping methods.

Map Color, Tex Color Scale, and Tex Color Offset **Map Color** must be checked for the tube to carry a texture bitmap. If **Map Color** is unchecked, the tube color is derived solely from the **Color1** attribute, which is found in the Shading section.

Tex Color Scale serves as a scaling factor that multiplies the texture color by the **Color1** color. If **Map Color** is checked and **Tex Color Scale** is set to 1, the texture is tinted the **Color1** color. If **Tex Color Scale** is less than 1, the texture color and **Color1** color are averaged. If **Tex Color Scale** is set to 0, only the texture color is used and **Color1** is ignored. **Tex Color Offset** serves as an offset for the **Tex Color Scale** calculation. The higher the **Tex Color Offset** value, the more white is introduced into the color.

Tex Color1 and Tex Color2 **Tex Color1** is the first color used by the **Texture Type** attribute. **Tex Color2** is the second color. If **Texture Type** is set to File, **Tex Color1** tints the highest values in the bitmap and **Tex Color2** tints the lowest values. If **Texture Type** is set to Checker, U Ramp, V Ramp, or Fractal, **Tex Color1** and **Tex Color2** provide the colors for the resulting pattern.

Map Opacity, Tex Opacity Scale, and Tex Opacity Offset If checked, **Map Opacity** supports alpha information provided by the texture determined by **Texture Type**. If **Texture Type** is set to Checker, U Ramp, V Ramp, or Fractal, the RGB values of the texture are interpreted as alpha (by default, black becomes transparent). If **Map Opacity** is unchecked, opacity is determined by the **Transparency1** attribute, which is found in the Shading section. **Tex Opacity Scale** is a scaling factor that multiplies the texture's alpha values by the **Transparency1** value. **Tex Opacity Offset** serves as an offset for the **Tex Opacity Scale** calculation.

Tex Alpha1 and Tex Alpha2 **Tex Alpha1** defines the opacity values of pixels in the texture that possess the highest RGB values. **Tex Alpha2** defines the opacity values of pixels in the texture that possess the lowest RGB values. To reverse the transparency of a tube, set **Tex Alpha1** to 0 and **Tex Alpha2** to 1.

Map Displacement, Displacement Scale, and Displacement Offset If checked, **Map Displacement** displaces the tube geometry using the texture defined by **Texture Type**. **Displacement Scale** sets the amount of displacement relative to the tube width. Higher values create greater displacement. If the RGB values within the texture are less than 0.5, the tube is displaced inward. You can reverse this effect by using a negative **Displacement Scale** value. **Displacement Offset** determines the amount of additional displacement that is independent of the tube width. Displacement is supported only by "mesh"-style brushes.

Bump Intensity and Bump Blur If **Map Displacement** is checked, a bump mapping effect is created with the texture defined by **Texture Type**. The higher the **Bump Intensity** value, the more intense the bump mapping. **Bump Blur** softens the bump map. To see the bump map by itself, set **Displacement Scale** and **Displacement Offset** to 0. For the bump map to appear, you must also check **Per Pixel Lighting**, which is found in Mesh section. **Per Pixel Lighting** forces the tube lighting calculation to be carried out on a per-pixel basis rather than a per-vertex basis.

SmearU, SmearV, and Smear **SmearU** and **SmearV** distort the texture in the U and V directions by applying a noise defined by the **Smear** attribute. The **Smear** value determines the frequency of the distorting noise. The higher the value, the higher the noise frequency, the finer the distortion detail, and the more obscured the original texture is. If **SmearU** and **SmearV** are set to 0, no distortion occurs.

Blur Mult Defines the amount of anti-aliasing applied to the texture. A value of 1 produces fair results. Higher values create blurrier textures. A value of 0 turns the anti-aliasing off.

As a final note, **Color2** and **Transparency2** attributes, found in the Tube Shading subsection, are not available to all Paint Effects brushes. If they are available, they determine the color and opacity of the tube tips. In addition, their values are subject to calculations involving **Tex Color Scale**, **Tex Color Offset**, **Tex Opacity Scale**, and **Tex Opacity Offset**.

■ Industry Tip: Rendering ZBrush Displacement Maps in Maya

Pixologic ZBrush is fast becoming an important modeling tool in the 3D visual effects and gaming world. Since the program is fairly new, integration with Maya remains somewhat unintuitive. In particular, importing displacement maps and rendering them properly is fraught with peril. Rocky Bright, Jr., a media arts and animation instructor at the Art Institute of Las Vegas, offers the following steps for avoiding displacement headaches. Many of the individual tips in this section were originally put forward by such animators as Sunit Parekh, Scott Spencer, and others posting to the ZBrush Central forum (www.zbrushcentral.com).

The first two steps prepare the displacement map within ZBrush and Photoshop:

1. Create a displacement map within ZBrush. In short, this involves the creation of a low-resolution object, the tessellation of the object through the Divide tool, the painting of detail, and the exportation of the displacement bitmap. If you're new to ZBrush, you can find tutorials within the ZBrush help topics. Aside from standard ZBrush procedures, three special steps are recommended:

   ■ While the displaced object remains low resolution, export it out as an OBJ file through the **Tool → Export** menu. The file will be loaded into Maya in step 3.

   ■ Before the bitmap is exported, open the **Alpha** menu and note the value beside the **Alpha Depth Factor** attribute; this number is required in step 5.

   ■ Save the displacement bitmap in the TIFF file format.

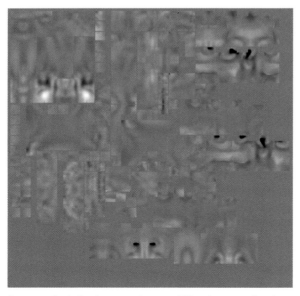

An exported displacement map. ZBrush saves the image in 16-bit grayscale.

2. Open Adobe Photoshop or a similar digital paint program. Double-check the color management profile. Ideally, you *do not* want the program to apply color management to any opened displacement bitmap. If the program does, the bitmap's grayscale may shift in value and the displacement may be thrown off. To turn off the color management in Photoshop CS2, for example, choose **Edit → Color Settings**. In the Color Settings window, set the Working Spaces **RGB** drop-down menu to sRGB IEC61966-2.1. Set the Color Management Policies **RGB** and **Gray** drop-down menus to Off.

Open the displacement TIFF. Popular paint programs, such as Photoshop CS2, correctly recognize the bitmap as a 16-bit grayscale image. Convert the bitmap to 16-bit RGB. The displacement must be converted to RGB for Maya to interpret it correctly. In CS2, choose **Image → Mode → RGB Color**.

If you did not flip the image vertically in ZBrush, do so now. If the image is not flipped, it will appear upside down on the model.

Save the image. The bitmap must be saved as 16-bit. If the bitmap is inadvertently converted to 8-bit, banding and stair-stepping will occur over the entire model.

The remaining steps occur within Maya:

3. Create a new scene. Import the low-resolution OBJ file created in ZBrush. If the object imported into Maya is faceted, switch to the Polygons menu set and choose **Normals → Soften Edge**. Delete the history by choosing **Edit → Delete By Type → History**.

4. Open the Hypershade and assign a Blinn, Phong, or Phong E material to the object. Using a material with specular quality makes the displacement detail easier to adjust. Open the material's Attribute Editor tab. Switch to the shading group node tab by clicking the Go To Output Connection button (beside the Presets button). Click the Map button beside the **Displacement Mat.** attribute. In the Create Render Node window, click the File button. Open the new file node in the Attribute Editor, click the file browse button beside **Image Name**, and load the displacement TIFF.

5 In the Color Balance section of the file node's Attribute Editor tab, change the **Alpha Gain** to the same value that was listed for **Alpha Depth Factor** in ZBrush. To determine a correct **Alpha Offset** value, use this formula:

```
Alpha Offset = (Alpha Gain / 2) * -1
```

The purpose of this formula is to remap 50 percent gray values to 0. Thus, what represents zero displacement in ZBrush equals zero displacement in Maya. By default, the **Alpha Gain** and **Alpha Offset** attributes control the intensity of all displacement maps within Maya. **Alpha Gain** is a multiplier and **Alpha Offset** is an offset factor, much like **Color Gain** and **Color Offset**.

6. With the polygon object selected, choose **Window → Rendering Editors → mental ray → Approximation Editor**. With the mental ray renderer, approximation is the process by which NURBS are converted to polygons and polygons are triangulated for displacements. (Approximation is roughly equivalent to the tessellation of NURBS undertaken by the Maya Software renderer).

The mental ray Approximation Editor

With the polygon object selected and the mental ray Approximation Editor window open, check the **Show In Hypergraph** check box. Click the Create button beside the **Subdivision Approx.** attribute. The Hypergraph window automatically opens and displays a new mentalraySubdivApprox1 node connected to a mentalrayItemsList node. Click the Edit button that appears to the immediate right of the Create button in the mental ray Approximation Editor window. The Attribute Editor tab for the mentalraySubdivApprox1 node is loaded. Change the **Approx Method** attribute to Spatial.

7. Open the Render Settings window. Switch **Render Using** to mental ray. Render a test.

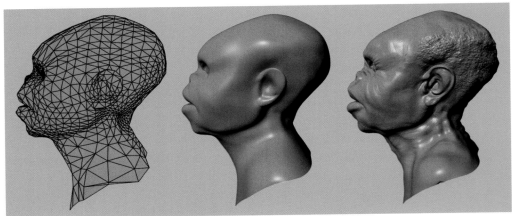

(Left to right) Triangulated low-resolution head; same head with the Soften Edge tool applied; final render of displaced head. You can download this model, along with the matching displacement map, at www.pixologic.com.

If the displacement is too subtle, increase the **Alpha Gain** value and change the **Alpha Offset** accordingly. If the displacement detail is not fine enough, you can increase the mentalraySubdivApprox1 node's **Min Subdivisions** and **Max Subdivisions** attributes.

Occasionally, imported displacement bitmaps cause triangular artifacts or unusual creases to appear on the model. Should this happen, you can apply the Smooth tool. Select the object and choose **Mesh → Smooth** with the default options. Since the polygons are subdivided, this can significantly slow the render.

If rendering artifacts persist or the model appears puffy and balloonlike, double-check the displacement TIFF to ensure that the colors have not been shifted by incorrect color profile management or bit depth. Slight variations in RGB values can lead to major changes in the displacement.

If the camera is destined for animation, open the mentalraySubdivApprox1 Attribute Editor tab and uncheck **View Dependent**. If **View Dependent** is left checked, render "pops" may occur on the displacement. Also, if the rendering is bogging down, one way to save a time is to uncheck **Ray Tracing** in the mental ray tab of the Render Settings window.

It's possible to render ZBrush displacement maps with the Maya Software renderer. However, the results are generally inferior. If you do choose this route, you can refine the displacement by increasing the **Initial Sample Rate** and **Extra Sample Rate** values (found in the Displacement Map section of the surface's Attribute Editor tab).

ROCKY BRIGHT, JR.

Rocky is a lead instructor at the Art Institute of Las Vegas, where he specializes in texturing, lighting, and visual effects classes. Before joining the institute, he worked as a modeler for Tri-Dimensional Studios in Tampa, Florida, and Trevi Manufacturing, Inc. in Las Vegas, Nevada. To learn more about Rocky's work, visit www.thingamatoon.com.

Lighting

7

LIGHTING IS WHERE the magic happens. Although an excellent model, clever rigging, strong character animation, and fine textures can make a project impressive, it's the lighting that makes the viewer believe that the 3D might actually be *real*. When surveying the wealth of literature on the subject of lighting, 3-point lighting is encountered repeatedly. Despite this, 1-point, 2-point, and naturalistic lighting remain equally valid. Although a good portion of lighting technique deals with aesthetic issues of light placement, color, and intensity, many technical issues are present, such as, for example, the creation of high-quality shadows and the control of light decay.

This chapter's topics are organized into the following techniques:

- Mastering 1-, 2-, and 3-Point Lighting
- Mastering Naturalistic Lighting
- Setting the Mood with Light Color and Position
- Setting Up Believable Lamp Light
- Forcing Decay on Directional and Ambient Lights
- Industry Tip: Unusual Lighting Techniques
- Producing Quality Depth Map Shadows

▣ Mastering 1-, 2-, and 3-point Lighting

Generally, when books cover 3D lighting, they begin with the 3-point technique. Although 3-point lighting is appropriate for many scenarios, there are an equal number of scenarios where it falls short. Naturalistic, 1-point, and 2-point lighting are therefore equally valid approaches. Whereas 1- and 2-point lighting are related, naturalistic lighting is in its own category. Hence, this section starts with 1-point lighting, while naturalistic lighting is reserved for the next section.

A single key light is used for 1-point lighting. In this situation, no appreciable fill exists. The style is appropriate for dark, moody pieces. In the world of art, examples of 1-point lighting include the paintings of Rembrandt (1606–1669) and Caravaggio (1573–1610). In the world of motion pictures, film noir and similarly stark styles typify 1-point lighting.

(Left) Rembrandt. *The Syndics of the Clothmakers' Guild*. 1662. Oil on canvas. Rijksmuseum, Amsterdam. (Right) Still from the 1950 motion picture *The Miniver Story*. Arrows indicate key direction. *Photos © 2007 Jupiterimages Corporation.*

Spot lights and directional lights generally make the best key lights in Maya. This is due to their default lack of decay and well-defined shadows. When setting the key for 1-point lighting, choose a position that allows important parts, such as the face, to be seen. In addition, choose a position that generates the most interesting shadows. Although standard 3-point lighting suggests that the key be placed approximately 45 degrees off the axis of the camera, this is by no means mandatory.

When setting the **Intensity** attribute of the key light, choose a value that appropriately exposes the subject without allowing some parts to go pure white.

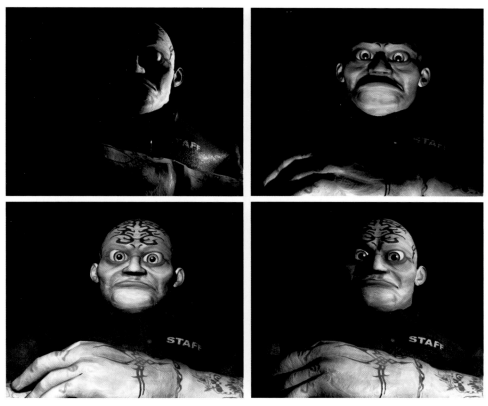

Four different key placements create significantly different results. The lower-right image uses a classic portraiture technique that places a triangular *Rembrandt patch* on the character's right cheek.

(Left to right) A key with a low **Intensity** value; a key with a proper **Intensity** value; a key with an inappropriately high **Intensity** value

Adding the Second Light

A key light and fill light are necessary for 2-point lighting. Fill light is simply the sum of all reflected light rays arriving from a particular direction. Maya ambient lights make excellent fill lights. This is due to their default combination of omnidirectional and directional light rays.

You can replicate many naturally occurring lighting scenarios with two lights. For instance, a character walking down a sidewalk receives key light from the sun and fill light in the form of light reflected up from the concrete. A second scenario involves a brightly lit interior. Key light arrives as sunlight through a window, while equally bright fill light arrives from large banks of fluorescent lights on the ceiling.

An indoor and an outdoor scene display 2-point lighting. *Photos © 2007 Jupiterimages Corporation.*

Painted portraits from the early Renaissance to modern times often display 2-point lighting. In these paintings, there is generally a strong key light, usually in the form of diffuse sunlight, and an even more diffuse fill arriving from the opposite side or from all other points in the scene.

If the source of the fill light is not defined, position the light opposite the key. If the fill light has a specific source, such as a window on a set, place the fill light in a position that mimics that source. Although standard 3-point lighting suggests that the fill light intensity should be approximately half the key, there is a great deal of flexibility. Choose an intensity that creates the most aesthetic result and/or best matches the location.

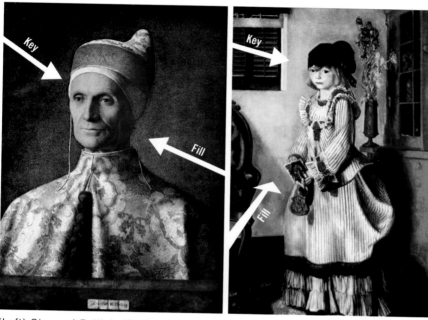

(Left) Giovanni Bellini. *The Doge Leonardo Loredan.* 1501. Oil on wood. The National Gallery, London. (Right) George Bellows. *Lady Jean.* 1924. Oil on canvas. Yale University Art Gallery, New Haven. *Photos © 2007 Jupiterimages Corporation.*

(Left) Fill light with a low intensity (referred to as a high key-to-fill ratio). (Right) Fill light with a high intensity (referred to as a low key-to-fill ratio). *Photos © 2007 Jupiterimages Corporation.*

Adding the Third Light

A rim light (also called a hair light or back light) is added to the 3-point lighting scenario. Naturally occurring rim lights are relatively rare in the world. They are most likely to occur when sunlight is arriving from behind the subject; in this case, the sun is actually the key and the remaining light is the fill.

Naturally occurring rim light provided by the sun. *Photos © 2007 Jupiterimages Corporation.*

Painting and other fine art rarely displays 3-point lighting. Historically, 3-point lighting was developed by the motion picture industry as an efficient method to light actors on a sound-stage. Rim lights, in particular, were added as a means to separate subjects from their background and a way to impart fantastic, glamorous glows to the hair of heroes and heroines.

Katharine Hepburn and James Stewart in a still from the 1940 motion picture *The Philadelphia Story*. Rim light appears on their profiles and hair. *Photo © 2007 Jupiterimages Corporation.*

Should a third light become necessary, place it behind the subject so that it barely grazes the subject's edge. You may find it necessary to raise the Intensity of the rim to a value 5 or 10 times greater than the key.

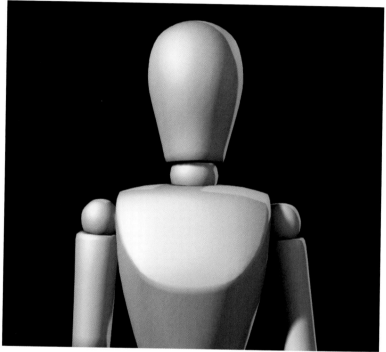

A red rim light grazes the screen right side of a character lit by 3-point lighting.

Mastering Naturalistic Lighting

Naturalistic lighting is not dependent on a particular number of lights. Instead, the technique strives to match the lighting of the real world, whatever it might be. Every naturalistic lighting setup is different. Therefore, specific steps for achieving good naturalistic lighting cannot be written in stone. Nevertheless, some general guidelines are appropriate:

- First, identify the strongest source of light and determine its origin. Is the light coming from a recognizable object, such as a lamp? Is the light actually reflected from a floor, wall, or ceiling? If you're lighting a 3D scene that doesn't actually exist, think of a location in the real world that is a relatively close match. Once you've determined what the source is, place a key light that replicates its quality. For example, sunlight is best replicated with a directional light, a flashlight is best replicated with a spot light, reflected light from a large wall is best replicated with an area light, and so on.

■ Shadows offer clues to the nature of the light source. For example, if a row of windows is shadowed and the shadows are hard-edged and all in parallel, the source is direct sunlight. If the shadows are fairly distinct but are skewed, the source is an artificial light fairly close by. If shadows are extremely soft and diffuse, the source either is very broad or consists wholly of reflected light. If you are lighting a scene that has a particular time of day or specific interior location, make sure your shadows match accordingly.

(Left) Sunlight creates parallel shadows of windows on a floor. (Middle) An artificial light creates heavily skewed shadows of a fence. (Right) A photographer's light umbrella creates a broad source of light and thus an extremely soft shadow.

■ Color can also give clues to the nature of a light source. Natural sunlight has a blue cast when seen during the day. This is due to shorter wavelengths of light being more efficiently scattered by atmospheric molecules than longer wavelengths. As such, the human eye responds to these shorter wavelengths and the brain interprets the color as blue. In contrast, sunsets and sunrises appear more reddish because longer wavelengths have survived the trip through the atmosphere while the shorter wavelengths have been scattered away. As for artificial light sources, incandescent bulbs tend to produce reddish or yellowish light. Other bulbs, such as fluorescent and tungsten, may have blue casts. On a more technical level, light color is indicated by specific color temperatures, as measured in kelvins. If you are lighting a scene that has specific light sources, such a wall sconces, skylights, or even candles, make sure your light colors are appropriate.

■ Once the key light is adjusted, continue on to the second strongest source of light. Determine its origin and its nature. Place a light to match. Continue the process, adding one light at a time. If it becomes difficult to tell what a particular Maya light is contributing to the scene, temporarily turn off all the other lights by unchecking their **Illuminates By Default** attributes.

One way to practice naturalistic lighting is to reverse-engineer photographs. That is, select a photo and try to determine what the light sources were at the time of the photography. For example, a sunlit scene makes for good exercise.

A girl is lit by direct and reflected sunlight.

Based on the shadow of the girl's chin on her neck and the slight rim on her right shoulder, it's apparent that sunlight is arriving from screen left and from behind. The light is not strong, however. This could be due to an overcast day or the fact that nearby buildings are reducing the total amount of sunlight. Shadows on the screen right wall and window also indicate that bushes or other foliage may be reducing the light. A strong fill arrives from the photographer's position. Based on the light color and diffuse quality of the shadows, it's apparent that this light is reflected sunlight. The concrete, the white wall, and the etched glass of the window make excellent reflectors. In fact, the window is contributing a small amount of light to the edge of her left cheek, which fails to become overly dark.

Setting the Mood with Light Color and Position

You can establish the mood of a lit scene by carefully choosing a light's color, position, and shadow quality. Many lighting scenarios encountered in everyday life have specific looks that we are subconsciously familiar with. Additional lighting scenarios have been stylistically established by motion pictures, television, and video games.

As an example, a single set is lit to emulate a warm sunset, a bright day, a moonlit night, and a scary hellhole.

To create a warm sunset, a directional light is used as a key. The directional is placed at a low angle to one side to replicate the sun low to the horizon. The directional's **Intensity** is set to 1.3 and its **Color** is set to a saturated orange. The directional has **Use Depth Map Shadows** checked, with the **Resolution** attribute set to 512 and the **Filter Size** attribute set to 12. This creates a diffuse shadow, appropriate for sunset light. (For more information, see the section "Producing Quality Depth Map Shadows" later in this chapter.) A single ambient light is added as a fill. The ambient's **Intensity** is set to 0.2, preventing solid blacks from appearing in the corners.

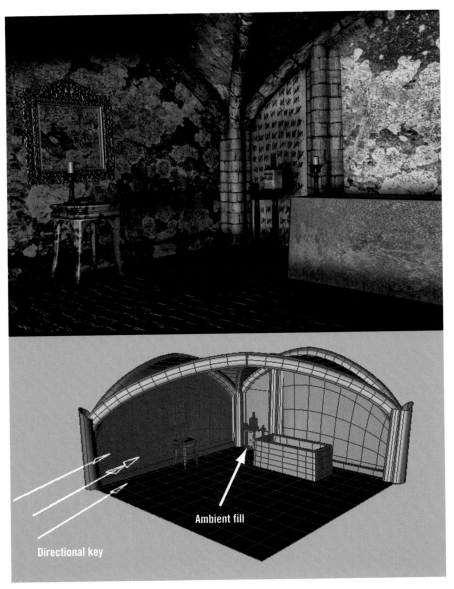

A warm sunset

To create a bright, sunlit day, a spot light is used as a key. The spot light is placed high and is pointed straight down, thus emulating a noonday sun. The **Intensity** of the spot light is set to 1.75 and its **Color** is set to an extremely pale blue. The spot light's depth map shadow is given a sharp edge by setting the **Resolution** value to 2048 and the **Filter Size** value to 1. The spot light's **Cone Angle** is set to 100. The light is also given a fog cone by activating the **Light Fog** attribute. The resulting fog is given a low **Density** value of 0.2. This subtle addition of fog emulates the hazy scattering of intense sunlight, much of which is caused by dust and particulate matter in the air. A single ambient light is placed in the room's center and serves as a fill with an **Intensity** value set to 0.5. Since the sunlight is intense, a significant amount of reflected light would normally reach the ceiling and other shadowed areas.

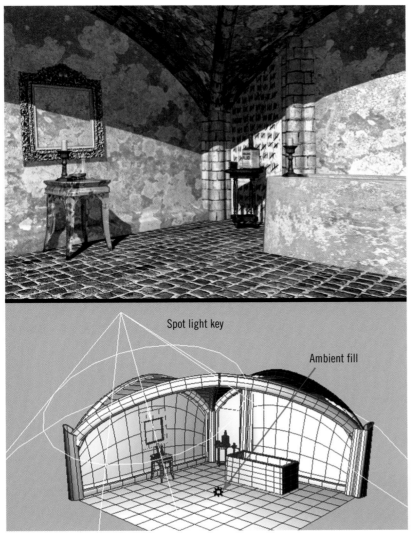

Spot light key

Ambient fill

A bright day

When switching between lighting setups, you may find that a material or texture no longer works. It may be too bright or too dark, possess too much contrast or too little, or have an inappropriate saturation or color tint. Hence, it becomes necessary to adjust the materials as the lights are adjusted. Such an adjustment should not be considered some kind of lighting cheat. Although large productions, such as animated feature films, go to great lengths to create materials and textures that work in all lighting situations, it is not always possible on smaller productions or projects. For example, generic rust, stone, and dirt bitmaps, few of which have been customized, are used as textures for the set featured in this section. The surfaces are assigned to standard Blinn materials. Hence, when switching from a sunset to daylight, the floor became too bright and green. The **Diffuse** attribute of the floor material and the **Color Gain** of the floor's texture were therefore adjusted. In addition, the walls became too bright and possessed too much contrast. The **Diffuse** attribute of the walls' material was lowered. The **Color Gain** of the wall texture was also lowered, and the **Color Offset** was raised, thus reducing the contrast.

To create a moonlit night, a movie convention is applied. When shooting a night scene, cinematographers are unable to expose the film with real moonlight regardless of the moon's fullness. Rather, the crews provide lights with blue gels. Audiences associate this artificial blue with nighttime scenes. On older films shoots, it was necessary to shoot *day for night* by placing a filter over the camera lens and shooting in sunlight. Although the resulting scenes were appropriately dark, the shadows were unnaturally black and well defined. As for the 3D scene, a directional light is made the key, its **Color** is set to a saturated blue, and it's placed high and at a moderate angle. The directional's depth map shadows are made extremely soft by setting the **Resolution** attribute to 256 and the **Filter Size** attribute to 24. Soft shadows accurately replicate the diffuse nature of moonlight. For this lighting setup, no additional lights are created.

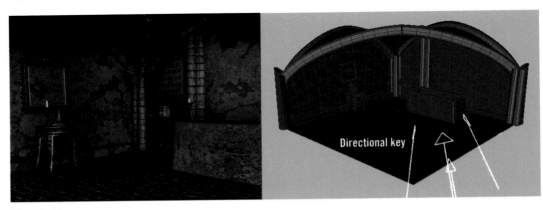

Moonlight

Creating Stylistic Lighting

Although the moonlit scene is somewhat unrealistic, it's intended to represent a real lighting scenario. You can make the lighting truly stylistic by divorcing it from any semblance of real-world lighting. For example, when lighting a scene that is intended to be spooky, scary, or disturbing, you can add lights that create unnatural shadows and utilize strange, saturated colors.

To make the example scene a scary hellhole, a spot light is used as a key. Its **Color** is set to a supersaturated red, its **Cone Angle** is set to 120, its **Intensity** is set to 20, and its **Decay Rate** is set to Linear. The decay weakens the light as it travels and allows various corners of the set to slowly go dark. The spot light is placed directly behind the table on screen left and is pointed toward to ceiling. This low-angle approach mimics a classic technique employed by horror films running all the way back to *Frankenstein* (1931). The end result is a set of strange, enlarged shadows.

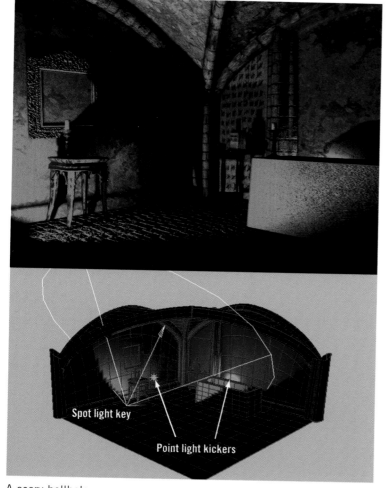

A scary hellhole

Two additional point lights are added to accent various parts of the set. One is placed behind the table opposite the spot light. A second is positioned behind the stone coffin at screen right. Both lights have a supersaturated green for **Color** and a **Decay Rate** set to Linear. The point light behind the table has an **Intensity** of 1. The point light behind the coffin has an **Intensity** value of 5; this light also has **Use Depth Map Shadows** checked and creates the shadow of the bottle at the center of the image. Although the two point lights serve as a type of fill, their intensity and limited throw make them similar to rim lights. Perhaps the term *kicker* fits them best — they kick specific areas of the render to the forefront.

In each of the lighting examples in this section, no more than three lights were used. If characters had been positioned on the set, additional lights might be required. If it was necessary to emulate candlelight emanating from the two candle models on the set, separate lights would be needed for a flame effect. If you'd like to practice lighting this scene, a simplified version is included as `light_set.mb` in the Chapter 7 scene folder on the CD.

Setting Up Believable Lamplight

Table lamps, although seemingly innocuous, can present lighting challenges. Placing a single point light in the center of the lamp rarely produces a satisfactory result. Rather, multiple lights tend to work best. In addition, creating an appropriately illuminated lamp shade often requires special manipulation of the lamp shade material.

As an example, a modern table lamp is built in 3D. Five lights are used to illuminate the table and wall. Two spot lights are tucked inside of the lamp shade, pointing down at the table and pointing up at the ceiling. **Use Depth Map Shadows** is checked for both. The shadow edges are made soft with low **Resolution** values (256 for both) and high **Filter Size** values (18 for the up-pointing and 30 for the down-pointing). With such settings, a shadow of the lamp shade's wire support is barely visible on the table. The **Receive Shadows** attribute for the lamp socket geometry is unchecked, which prevents the socket from creating an unneeded shadow on the lamp base. The socket is useful, however, since it is visible through the shade as a slightly dark spot. Each spot light has a **Decay Rate** set to Linear and an **Intensity** value of 6.

A table lamp in 3D

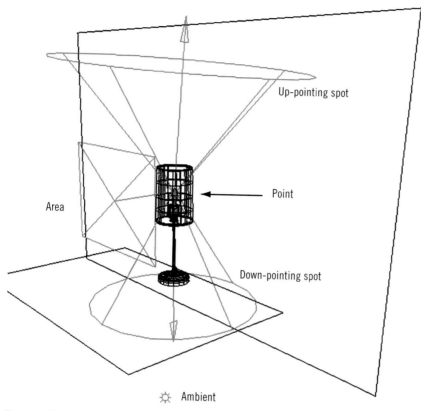

Up-pointing spot

Point

Area

Down-pointing spot

☼ Ambient

The five lights

A point light is placed where the lightbulb would normally sit. The **Light Glow** attribute is activated for the light. The corresponding Optical FX utility has **Glow Type** set to Ball, **Star Points** set to 0, **Glow Intensity** set to 0.8, **Glow Spread** set to 0.6, and **Glow Opacity** set to 0.5. The Optical FX utility thereby creates a hot spot in the center of the lamp shade. The various attributes of the utility must be balanced with the attributes of the material assigned to the lamp shade; slight changes make the glow too intense or too dull.

An area light is positioned in front of the lamp between the camera and the wall. The light brightens the wall directly behind the lamp shade. Although the **Intensity** of the point light is set to 0.2, the hot spot it creates on the wall is too small to look good by itself. The area light **Intensity** is set to 0.125. Finally, an ambient light is positioned behind the camera, thus raising the overall brightness of the scene. The ambient light Intensity is 0.2. Each of the five lights has its Color attribute set to a pale orange.

The lamp shade geometry is assigned to a Lambert material. Ambient Color is set to a dark gray. **Diffuse** is set to 0, thereby skipping the diffuse contribution of the scene's lights. **Transparency** is raised slightly above 0, allowing the socket and wire support to peek through. **Translucence** is set to an artificially high value of 5.5, encouraging the light from the spot lights and point light the pass through the surface. **Translucence Depth** is set to 5 and **Translucence Focus** is set to 0.4, spreading the translucent light out over the majority of the shade surface.

The Lambert material's **Color** attribute is provided by a custom network. A Condition utility switches between a File with a loaded cloth bitmap and solid white. The input for the Condition utility is the **Flipped Normal** attribute of a Sampler Info node. With this setup, the flipped side of the surface receives the white and the nonflipped side receives the cloth texture. Thus, the inside of the lamp shade is rendered white, as can be seen at the top of the lamp, while the outside is rendered as cloth. (In Maya, the flipped side becomes invisible when the **Double Sided** attribute of the surface is unchecked.)

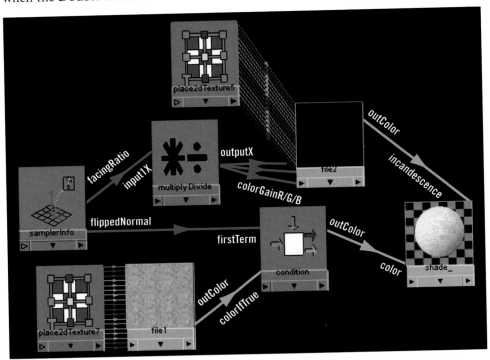

The shade material's custom shading network

The Lambert's **Incandescence** attribute is also connected to a custom network. In this case, the **Facing Ratio** attribute of the Sampler Info utility is fed into a Multiply Divide utility before it is connected to **Incandescence**. In short, this creates the greatest amount of incandescence on the faces of the surface that point toward the camera. Thus, the sides of the lamp shade are slightly darker.

As a final trick, a duplicate of the lamp shade is scaled down slightly and assigned to a Lambert material with 100 percent white **Transparency**. Although this prevents the duplicate from rendering, it allows it to be shadowed by the spot lights. If the duplicate lamp shade is removed, the original lamp shade would receive the light of the spot lights in an uneven manner.

A final version of this scene is included as lamp.mb in the Chapter 7 scene folder on the CD.

Forcing Decay on Directional and Ambient Lights

By default, directional and ambient lights do not possess decay. You can create a custom shading network, however, to control the distance a directional or ambient light can travel.

If you're familiar with custom connections in Maya, you need only replicate the following network.

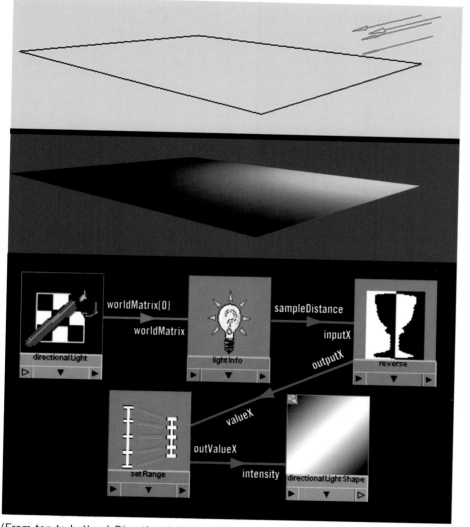

(From top to bottom) Directional light next to a plane; render with custom decay shading network; shading network in Hypershade

With this network, a Light Info utility reads the distance from the light to the shaded surface point. The distance is made negative with a Reverse utility and its range of values is rescaled with a Set Range utility. For example, the Reverse utility converts a distance of 20 into –19 and a distance of 5 into –4. In turn, the Set Range utility rescales the Reverse utility's output of –19 to 0 and –4 to 1. Thus, points far away from the light are given small values, which are ultimately fed to the light's **Intensity** attribute. Points close to the light are given higher values.

If you've never created custom connections, follow these steps:

1. Create a new scene. Create a NURBS plane. Open the Hypershade and Hypergraph Input And Output Connections windows. In the Hypergraph, select the directionalLightShape1 node and MMB drag it into the Hypershade work area. Switch to the scene view by choosing **Graph → Scene Hierarchy** from the Hypergraph menu. Select the directionalLight1 transform node and MMB drag it into the Hypershade work area.

2. Close the Hypergraph window. In the Hypershade, MMB drag a Light Info utility, a Reverse utility, and a Set Range utility into the work area. (You can find the utilities in the General Utilities section of the Create Maya Nodes menu). MMB drag the directionalLight1 node on top of the lightInfo1 node. Choose Other from the Connect Input Of menu. The Connection Editor opens. In the left column, highlight **World Matrix**. In the right column, highlight **World Matrix**. A connection is made. Close the Connection Editor.

3. MMB drag the lightInfo1 node on top of the reverse1 node and choose Other from the Connect Input Of menu. In the Connection Editor, highlight **Sample Distance** in the left column and **InputX** in the right column. Close the editor. MMB drag the setRange1 node on top of the directionalLightShape1 node and choose Other from the Connect Input Of menu. In the Connection Editor, highlight **Out ValueX** in the left column and **Intensity** in the right column. Close the editor.

4. MMB drag the reverse1 node on top of the setRange1 node and choose Other from the Connect Input Of menu. In the Connection Editor, highlight **OutputX** in the left column and **ValueX** in the right column. Close the editor. Select the setRange1 node and open its Attribute Editor tab. Change **Max X** to 5 and **Old Min X** to –5. Render a test frame. The light illuminates the plane unevenly, ultimately fading out within 5 world units. To increase the overall intensity of the light, raise the **Max X** value. To increase the distance the light travels, reduce the **Old Min X** value; that is, enter a larger negative number, such as –20.

You can create the same network for an ambient light. Simply add ambientLight and ambientLightShape nodes to the network. In such a case, the **Ambient Shade** attribute, which normally mixes omnidirectional light rays with directional ones, is overridden. The values of the setRange1 node continue to determine the distance the light is able to travel. A sample scene using a directional light is saved as `directional_decay.mb` in the Chapter 7 scene folder on the CD. An ambient light version is included as `ambient_decay.mb`.

Industry Tip: Unusual Lighting Techniques

Although professional lighters tend to follow the same basic tenets of lighting theory, they each have their favorite techniques. One example is Joshua Perez, a environment artist at Spark Unlimited. Joshua offers his own set of unusual tips:

- Three-point lighting is one lighting option. However, it can pay to experiment. For instance, place two keys on the main subject. One key is a traditional key that emulates the main light source, such as the lamp. The second key is placed on the opposite side as a type of *kicker*, which helps outline the geometry. The kicker light is given a higher **Intensity** value than a normal fill light; in fact, it sometime rivals the key.

A stylized samurai. Note the strong key on the left and strong kicker on the right, as well as the use of colored lights. *Render courtesy of Joshua Perez.*

- If the scene you are lighting is destined to be a still image, consider rendering multiple passes and combining those passes into a digital imaging program. For example, if you cannot decide what colors to tint the various lights, render out different combinations as multiple frames. Bring those frames into Photoshop and flip through the layers. You can pick and choose specific areas of each frame by erasing various parts out.

- When it comes to fill light, never leave any part of your scene pitch black. Although a single fill light often does the trick, you are not limited to the number of lights you use. In fact, it can sometimes pay to use a large number of fill lights that have a limited throw due to the **Decay Rate** set to something other than None. In this situation, point lights will do the trick.

- Don't underestimate rim lights. Adding rims is a great way to lend depth to the 3D models. Rims also help draw the viewer's attention to specific parts of the frame. (For some great examples of rim lighting, watch *Monsters Inc.*).

JOSHUA PEREZ

Joshua graduated from the Art Institute of Las Vegas in 2006. Two days after graduation, he was hired as an environment artist by Spark Unlimited in Sherman Oaks, California. Spark Unlimited is best known for developing the *Call of Duty: Finest Hour* console game. The company is currently creating a new series of games based on the Unreal engine. While in the Media Arts and Animation program, Joshua specialized in lighting and developed his own unique approach in both 3ds Max and Maya. To learn more about Joshua's work, visit www.sparkunlimited.com or www.darknessraven.com.

Producing Quality Depth Map Shadows

Depth map shadows, although easy to apply and quick to render, can be frustrating to adjust. Here are a few tips for creating clean depth map shadows:

- If you want a sharp, hard-edged shadow, choose a high **Resolution** value and a low **Filter Size** value. If you want a soft depth map shadow, choose a low **Resolution** value and a high **Filter Size** value. These attributes are found in the Depth Map Shadow Attributes section of the light's Attribute Editor tab. Depth map shadows are available to all lights but ambient. Maya can handle **Resolution** sizes as large as 3000 and continue to render quickly. If you feel the need to choose a **Resolution** size larger than 3000, it may be best to switch to raytrace shadows.

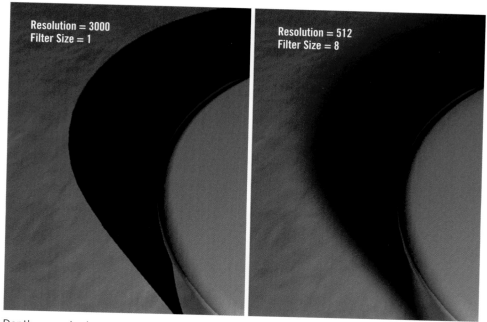

Depth map shadows

- If shadow artifacts are present, slowly raise the **Bias** attribute from 0.001 to 1. High **Bias** values may remove an artifact but are likely to erode other sections of the shadow.

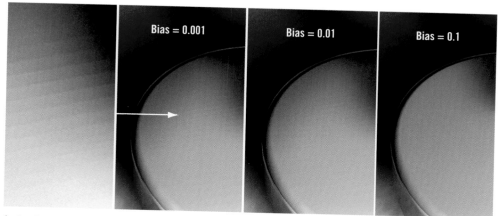

A depth map shadow artifact appears as banding across a surface. A **Filter Size** of 0.1 reduces the artifact significantly.

- If you want to emulate shadows created by the sun, choose a directional light with depth map shadows. Directional lights produce parallel light rays, whereas spot lights do not.

- By default, depth map files are destroyed after the rendered frame is complete. To force Maya to save a depth map, switch the **Disk Based Dmaps** attribute to Overwrite Existing Dmap(s). The depth maps are thereafter written to the default project directory as IFF files. You can choose your own depth map name by changing the **Shadow Map File Name** attribute.

- By default, two depth maps are created per shadow: a standard map and a MIDMAP. The standard map records all the first-surface intersections of the shadow rays. The MIDMAP records all the second-surface intersections of the shadow rays. MIDMAPs are a product of the **Use Mid Dist** attribute, which is checked by default. **Use Mid Dist** is able to average both maps and thereby reduce shading artifacts common to depth maps.

- To view a depth map written to the disk, choose **File → View Image** and browse for the depth map. The FCheck window opens. While the mouse arrow hovers over the FCheck window, press the Z key. The depth map is revealed as a grayscale image from the view of the light. Objects captured as lighter grays are close to the light. Objects captured as darker grays are farther from the light.

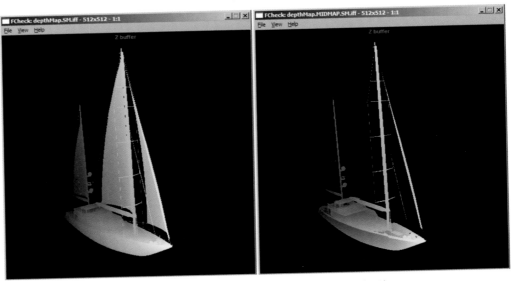

(Left) A standard depth map viewed in FCheck. (Right) A MIDMAP depth map.

Rendering

THE FINAL STEP in any 3D animation is rendering. Although rendering isn't glamorous, proper attention to the process can improve any project. In particular, you can save time and energy by splitting up renders based on objects or shading components. You can even separate shadows from the rest of the scene or temporarily assign objects to specialized materials through the Render Layer Editor. Careful attention to rendering can also prevent such problems as raytraced "black pits." Last, specialized rendering techniques, including those that involve the Maya Vector renderer and the Hardware Render Buffer window, can expand the presentation possibilities of a demo reel.

8

This chapter's topics are organized into the following techniques:

- Splitting Up Renders per Object
- Rendering Interlocking Characters in Separate Passes
- Splitting Up Renders per Shading Component
- Rendering Lone Shadows
- Rendering Multiple Passes with the Render Layer Editor
- Mastering Render Layer Editor Intricacies
- Avoiding Raytraced "Black Pits"
- Rendering a Wireframe for Your Reel
- General Rendering Tips for Your Reel

Splitting Up Renders per Object

On professional productions, finished animation is rarely rendered in a single pass. Rather, the animation is split into multiple passes. That is, various objects are rendered separately, producing multiple sets of frames. The advantages are as follows:

- Individual frames render more quickly since less geometry is involved.

- You can render static parts of the scene, such as a background set, as a single frame, saving a significant amount of render time.

- If there is a glitch that only affects one object in a render, you can render that object by itself. Other objects that rendered cleanly need not be re-rendered.

- Splitting up a render allows for greater flexibility in the composite. For instance, you can adjust the color or brightness of a character independently of the set.

- You can independently reposition and rescale objects rendered separately. For instance, during the composite, you can slide one character screen left and rescale a second character by 5 percent to improve the end composition.

Five separate render passes (outlined in green) are composited together to create a final frame (outlined in red).

A simple method for splitting renders employs layers through the Display Layer Editor, which is found at the bottom of the Channel Box.

To create a new layer, click the Create A New Layer button (which features a small yellow gear over a plane). To assign a selected object to a layer, RMB click the layer name and choose Add Selected Objects from the shortcut menu. You can hide a layer, and the objects that belong to it, by clicking off the *V* to the left of the layer name. If a layer is hidden, its objects will not appear in the Render View window or in the frames of a batch render. To remove a selected object from a layer, RMB click the layer name and choose Removed Selected Objects from the shortcut menu. You can delete a layer at any time by choosing Delete Layer from the shortcut menu.

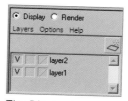

The Display Layer Editor with two layers

Although the Display Layer Editor is convenient, it does not have the power to assign specialized materials to the assigned objects. Such materials are useful when isolating shadows or dividing a render into shading components. The Render Layer Editor, however, can achieve this and is described later in this chapter.

Rendering Interlocking Characters in Separate Passes

Many times, characters in a shot interact closely — so closely that they interlock. They hug, shake hands, wrestle, kiss, dance, and so on. In this situation, the Display Layer Editor is unable to record proper screen position. While you can assign each character to a separate layer, the rendered layers will not "fit" together in the composite.

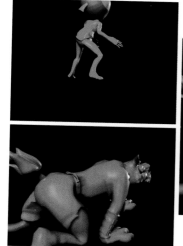

Two characters are assigned to separate layers and rendered separately. They do not "fit" in the resulting composite.

You can avoid this pitfall by temporarily assigning the characters to Use Background materials. As a simple demonstration of this process, you can follow these steps:

1. Create two primitive toruses. Rotate and position the toruses so that they interlock like links of a chain. Assign the toruses to two materials of your choice. Save the scene as torus_clean.mb.

2. Assign the left torus to a Use Background material. Render a frame through the Render View window. Save the frame as torus_right.tga by choosing **File → Save Image** from the Render View window menu.

3. Open torus_clean.mb. Assign the right torus to a Use Background material. Render a frame through the Render View window. Save the frame as torus_left.tga by choosing **File → Save Image** from the Render View window menu.

4. Open a compositing program, such as After Effects. Import torus_right.tga and torus_left.tga and drop them on top of each other in the composite. Assuming that the alpha is correctly interpreted as premultiplied, the toruses fit together perfectly.

Interlocking toruses temporarily assigned to a Use Background material fit together in the composite.

The Use Background material serves as an "alpha punch," cutting holes into objects that lie behind the object assigned to the material. In actuality, this is merely a side effect. Use Background is designed to derive its RGB and alpha color information from the **Background Color** attribute of the camera. If the **Background Color** is black, as is the default, the RGB and the alpha of the assigned object renders black. In Maya, a black alpha value indicates 100 percent transparency.

Unfortunately, no automated method exists in Maya that produces renders similar to this example. Although it may be tempting to create a Use Background material preset in the Render Layer Editor, the preset will not produce the needed results. In any case, when the technique described in this section is applied to a scene with interlocking, it is impossible to tell that the characters were rendered separately.

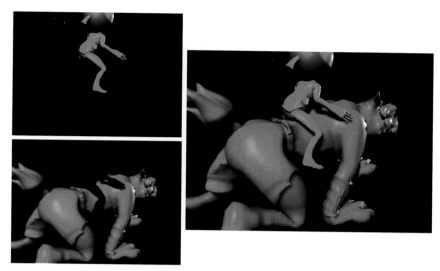

Interlocking characters temporarily assigned to a Use Background material fit together in the composite. Note that the shadows are carried through properly.

■ Splitting Up Renders per Shading Component

You can split renders per shading component, giving you a great deal of flexibility during the compositing process. For example, you can render the diffuse component of an object separate from the specular component. The term *component* refers to one element of a shading model equation. In simpler terms, you can think of a shading component as a particular visual element of a render. For instance, the specular component of a shiny surface is the specular highlight.

Material and light attributes determine the quality of a shading component. Any given component requires more than one attribute. For example, the diffuse component of a surface is determined by the **Diffuse** attribute of the assigned material and the **Intensity** attribute of the light hitting the surface. If the surface is assigned to a Blinn material, the specular component is determined by **Eccentricity**, **Specular Roll Off**, and **Specular Color** attributes, as well as the light's **Intensity** attribute.

To render out a shading component by itself, follow these steps:

1. Switch to the Render Layer Editor by checking Render radio button in the Layer Editor (the Layer Editor contains both the Display Layer Editor and Render Layer Editor). To assign an object to a new render layer, select the object and click the Create New Layer

And Assign Selected Objects button (the rightmost button with a yellow gear and blue sphere). The new layer is added to the list. The master layer, named masterLayer, is also revealed. All objects belong to the master layer by default.

2. Click the flag icon beside the new layer name. The render layer's Attribute Editor tab opens. Expand the Render Pass Options section. By default, the **Beauty** attribute is checked. When the layer is rendered, all the standard shading components are included.

The Render Layer Editor with a custom render layer and the master layer

The Render Pass Options section of a render layer's Attribute Editor tab

3. To render the diffuse component by itself, uncheck **Beauty** and check the **Diffuse** attribute in the Render Pass Options section. Render a test frame. The specular component, assuming the object is assigned to a Blinn, Phong, Phong E, or Anisotropic material, is missing.

(Left to right) Render with the **Beauty** attribute checked; render with the **Diffuse** attribute checked; render with the **Specular** attribute checked

The Render Pass Options section includes the following attributes: **Beauty**, **Color**, **Diffuse**, **Specular**, and **Shadow**. As demonstrated in step 3, **Beauty** allows the renderer to output all the standard shading components and include cast and raytrace shadows. The **Color** attribute, on the other hand, forces the renderer to ignore all shadows. The **Diffuse** attribute forces the renderer to ignore all shadows and skip the specular component. The **Specular** attribute forces the render to output only the specular component. Although **Beauty**, **Color**, and **Diffuse** attributes allow the renderer to output proper alpha channels, **Specular** forces the renderer to ignore the alpha information. In contrast, the **Shadow** attribute forces the renderer to ignore the RGB channels and is described in the next section.

Rendering Lone Shadows

Render splitting is not limited to objects and shading components; it can also be applied to shadows. The quickest method by which to achieve this is to check the **Shadow** attribute, by itself, in the Render Pass Options section of a render layer's Attribute Editor tab. In this case, the RGB is rendered black and the shadow is rendered as white in the alpha channel.

A shadow isolated in the alpha channel. *Engine modeled by Ian Wilmoth.*

When batch-rendering, set the **Image Format** attribute to Tiff or Targa so that the alpha survives. In addition, set the camera's **Background Color** attribute to black; otherwise, the premultiplication of the alpha will trap color along the edges of the shadow. Once the shadow is rendered by itself, you can composite it on top of a render that lacks a shadow, such as a static frame of a set.

(Left) Engine and ground rendered without a shadow. (Right) Same render composited with a shadow render provided by the **Shadow** attribute.

A second method of isolating a shadow involves the use of the Use Background material and the following steps:

1. Save the scene you want to render. It is important to keep a clean copy in which all the original materials remain assigned. Select the object onto which the shadow falls, such as the floor plane. Assign the object to a Use Background material.

2. Select the object that casts the shadow and assign it to a 100 percent transparent Lambert material. While the object remains selected, open its Attribute Editor tab. In the Render Stats section, uncheck **Receive Shadows**. This prevents the object from casting a shadow onto itself, which can sometimes interfere with the compositing process. If more than one object casts the shadow, you can turn off **Receive Shadows** in the Attribute Spread Sheet (select all the objects, choose **Window → General Editors → Attribute Spread Sheet**, and switch to the Render tab). Render a frame with the Render View window. Click the alpha button (a white dot in a black square). The alpha channel reveals the isolated shadow.

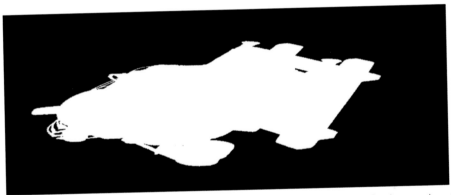

A shadow isolated in the alpha channel. This render utilizes the Use Background material. **Receive Shadows** is turned off for all the engine surfaces.

Rendering Multiple Passes with the Render Layer Editor

With the Render Layer Editor, you can temporarily assign a material to an object assigned to a layer. This assignment does not affect the materials assigned outside the layer. This is particularly useful when rendering an object with a specialized look that requires multiple render passes. As an example, a psychedelic sphere is created. Aside from an unusual color combination, the final frame features a slightly offset red. That is, the red is out of line with the other colors, similar to an offset printing mistake.

A psychedelic sphere is constructed from multiple render passes.

Before describing the step-by-step process, a look at the final Render Layer Editor and its various parts is in order.

Components of the Render Layer Editor

To create a similar setup, follow these steps:

1. Open sphere.mb from the Chapter 8 scene folder on the CD. Switch to the Render Layer Editor by checking the Render radio button in the Layer Editor (at the bottom of the Channel Box). Select the sphere, ground plane, and two lights and click the Create New Layer And Assign Selected Objects button four times. Four new layers are created. The master layer, masterLayer, is also revealed. Rename the new layers Base, Shadow, Offset-Color, and Specular. You can rename a layer by double-clicking the layer name, entering a name into the **Name** field of the Edit Layer window, and clicking the Save button.

2. Select the Base layer. The layer selection is indicated by a blue bar across the layer name. Click the controls icon to open the Render Settings window (see the illustration before step 1). Switch to the Maya Software tab. Check **Raytracing** in the Raytracing Quality section. With the mouse arrow hovering over the check box, RMB click and choose Create Layer Override from the shortcut menu. The word *Raytracing* turns orange, indicating that the attribute is overridden for this particular layer. The override is also indicated by a colored controls icon in the Render Layer Editor.

3. While the Base layer remains selected, open the Hypershade window by choosing **Window → Rendering Editors → Hypershade**. Select the Blinn material named Green and assign it to the sphere. Select the Blinn named Yellow and assign it to the ground plane. The reassignment of materials, in this case, only occurs on the selected layer. If you return to the master layer, the sphere and plane remain assigned to the default Lambert material.

4. While the Base layer remains selected, RMB click the layer name and choose Attributes from the shortcut menu. The layer's Attribute Editor tab opens. In the Render Pass Options section, uncheck **Beauty** and check **Color**. This forces the renderer to skip all the shadows. Return to the Render Layer Editor and turn off the *R* beside each layer name. Turn the *R* back on for the Base layer. Render a test frame. A green sphere on a reflective yellow ground is rendered.

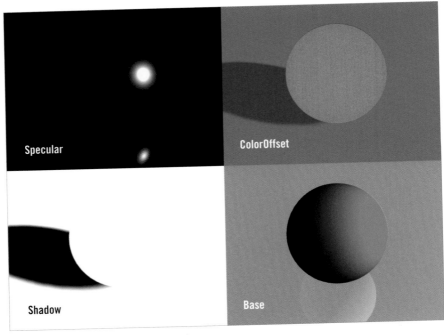

The four layers rendered separately

5. Select the Shadow layer. RMB click the layer name and choose Attributes from the short-cut menu. In the Render Pass Options section of the layer's Attribute Editor tab, uncheck **Beauty** and check **Shadow**. This forces the renderer to output only the shadows for the layer. Return to the Render Layer Editor. Turn on the *R* for the Shadow layer. Render a test frame with the Render View window. The Base layer is rendered first and displayed, the Shadow layer is rendered second and displayed, and the composite of the two layers is displayed last.

6. Select the ColorOffset layer. Select the sphere and make a duplicate with the Duplicate tool. Move the duplicate sphere to the right slightly. The duplicate sphere will create the illusion of offset color. Select the original sphere, RMB click the ColorOffset layer name in the Render Layer Editor, and choose Remove Selected Objects from the shortcut menu. This removes the original sphere from the layer. Select the duplicate sphere, RMB click the Base layer name, and choose Remove Selected Objects from the shortcut menu. This removes the duplicate sphere from the Base layer. Repeat the process with the dupli-cate sphere for the Shadow and Specular layers. The duplicate sphere should only appear in the ColorOffset layer. The original sphere should appear in the remaining layers.

7. Select the ColorOffset layer. Select the duplicate sphere, open the Hypershade, and assign the sphere to the flatRed Blinn material. Select the ground plane and assign it to the flat-Blue Blinn material. In the Render Layer Editor, turn on the *R* for the ColorOffset layer. Switch the blend mode drop-down menu from Normal to Screen. The blend mode deter-mines how a layer will be combined with the layer below it. The Screen mode takes the inverse colors of the layer and multiplies them by the lower layer. The result, with this example, is an orange sphere and a blue shadow. The flatRed and flatBlue materials pos-sess intense, saturated **Ambient Color** values, which make the colors of the ColorOffset layer flat and bright.

8. Select the Specular layer. Select the sphere, open to the Hypershade, and assign the sphere to the Blinn material named Yellow. In the Render Layer Editor, RMB click the layer name and choose Attributes from the shortcut menu. In the Render Pass Options section of the layer's Attribute Editor tab, uncheck **Beauty** and check **Specular**. This forces the renderer to output the specular component for the layer by itself. Return to the Render Layer Editor. Switch the blend mode drop-down menu to Screen. (The Normal blend mode will not work since the specular render does not produce an alpha channel.) Turn on the *R* for the Specular layer. Render a frame with the Render View window. The render is complete. A finished version is included as `offset_final.mb` in the Chapter 8 scene folder.

Mastering Render Layer Editor Intricacies

For a small window, the Render Layer Editor is quite complex. Therefore, the following additional tips are recommended for its general use:

- When a layer is selected by clicking on the layer name, only the objects assigned to the layer are visible in the workspace views. Each workspace view indicates which layer it displays by adding the layer name to the window name — for example, front(Base).

- The Render Layer Editor can employ a different renderer for each layer. To choose a different renderer, click the controls icon to bring up the Render Settings window, switch the **Render Using** attribute to the renderer of your choice, RMB click over the words *Render Using*, and choose Create Layer Override from the shortcut menu. **Render Using** turns orange to indicate a render override.

- The contents of the Render Settings window change based on the layer currently selected. The Render Settings window indicates this by adding the layer name to the window title—for example, Render Settings(Base). The settings found in the master layer Render Settings window are propagated to *all* the layers *until* a layer has a render override created. If an attribute never has an override created, it always takes its value from the master layer Render Settings window. All render overrides are indicated by orange text. When viewing the master layer Render Settings window, each renderer has a representative tab.

- The shader icon in the Render Layer Editor window becomes colored when a material preset is applied to a layer. To choose a material preset, RMB click the layer name and choose **Presets → Preset Name** from the shortcut menu. When a preset is chosen, all the objects assigned to the layer are assigned to the preset material. Although only seven material presets are provided, you can create your own from any Maya or mental ray material. To do so, RMB click the layer name and choose **Create New Material Override → Material Name**. Once the override material exists in the Hypershade, you can modify its attributes. In fact, you can convert the modified override material into your own custom preset by choosing **Presets → Save Preset** from the shortcut menu in the Render Layer Editor. You can also assign an existing material override to another layer by choosing **Assign Existing Material Override → Material Override Name** from the shortcut menu.

- You can turn any preexisting material in the Hypershade into a material override. While in the Hypershade, RMB click a material icon and choose Assign Material Override For *Layer Name* from the marking menu. The selected material becomes the material override for all the objects assigned to the currently selected layer.

- You can remove a material override at any time by selecting a layer name in the Render Layer Editor, RMB clicking, and choosing Remove Material Override from the shortcut menu. (This will not affect materials that were manually assigned to individual objects through the Hypershade.) Along those lines, you can remove render overrides for a selected layer by choosing Remove Render Setting Overrides from the shortcut menu. Once a render override is removed, the attribute values are reset to the same values that are found in the Render Settings window for the master layer.

- The flag icon becomes colored when an override is selected from the Member Overrides section of a layer's Attribute Editor tab. (You can open the tab by simply clicking the flag icon.) Member overrides include common object attributes known as *render flags* (for example: **Double Sided**, **Casts Shadows**, **Receive Shadows**, and so on). The override only affects the objects on the layer for which the override is checked. The attributes found within the Render Pass Options section do not affect the color of the flag icon.

- By default, the Render View window temporarily displays rendered layers when multiple layers are rendered at one time. You can change this behavior by choosing **Options → Render All Layers → ▢** in the Render Layer Editor. The Render All Layers Options window opens. If you check **Composite And Keep Layers**, the composited frame is displayed and a slider is added to the bottom of the Render View window. If you move the slider to the right, the layers are displayed one at a time. If you check **Keep Layers**, the topmost layer is displayed and a slider is added to view the remaining layers. Storing numerous layers in the Render View window can adversely affect the performance of Maya. Periodically, choose **File → Remove All Images From Render View** in the Render View window to reduce the memory load.

- You can force Maya to save out each layer as a layer within a Photoshop PSD file. Select the master layer, open the Render Settings window, switch **Image Format** to PSD Layered and choose appropriate **File Name Prefix**, **Start Frame**, and **End Frame** values. In the Render Layer Editor, choose **Options → Render All Layers → ▢**, check **Keep Layers**, and click the Apply And Close button. Switch to the Rendering menu set and choose **Render → Batch Render**. The PSD file renders to the default project directory. Each layer of the Render Layer Editor is given its own layer in the PSD file with the appropriate blend mode selected. In addition, a background layer that possesses the same color as the camera's **Background Color** attribute is added. Note that Photoshop converts the alpha information into transparency. A sample PSD file is included as offset_final.psd in the Chapter 8 images folder.

The five layers of a PSD file, as seen in Photoshop CS

Avoiding Raytraced "Black Pits"

When raytracing reflective and refractive surfaces with either the Maya Software or mental ray renderer, "black pits" often appear. There are several steps you can take to reduce or eliminate the pits.

First, increase the **Reflections** and **Refractions** attributes to their maximum limit. These are found in the Raytracing Quality section of the Maya Software tab or the Raytracing section of the mental ray tab within the Render Settings window. These attributes allow each light ray to reflect and refract a greater number of times before being killed off, thus increasing the chance that they will encounter nonreflective/nonrefractive surfaces. Such nonreflective/nonrefractive surfaces are able to contribute their color to the pixel color calculation and thereby prevent the use of the **Background Color** attribute. In addition, you can increase **Max Trace Depth** for mental ray, which is also found in the Raytracing section. **Max Trace Depth** determines the maximum number of times a ray can reflect or refract.

If necessary, also increase the **Refraction Limit** and **Reflection Limit** attributes, which are found in the Raytrace Options section of the material assigned to the reflective/refractive surface. Ultimately, these attributes override **Reflections** and **Refractions** on a per-material basis.

If the pits persist, surround the rendered object with a complete 3D set. Ideally, the object should be surrounded on all six sides. Any side that does not have geometry, even if it is behind the camera, will contribute the camera's black **Background Color** to the color of the reflections and refractions. If time does not permit the addition of geometry, you can change the **Background Color** to a color that matches the textures in the scene. You can find the **Background Color** attribute in the Environments section of the camera's Attribute Editor tab.

(Left) Black pits appear in a raytrace. (Right) Black pits are disguised by changing the **Background Color** to brown.

Occasionally, small black pits appear even if the object is fully surrounded by 3D geometry and the various raytrace attributes are raised to their limits. This is due to rays reflecting and refracting in such a way that they are unable to reach nonreflective/nonrefractive surfaces. This occurs most commonly with convoluted, complex models. Since the pits are small, however, changing the **Background Color** attribute from default black to another color generally works.

If a non-default **Background Color** is not satisfactory for large pits, you can employ a mental ray environment shader. The shader is able to impart a greater detail to areas suffering from the black pits. Using the glass_pits.mb sample scene included in the Chapter 8 scene folder, follow these steps:

1. Select the persp camera and open its Attribute Editor tab. Expand the mental ray section. Click the Map button beside the **Environment Shader** field. The Create Render Node window opens with the mental ray tab visible. Switch to the Textures tab. Click the Env Sphere button in the Environment Textures section.

2. The **message** of an envSphere node is connected to the **miEnvironmentShader** attribute of the camera. The envSphere is an infinite sphere from which a texture is projected. The transforms of the envSphere are controlled by a 3D Placement utility, which is automatically connected; the utility, named place3dTexture1, is represented by a placement icon formed out of two interlocking circles. The scale and translation of the placement icon does not affect the projection—however, the rotation does.

3. In the Hypershade, MMB drag a File texture into the work area and drop it on top of the envSphere node. The Connect Input Of menu appears. Choose Other. The Connection Editor opens. In the left column, highlight **Out Color**. In the right column, highlight **Image**. Close the Connection Editor.

4. Open the file node's Attribute Editor tab. Click the file button beside **Image Name** and browse for a bitmap. A sample bitmap is included as background.jpg in the Chapter 8 textures folder. Render a test frame with the mental ray renderer. The areas that were once black pick up the bitmap. Adjust the **Color Gain** and **Color Offset** values of the file node to create a more believable integration. If necessary, select different colors for the **Color Gain** and **Color Offset** attributes.

To increase the intensity of the bitmap reflection, raise the glass material's **Reflectivity**. High **Reflectivity** values allow the bitmap to be seen throughout the body of the glass. Use caution, however, or the glass will become overexposed. Ideally, you should map a bitmap to the envSphere that matches the 3D scene. For example, if the 3D replicates a dark interior of a restaurant, find a bitmap that represents the same location. A sample scene file that utilizes an envSphere is included as pit_environment.mb in the Chapter 8 scene folder.

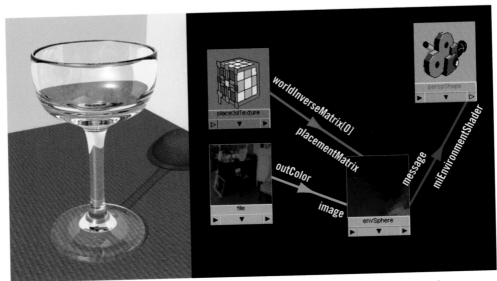

(Left) The black pits are alleviated with the use of a mental ray environment shader.
(Right) The resulting shading network.

Rendering a Wireframe for Your Reel

When constructing a demo reel—particularly one that shows off 3D modeling—it is necessary to render out wireframe views. The most efficient renderer, in this situation, is the Maya Vector renderer. To render out a wireframe, follow these steps:

1. Choose **Window → Rendering Editors → Render Settings**. Change **Render Using** to Maya Vector. Switch to the Maya Vector tab.

2. In the Edge Options section, check **Include Edges**. Switch **Edge Style** to Entire Mesh. Render a test frame. The surface, even if it's a NURBS or subdivision surface, renders as triangulated polygons. To increase the size of the rendered lines, change **Edge Weight Preset** from Hairline to a specific point size. To change the color of the lines, select a color through the **Edge Color** swatch. The color of the surface is determined by the assigned material's **Color** attribute. If a texture is mapped to the **Color** attribute, the colors are averaged into a single color.

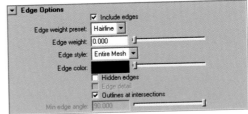

The Edge Options section of the Maya Vector tab in the Render Settings window

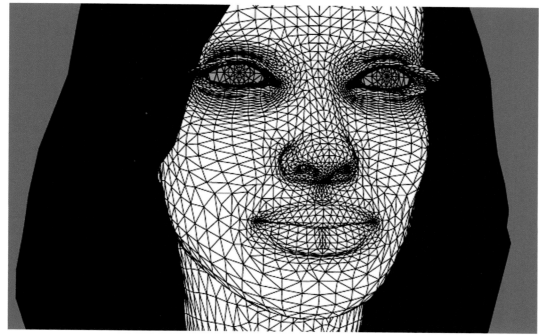

A polygon wireframe produced by the Maya Vector renderer

Rendering a Wireframe with the Hardware Render Buffer

The Maya Vector renderer can only render surfaces with triangulated faces. If you would like to keep quadrilateral faces on a polygon model, or keep a high degree of curvature on a NURBS surface, use the Hardware Render Buffer window. Follow these steps:

1. Select the view you would like to render. Choose **Window → Rendering Editors → Hardware Render Buffer**. In the Hardware Render Buffer window, choose **Render → Attributes**. The render settings for the buffer open in the Attribute Editor (the tab is named defaultHardwareRenderGlobals).

2. In the Render Modes section, change **Draw Style** to Wireframe. Render a test frame by choosing **Render → Test Render** in the Hardware Render Buffer window. The wireframe, just as it appears in a workspace view, is rendered. However, by default the background is black and the wire is blue.

To change the background, choose a different color through the **Background Color** swatch (found in the Display Options section of the defaultHardwareRenderGlobals Attribute Editor tab). To change the color of the wire, you must open the Color Settings window.

Choose **Window → Setting/Preferences → Color Settings**, switch to the Inactive tab (assuming the objects are unselected), expand the Objects section, and adjust the color sliders labeled **NURBS Surfaces**, **Polygon Surfaces**, and **Subdivision Surfaces**.

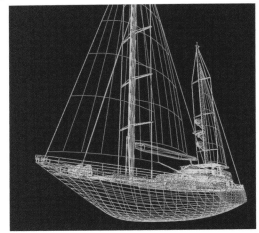

To refine the quality of the wire, check on **Multi Pass Rendering** in the Multi-Pass Rendering Options section of the defaultHardwareRenderGlobals Attribute Editor tab. You can increase the **Render Passes** setting to increase the quality further. If an increased **Render Passes** setting fails to improve the smoothness of the wire, choose a larger render size through the **Resolution** attribute (in the Image Output Files section). Keep in mind that the quality of the render is dependent on the graphics card installed on the system.

A polygon wireframe produced by the Hardware Render Buffer window. The wire colors are adjusted through the Color Settings window.

Rendering a Wireframe with a Custom Shader

An alternative solution for the render of a polygon wireframe involves a custom shading network. To create a relatively simple one, follow these steps:

1. Select the polygon object you would like to render as a wireframe. (Before you proceed, make sure that you have a clean copy of the scene saved.) Choose **Window → UV Texture Editor**. In the UV Texture Editor, choose **Polygons → Unitize**. Each polygon face is given 100 percent of the UV texture space. Thus, all the polygon faces overlap.

2. Open the Hypershade window. MMB drag a new Surface Shader material into the work area and assign it to the polygon object. Open the surfaceShader node's Attribute Editor tab. Click the Map button beside the **Out Color** attribute. Click the Ramp button in the Create Render Node window.

3. Open the new ramp node's Attribute Editor tab. Delete the middle ramp handle. Change **Type** to Box Ramp and **Interpolation** to None. Move the top ramp handle down slightly. Render a test frame. The polygon edges are rendered with a blue line.

To thicken the polygon edge lines, lower the top ramp handle. To change the edge line color, change the top handle's **Selected Color** attribute. To change the color of the faces, change the bottom handle's **Selected Color** attribute. If you'd like to give the object transparency along the edges, but not the center, follow these additional steps:

4. MMB drag a Sampler Info and a Reverse utility into the work area. You can find both utilities in the General Utilities section of the Create Maya Nodes menu. Connect the **facingRatio** of the samplerInfo node to **inputX**, **inputY**, and **inputZ** of the reverse node.

5. Connect the **output** of the reverse node to the **outTransparency** of the surfaceShader node. Render a test frame. The object is semitransparent along the edges and opaque in the center.

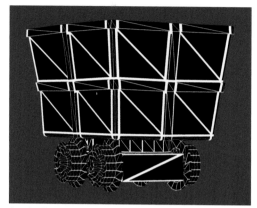

A wireframe rendered with a custom shading network. *Model created by RadishWorks.*

For more information on creating custom connections, see the previous chapter.

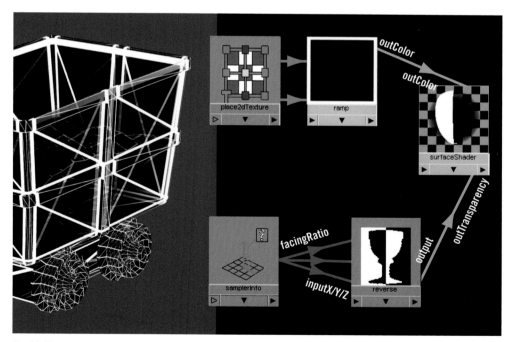

(Left) The custom wireframe with edge transparency added (Right) The shading network

General Rendering Tips for Your Reel

When preparing renders for a demo reel, you want to maintain the maximum degree of quality. Here are a few tips for achieving this goal:

- Render out as large as time permits. Even if your reel is destined for video, you are not required to render 640×480 frames. Rather, you can render any multiple of the 1.33 aspect ratio. For instance, rendering 1280×960 frames produces greater render quality. You will have to shrink the frames down to a proper video resolution; however, the process of image reduction acts as an additional layer of anti-aliasing. In other words, a 640×480 render is always inferior to a 1280×960 that has been shrunk down to 640×480.

- Never render non-square pixels out of Maya. If you plan to cut your reel as digital video, render out 720×540 square pixel images, not 720×480 non-square pixel images. By rendering out square pixels, you gain render quality. After all, the 720×540 render produces an extra 60 vertical lines of resolution. You can easily convert square pixels into non-square pixels in a compositing program. For instance, you can fit a 720×540 image to a 720×480 NTSC DV composite in After Effects by scaling the image by 89 percent in the Y. Of course, the larger the square pixel render the better. As alluded to in the previous paragraph, a 1440×1080 render is superior to a 720×540 render.

- Never render with compression. To avoid compression artifacts, render a series of Targa images, which are uncompressed by default. By comparison, default JPEG and TIFF images, when rendered from Maya, are compressed.

- If you plan to cut your reel in Final Cut Pro, consider storing each composited shot as an uncompressed QuickTime movie. That is, import the rendered Targa frames into a compositing program, export the frames as a QuickTime movie with compression set to None, then import the QuickTime into Final Cut Pro. This guarantees that the maximum quality survives until the editing process. For additional tips covering the preparation animation for video, see chapter 10.

Advanced Rendering Techniques

BASIC RENDERING TECHNIQUES produce 8-bit, Low Dynamic Range (LDR) images. Yet Maya supports 16-bit and 32-bit floating-point High Dynamic Range (HDR) images for texturing, lighting, and rendering. You can render OpenEXR and `.hdr` image formats with the mental ray renderer, thus achieving dynamic ranges that approach those found in the natural world. In addition, you can import HDR bitmaps and apply them as textures; if the textures are rendered with mental ray, the full dynamic range is preserved. Better yet, you can light a scene with Final Gather and any LDR or HDR bitmap. Other advanced tools allow you to import normal maps, create normal maps with low- and high-resolution models, and make and break shadow links between lights and surfaces.

9

This chapter's topics are organized into the following techniques:

- Rendering OpenEXR and *.hdr* Images with mental ray
- Texturing with HDR Images
- Rendering Super-White Values with mental ray
- Choosing between 16-Bit and HDR Formats
- Lighting with LDR and HDR Images
- Importing ZBrush Normal Maps
- Normal Mapping in Maya
- Linking and Unlinking Shadows

■ Rendering OpenEXR and *.hdr* Images with mental ray

When you're rendering in Maya, numerous image formats are available. Common formats, such as JPEG, TIFF, and BMP, provide 8-bit color space. That is, the red, green, and blue channels each possesses 8 bits of storage, providing a total of 24 bits and potentially providing 16,777,216 different colors. Several of the formats, on the other hand, provide HDR accuracy and are available to the mental ray renderer.

HDR stands for High Dynamic Range. An HDR image stores 32 bits per channel and utilizes a *floating point*. A floating point takes a fractional number (known as the *mantissa*) and multiplies it by a power of 10 (known as the *exponent*). For example, a floating-point number may be expressed as 9.935e+9, where e+9 is the same as $\times 10^9$. In other words, 9.935 is multiplied by 10^9, or 1,000,000,000, to produce a value of 9,935,000,000. Hence, a floating point has the advantage of storing a huge value with a limited number of digits. If the exponent uses a negative sign, such as e–9, the decimal travels in the opposite direction and produces 0.000000009935 (e–9 is the same as $\times 10^{-9)}$. Because HDR images use floating points, there is no practical limit to the number of colors, or tonal steps, they can provide.

HDR images are used to store multiple exposures captured by a digital camera within a single file. As a result, the HDR file properly exposes all areas of the photographed scene regardless of the dynamic range that is present. Dynamic range represents the minimum to maximum luminous values present. For example, a brightly lit window in an otherwise dark room might create a dynamic range of 10,000:1, where the light outside the window is 10,000 times more intense than the light reflected from a dark corner.

In contrast, standard digital photographs use an LDR, or Low Dynamic Range, image format. A single exposure is captured and stored in its own file. Many cameras write the files as 8-bit TIFFs or JPEGs. An 8-bit LDR image can display a maximum dynamic range of 255:1 (the maximum number of separate tonal steps available to an 8-bit channel is 255). The average CRT monitor fares even worse, displaying dynamic ranges as low as 100:1.

Although HDR images are routinely used in digital photography, they are also useful for 3D texturing, lighting, and rendering. In terms of Maya image formats, you have the option to output .hdr and OpenEXR files. Aside from describing High Dynamic Range images, the letters *HDR* describe a specific image format that is based on RGBE Radiance files. To differentiate between HDR as a style of image and HDR as the specific image format, I will refer to the image format by its .hdr extension.

OpenEXR is an image format developed by Industrial Light and Magic that carries the .exr extension. OpenEXR is flexible enough to offer 16-bit and 32-bit variations plus carry an arbitrary number of additional attributes, channels, and render passes (camera color balance information, depth channels, specular passes, and so on). In Maya, OpenEXR is supported by a plug-in. To activate the plug-in, choose **Window → Settings/Preferences →**

Plug-In Manager and check the Loaded check box beside `OpenEXRLoader.mll`. You can also read 32-bit floating-point TIFFs in Maya by activating the `tiffFloatReader.mll` plug-in.

To render an OpenEXR or `.hdr` image, open the Render Settings window, change **Render Using** to mental ray, and change **Image Format** to OpenEXR or HDR. To take advantage of the dynamic range, you must launch a batch render by switching to the Render menu set and choosing **Render → Batch Render**. The Render View window, by comparison, can only display an 8-bit LDR version of the render. For specific applications of OpenEXR and `.hdr` images, see the following sections.

Viewing HDR Images

You can view HDR images with a program that explicitly supports the format. Even with such a program, a simplified version must be displayed.

For example, Photoshop CS2 supports OpenEXR, `.hdr`, and 32-bit floating-point TIFF formats. When an HDR image is opened, Photoshop displays a limited portion of the dynamic range (which I'll refer to as *exposure range*). Photoshop allows you to select different exposure ranges by providing 32-bit exposure and gamma controls. To apply these controls, choose **View → 32-Bit Preview Options** and adjust the Exposure and Gamma sliders. The Exposure slider selects different exposure ranges within the image. If a Maya-rendered

OpenEXR or `.hdr` image is opened in Photoshop CS2, the Exposure slider works in the same fashion. In simple terms, the Exposure slider controls the brightness of the image. The Gamma slider, in essence, controls the contrast of the image. The Exposure and Gamma sliders are measured in stops. A *stop* is the adjustment of a camera aperture that either halves or doubles the amount of light reaching the film. For the sliders, each stop is twice as intense, or half as intense, as the stop beside it (for example, +2 is twice as intense as +1 and four times more intense than 0).

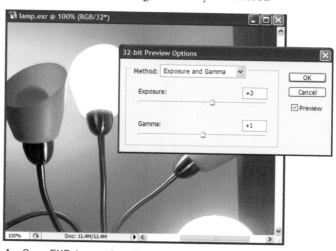

An OpenEXR image is adjusted with Photoshop's 32-Bit Preview Options window.

Once the Exposure and Gamma sliders are adjusted in Photoshop, you can save an LDR version by choosing **Image → Mode → 8 Bits/Channel**, clicking the OK button in the HDR Conversion window, and choosing **File → Save As**. A sample OpenEXR file is included as `lamp.exr` in the Chapter 9 images folder.

Several programs, such as Photomatix Pro (`www.hdrsoft.com`) and HDRShop (`www.hdrshop.com`) are specifically designed to create and manipulate HDR images. For example, when an OpenEXR or floating-point TIFF is opened in Photomatix Pro, a single exposure range is selected for display. So you can view different exposure ranges, a small HDR Viewer window is provided. Based on the contents of the viewer, the exposure range changes. The chosen range fits within a standard LDR range that can be displayed on a monitor.

Photomatix Pro with an HDR image previewed by the HDR Viewer window

To export an 8-bit LDR version of an HDR image while using Photomatix Pro, you must tone map the image. Tone mapping is the process by which the dynamic range is rescaled to fit within the standard 8-bit LDR dynamic range. In general, there are two methods by which this is achieved: global operator and local operator. With the global operator process, a pixel value is rescaled according to the global characteristics of the image; this tends to produce a more natural result. With the local operator process, the location of the pixel in the image is noted and compared to its surrounding pixels; this generally exposes all areas of the image equally. In Photomatix Pro, you can access the global operator process by choosing **HDR → Tone Mapping** and switching Method to Tone Compressor. You can access the local operator process by choosing **HDR → Tone Mapping** and switching Method to Details Enhancer.

(Left) HDR image viewed without exposure adjustment. (Middle) Same image tone mapped using global operator process. (Right) Same image tone mapped using local operator process.

HDRShop also displays a single exposure range when an HDR image is opened. To change the exposure range a stop at a time, you can use the + and – keys. To export an LDR version, you can choose **File → Save As** and select an LDR format. The exposure that is displayed is captured by the LDR. In addition, HDRShop provides an optional tone mapping plug-in. You can also tone map in Photoshop CS2 by switching Method to Equalize Histogram (global operator) or Local Adaptation (local operator) in the HDR Conversion window.

Texturing with HDR Images

Maya 8.0 supports the use of OpenEXR, .hdr, and floating-point TIFFs as texture bitmaps (assuming that OpenEXRLoader.mll and tiffFloatReader.mll plug-ins have been activated). If you load an OpenEXR or floating-point TIFF into a File texture, however, the texture swatch may appear solid white or black. You can adjust the exposure range of the swatch by expanding the High Dynamic Range Image Preview Options section of the file's Attribute Editor tab and switching the **Float To Fixed Point** attribute to Clamp, Linear, and Exponential. The Clamp option takes all the color values above the 0 to 1 range and clamps them to 1. The Linear option normalizes all colors to the 0 to 1 range (the color curves are not clamped but are rescaled to fit the LDR

range). The Exponential option allows you to choose a specific exposure range by changing the **Exposure** attribute slider. Generally, the Exponential option provides the best results.

The High Dynamic Range Image Preview Options section of a file's Attribute Editor tab

When an OpenEXR or floating-point TIFF texture is rendered with the Maya Software renderer, Maya derives the exposure of the texture from the **Float To Fixed Point** attribute. In other words, the full dynamic range of the image is not used. When an .hdr texture is rendered with the Maya Software renderer, a median exposure is arbitrarily selected.

The mental ray renderer, on the other hand, gives you the ability to render out the full dynamic range of an OpenEXR, .hdr, or floating point TIFF texture. To do so, follow these steps:

1. Open the Render Settings window and change the **Render Using** attribute to mental ray. Change the **Image Format** attribute to HDR or OpenEXR.

2. Switch to the mental ray tab. Expand the Framebuffer section. In the Primary Framebuffer subsection, change **Data Type** to RGBA(Float) 4x32 Bit. Launch a batch render by switching to the Render menu set and choosing **Render → Batch Render**.

The Primary Framebuffer subsection of the mental ray tab in the Render Settings window

To test whether the rendered .hdr or OpenEXR image possesses a high dynamic range, open it in Photomatix Pro, HDRShop, or Photoshop CS2. Photomatix Pro offers the advantage of an easy-to-read histogram (choose **HDR → HDR Histogram**), which displays the low and high tonal values and an estimation of the dynamic range.

In a sample scene, birdbath.exr is loaded into a File texture. The File texture is mapped to a Surface Shader material, which is assigned to a primitive plane placed outside a modeled window. The scene is batch-rendered in two passes with mental ray. The first pass contains only the plane. When the resulting OpenEXR image is opened in Photomatix Pro, the HDR Histogram reveals the following:

Low value = 9.02e–04 (0.000902)

High value = 211

Dynamic range = 1,964:1

Although the high value is only 211, the dynamic range far exceeds a typical LDR image. The second render pass contains only the window geometry. The two passes are composited together for the final result. The latest version of Adobe After Effects and Autodesk Combustion support HDR images. Thus, the exposure of the plane render can be adjusted during the compositing phase (for more information, see the section "Choosing Between 16-Bit and HDR Formats" later in this chapter).

(Top) OpenEXR render of plane mapped with birdbath.exr. (Middle) TGA render of window. (Bottom) The two renders composited together. The exposure of the OpenEXR render is adjusted during the compositing phase.

If the plane is rendered with the window geometry, the plane appears dark. Although a high dynamic range of birdbath.exr remains present, an adjustment to the exposure would ruin the exposure of the window, which is lit for an LDR render. In order to create an acceptable exposure for the plane and the window in one render pass, an 8-bit LDR render is necessary; the exposure range of the plane would then be set by the attributes within the High Dynamic Range Image Preview Options section of the file's Attribute Editor tab.

This sample scene is included as HDR_render.mb in the Chapter 9 scene folder on the CD. birdbath.exr is included in the Chapter 9 images folder. The two render passes, plane.exr and window.tga, are also included in the images folder.

Previewing HDR Images in the Render View Window

Although a mental ray batch render creates an .hdr or OpenEXR image with the correct dynamic range, the mental ray preview within the Render View window can only provide an LDR version. Nevertheless, you can temporarily view a different exposure range in the Render View window with the following steps:

1. In the Primary Framebuffer subsection of the mental ray tab of the Render Settings window, change **Data Type** to RGBA(Byte) 4x8 Bit. Render a test frame with the Render View window.

2. Adjust the **Gamma** attribute, also found in the Primary Framebuffer subsection, and render additional tests. Lower **Gamma** values will force the renderer to select lower exposure ranges. If the default minimum of 0.2 doesn't lower the range sufficiently, open the File texture's Attribute Editor tab and lower the **Color Gain** value.

3. When you're ready to batch-render, return **Data Type** to RGBA(Float) 4x32 Bit, **Gamma** to 1, and **Color Gain** to its prior value.

Rendering Super-White Values with mental ray

Aside from rendering HDR textures with their full dynamic range, the mental ray renderer is able to render super-white values generated by intense lights or high material attribute values. *Super-white* refers to any value in Maya that exceeds the bounds of the 0 to 1 color range. You can push the majority of attributes in Maya past 1. Even if the attribute is represented by a slider with a default maximum of 1, you can push the slider past 1 by entering a higher value into the attribute field. For example, if you enter 10 into the **Diffuse** attribute field of a Blinn material, the slider resets itself to run between 0 and 20. To avoid super-white values during a render, the Maya Software renderer clamps any color values above 1 to 1. In a similar fashion, if the mental ray renderer is set to render an LDR image, such as a JPEG or BMP, it clamps any values above 1 to 1.

If mental ray is set to render an .hdr or OpenEXR image, values above 1 are supported. For example, a primitive polygon shape is assigned to a Blinn material. The Blinn's **Specular Color** is set to 10. (You can set color swatches above 1 by double-clicking the swatch and entering a high numbers into the H, S, or V fields of the Color Chooser window.) A directional light is added with a default **Intensity** value. In the Render Settings window, **Render Using** is set to mental ray, **Image Format** is set to HDR, and **Data Type** is set to RGBA(Float) 4x32 Bit. The resulting batch render retains super-white values and an extra high dynamic range. When the image is viewed with the Photomatix Pro HDR Histogram, the following numbers are revealed:

Minimum value = 5.23e–04 (0.000523)

Maximum value = 2,688

Estimated dynamic range = 838:1

This example is included as superwhite.mb in the Chapter 9 scene folder on the CD.

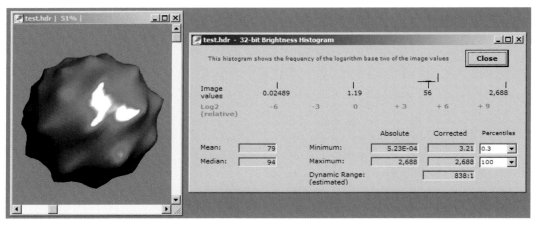

A primitive with a super-white specular highlight, as viewed in the 32-Bit Brightness Histogram window of Photomatix Pro

Maya 8.5 adds a mental ray tone-mapping shader, Mia_exposure_simple. The shader, when mapped to the **Lens Shader** attribute of a rendered camera's shape node, provides a means to select and render a specific exposure range of HDR textures and materials with super-white values. The Mia_exposure_simple shader provides five attributes with which to control the rendered range. **Gain** is equivalent to the Exposure control found with Photomatix Pro or Photoshop CS2. **Gamma** is designed to match the current gamma value of the computer's monitor. You can find the **Lens Shader** attribute in the mental ray section of a camera shape node's Attribute Editor tab.

Choosing Between 16-Bit and HDR Formats

The Maya Software renderer supports 16-bit IFF and TIFF image formats. The red, green, and blue channels each possesses 16 bits of storage, providing a total of 48 bits and potentially providing $2.81474977 \times 10^{14}$ colors. Hence, 16-bit renders are often sufficient for many projects. The disadvantage of the 16-bit bit image format is its inability to be manipulated by specialized HDR tools. For example, the exposure range of a 16-bit image cannot be adjusted in Maya, Photomatix Pro, or Photoshop CS2. In addition, while trillions of colors may sound sufficient, a 16-bit image is limited to a dynamic range of 65,535:1. Many naturally occurring events produce dynamic ranges that are greater.

To render a 16-bit TIFF, change the **Image Format** attribute to Tiff16. To render a 16-bit IFF, change the **Image Format** attribute to Maya16 IFF. mental ray can also render a 16-bit TIFF if the **Data Type** attribute is changed to RGBA(Half) 4x16 Bit.

Compositing 16-Bit and HDR Images

- Greater dynamic ranges allow for more precise integration of 3D elements with live-action background plates. While the dynamic range of an 8-bit image is 255:1, the dynamic range of a 16-bit is 65,535:1. In fact, 35mm motion picture film is often scanned and converted to 16-bit TIFFs. Since the dynamic range of motion picture film varies from 10,000:1 to 100,000:1, 16-bit scans offer a significant improvement over 8-bit scans. Nonetheless, HDR images can cover the entire dynamic range, whatever it may be. Thus, contemporary visual effects are occasionally composited at HDR resolution. Examples include shots from *Hellboy* (2004) and *The Day After Tomorrow* (2004) that were created by The Orphanage (www.theorphanage.com).

- Compositing filters operate more accurately at higher bit depths. Lower bit depths can produce banding and posterization.

- Rendering 3D elements with super-white values allows highlights to maintain greater detail. LDR images are forced to clip excessively high values. Highlights are not limited to the specular highlights but can include electrical arcs, sparks, flames, light glows, and sunbeams.

Adobe After Effects Professional 7.0, as well as Photoshop CS2, has integrated support for 16-bit and 32-bit images. In After Effects, you can change a project to 16 or 32 bits by choosing **File → Project Settings** and changing the Depth setting in the Project Settings window. Once an HDR image is imported, After Effects provides exposure and gamma controls that are identical to those in Photoshop CS2. Other compositing programs, such as Autodesk Combustion 4, provide similar 16- and 32-bit support.

■ Lighting with LDR and HDR Images

Perhaps the most common use of HDR images within Maya is image-based lighting. Image-based lighting does not require lights but can derive lighting information from the pixels of a bitmap. In Maya, the mental ray renderer with Final Gather is able to achieve this. Although it's often assumed that you must use an HDR image for image-based lighting, you can also use an LDR image with equally successful results. Since LDR images are easy to prepare and preview, I'll start with the steps necessary for an LDR render:

1. Create a simple scene. Open the Render Settings window. Change **Render Using** to mental ray. Expand the Render Options section and uncheck **Enable Default Light**. Switch to the mental ray tab. Expand the Image Based Lighting section and click the Create button. A yellow IBL projection sphere appears at 0, 0, 0. The sphere is generated by a mental ray IBL shape node, which is named mentalrayIblShape1.

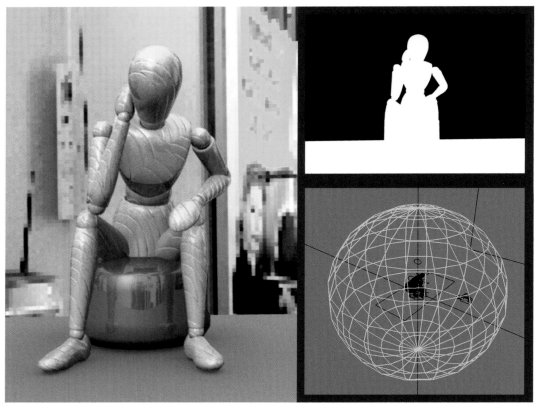

(Left) mental ray image-based lighting render using LDR bitmap. (Top right) Alpha channel of render. (Bottom right) Projection sphere created by IBL shape node. *Mannequin model created by Kristen Scallion.*

2. Open the IBL shape node's Attribute Editor tab. Load an LDR bitmap by clicking the file browse button beside the **Image Name** attribute. (The bitmap will not appear in the Hypershade.) Return to the mental ray tab in the Render Settings window and check **Final Gather** in the Final Gather section. Render a test frame.

    If the render appears too dark, raise the intensity of the bitmap by raising the **Color Gain** attribute of the IBL shape node. You can choose a super-white value by double-clicking the color swatch and entering a value greater than 1 in the V field of the Color Chooser window.
    Here are a few additional tips for the adjustment of the scene:

-   By default, the bitmap appears across the IBL projection sphere in the background of the render. Hiding the IBL projection sphere will not prevent it from rendering. Nevertheless, the alpha channel remains correct and does not contain the bitmap. The bitmap also appears in all reflections.

-   By default, the position and scale of the IBL projection sphere does not affect the render. However, this is no longer true if the **Infinite** attribute of the IBL shape node is unchecked. In both cases, the rotation of the sphere affects the render.

-   The IBL Shape node will not produce hard shadows. If hard shadows are needed, you can add standard Maya lights to the scene.

-   You can find the mentalrayIblShape1 node in the Lights tab of the Hypershade window.

    A sample scene is included as IBL_LDR.mb in the Chapter 9 scene folder. An LDR image of an office environment is included as office.bmp in the Chapter 9 images folder.
    If you'd like to replace the LDR image with an HDR image, follow these additional steps:

3. Load an HDR image by clicking the file browse button beside the **Image Name** attribute in the IBL shape node's Attribute Editor tab. Change the **Mapping** attribute to Spherical or Angular. HDR images designed for 3D lighting use various mapping techniques, which are described at the end of this section. If the HDR map is a panoramic or otherwise appears like a normal photograph, leave **Mapping** set to Spherical.

4. Render a test image. If the scene is too dark, adjust the **Color Gain** of the IBL shape node. If the Blinn material remains reflective and a portion of the reflection blows out to white, the renderer is clipping values above 1. If you'd like to maintain the entire dynamic range of the HDR image, batch-render an OpenEXR or .hdr image following the guidelines in the section "Rendering Super-White Values with mental ray." A sample scene is included as IBL_HDR.mb in the Chapter 9 scene folder. An HDR image of an office environment is included as office.hdr in the Chapter 9 images folder.

HDR images designed for 3D lighting are typically prepared with one of the following mapping techniques: angular (light-probe), latitude/longitude (spherical), horizontal cubic cross, and vertical cubic cross. `office.hdr` is a latitude/longitude (spherical) style HDR image. You can find other HDR images and additional HDR information at `www.debevec.org`. Paul Debevec is the pioneering developer of High Dynamic Range imaging.

Importing ZBrush Normal Maps

A normal map applies the surface normal values of a high-resolution polygon surface to a low-resolution variation of the same surface; in doing so, the low-resolution surface picks up the surface detail of the high-resolution surface. A bump map, although related, perturbs the normals of a surface so that the surface appears rough or bumpy. A bump map is not dependent on higher-resolution surfaces and can be generated from any bitmap. Neither normal maps nor bump maps are able to displace the edge of a surface. (A normal is a vector that is perpendicular to a surface face that helps determine how dark or light the face should render.)

Normal maps have two advantages over bump maps:

■ Bump maps store intensity values that represent the relative height of a pixel from the view of the camera. Normal maps store the direction of high-resolution surface normals relative to low-resolution surface normals. Thus, while a bump mapped surface renders a pixel as if it's displaced along a line drawn from the current surface normal, a normal mapped surface renders a pixel displaced in any number of different directions that are not dependent on the current surface normal. Ultimately, this allows normal maps to be more accurate and potentially better when rendering high peaks, deep valleys, and sharp corners.

■ Normal maps are not dependent on specific world units and thereby travel more easily between different 3D programs.

You can import normal maps from Pixologic ZBrush into Maya with a few specialized steps:

1. Export an 8-bit BMP, TIFF, or PSD normal map from ZBrush. The ZMapper plug-in, supplied by Pixologic, streamlines the process. The basic steps require that you set the model to its lowest possible subdivision setting, start the ZMapper plug-in, click the Tangent Space N.Map button, switch to the Normal & Cavity Map tab, and click the Create Normal Map button. Once the normal map is created, you can export it from the Texture palette by choosing the Export button. To create the normal map, ZMapper compares the low-resolution version of a model to the high-resolution, subdivided version through the normal mapping process. ZBrush also provides the option to convert a bump map to a normal map. For more information, visit `www.zbrush.info`.

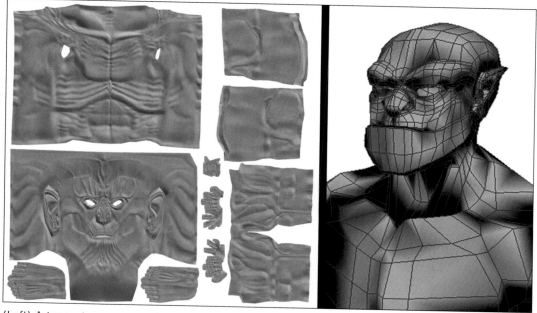

(Left) A tangent-space normal map exported from ZBrush. (Right) A matching low-resolution polygon model imported into Maya. *Normal map and model courtesy of Justin Patrick.*

2. Export a low-resolution version of the model to which the normal map belongs. ZBrush gives you the option to save an OBJ file by choosing Export from the Tool palette. An OBJ file stores UV texture space information, which is needed by the normal map.

3. In Maya, create a new scene. Import the low-resolution OBJ. If the model is faceted, switch to the Polygons menu set and choose **Normals → Soften Edge**. At this point, it is not necessary to increase the polygon resolution.

4. Open the Hypershade window. Create a new Blinn material and assign it to the model. Open the Blinn's Attribute Editor tab. Click the map button beside the **Bump Mapping** attribute. Click the File button in the Create Render Node window. A new bump2d1 node is loaded into the Attribute Editor. Change **Use As** to Tangent Space Normals.

5. Switch to the file1 node Attribute Editor tab. Load the normal map by clicking the file browse button beside the **Image Name** attribute. Render a test. The normal map bumps the surface. If the normal map appears upside down, open the place2dTexture1 node in the Attribute Editor and change **RepeatUV** to 1, –1. Render another test. If the normal map appears to be inverted (for instance, pushing out instead of in), change the **Bump Depth** attribute of the bump2d1 node to a negative number. If the normal map appears too strong, choose the **Bump Depth** value closer to 0.

The Maya Software renderer produces a fairly strong bumping effect with a normal map. The mental ray renderer, in comparison, smooths out the bump effect, making it appear less harsh.

(Left) Normal map rendered with Maya Software. (Right) Normal Map rendered with mental ray.

If you'd like to smooth out the low-resolution geometry and improve the overall quality of the normal map, you can choose one of two approaches:

- Select the model and choose **Mesh → Smooth**. This adds additional divisions to the polygon mesh. The quality of the render improves with both the Maya Software and mental ray renderers.

- Select the model and choose **Window → Rendering Editors → mental ray → Approximation Editor**. In the Approximation Editor window, click the Create button beside the **Subdivision Approx.** attribute. A mentalraySubdivApprox1 node is created and loaded into the Attribute Editor. Change **Approx Method** to Spatial. In the Render Settings window, switch **Render Using** to mental ray. Render a test. To increase the quality, gradually raise the **Min Subdivisions** and **Max Subdivisions** attributes, found in the mentalraySubdivApprox1 Attribute Editor tab. This process is similar to the one required for ZBrush displacement maps (see Chapter 6).

Some animators prefer to create the low-resolution model in Maya. This allows them to prepare the UV texture space in Maya. The low-resolution model is then imported into ZBrush, subdivided, and detailed. A normal map is then exported from ZBrush without the need to export the geometry.

Normal Mapping in Maya

Normal mapping refers to the preservation of high-resolution surface information in the form of a normal map. There are two ways to undertake normal mapping in Maya: apply the Normal Map preset in the Render Layer Editor or use the Transfer Maps window.

To apply the Normal Map preset, follow these steps:

1. Create a new scene. Build a model that can be successfully viewed in the front workspace view. It's best to create a model that has limited depth. For example, a brick wall, carved stone, or trelliswork is well suited for this technique. Interactively position the front view camera so that the model fills the view. If there are gaps in the model, such as the holes in the trelliswork, add a primitive plane behind the model. Empty space, when rendered as a normal map, will cause problems with the resulting bump. You can create the model with NURBS, polygons, or subdivision surfaces.

2. Switch to the Render Layer Editor by checking the Render radio button in the Layer Editor (see Chapter 8 for more information). Select all the surfaces that make up the model and click the Create New Layer And Assign Selected Objects button. A new layer, named layer1, is created. The master layer is also revealed.

3. RMB click the layer1 name and choose **Presets → Normal Map** from the shortcut menu. The preset creates a material override in which a Surface Shader material is assigned to all the surfaces included in layer1. A mental ray Mib_amb_occlusion shader is mapped to the **Out Color** of the Surface Shader.

4. Render the front workspace view in the Render View window. The view is converted to a tangent-space normal map. The Normal Map preset automatically creates a Render Settings override that uses mental ray as a renderer. You can open the appropriate Render Settings window by clicking the controls icon beside the layer name (it features a tiny motion picture clapboard). Once you're satisfied with the render, save the image by choosing **File → Save** from the Render View menu.

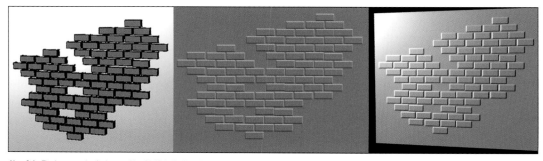

(Left) Polygon brick wall. (Middle) Wall rendered with Normal Map preset. (Right) Same render applied to a plane as a tangent-space bump map and re-rendered.

5. To test the normal map, click off the *R* beside the layer1 name. Switch back to the master layer by clicking on the masterLayer name. Click on the *R* beside masterLayer. Create a primitive plane. Assign the plane to a new Blinn material. Open the Blinn's Attribute Editor tab. Click the map button beside the **Bump Mapping** attribute. A new bump2d1 node is created and opened in the Attribute Editor. Change the **Use As** attribute to Tangent Space Normals. Switch to the file node's Attribute Editor tab. Load the saved normal map render by clicking the file browse button beside **Image Name**. Render a new test in the Render View window. The plane is given a bump effect by the normal map bump. A sample scene is included as wall_normal.mb in the Chapter 9 scene folder on the CD. A rendered normal map is saved as wallNormal.tga in the Chapter 9 textures folder.

The mental ray renderer produces superior results when rendering a normal map bump created in this fashion. The Maya Software renderer, in contrast, produces a noisy surface on each brick and is unable to produce as great a depth. If banding appears across the resulting bump with either renderer, you can improve the quality produced by the Mib_amb_occlusion shader. To do so, open the shader's Attribute Editor tab, raise the **Samples** value, and re-render layer1. Mib_amb_occlusion is designed as an inexpensive means to replicate global illumination. The Normal Map preset adds custom settings to the shader to capture tangent space normal information.

Normal Mapping with the Transfer Maps Window

The second method of normal mapping involves the use of the Transfer Maps window and the comparison of low- and high-resolution variations of the same polygon model. (In Maya 7.0, the Transfer Maps window is named the Surface Sampler window.) To apply this technique, follow these steps:

1. Create a new scene. Build low- and high-resolution variations of a single-surface polygon model. For instance, you can apply the Smooth tool to a low-resolution surface to create a high-resolution surface. If you are box modeling, an early version of the surface can serve as a low-resolution variation while the finished version can serve as the high-resolution variation.

2. Transform the low- and high-resolution surfaces to 0, 0, 0. It does not matter if they overlap. Select the low-resolution surface, switch to the Rendering menu set, and choose **Lighting/Shading → Transfer Maps**. The low-resolution surface shape node is listed automatically in the Target Meshes section of the Transfer Maps window. Click the Normal button (represented by the dimpled ball). Choose a destination for the normal map by clicking the file browse button beside the **Normal Map** attribute. Choose a file format. Normal maps can be written as any of the standard Maya formats. Choose **Map Width** and **Map Height** values in the Maya Common Output section. Click the Bake And Close button at the bottom of the window.

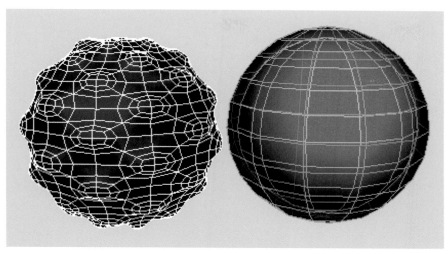

High- and low-resolution model with the search envelope rendered in red

By default, the high- and low-resolution surface must be located at the same point in world space. If the high-resolution surface is moved away from the low-resolution surface, the Transfer Maps tool does not consider it for the normal map. You can override this behavior by changing the **Transfer In** attribute, found in the Maya Common Output section, to Object Space; in this situation, each of the surfaces must have its transformations zeroed out with the Freeze Transformations tool.

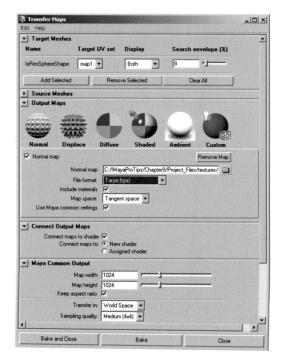

The Transfer Maps window with the low-resolution sphere listed in the Target Meshes section

3. When the Bake And Close button is clicked, the Transfer Maps window creates a new material, assigns it to the low-resolution surface, and loads the new normal map into a new bump2d node. Move the low-resolution surface away from the high-resolution surface. Render a test with mental ray. The low-resolution surface is bumped out. Although normal maps cannot displace the edge of an object, they can accurately duplicate bumpiness on the rest of the surface. The scene illustrated in this section is included as `transfer_normal.mb` in the Chapter 9 scene folder on the CD.

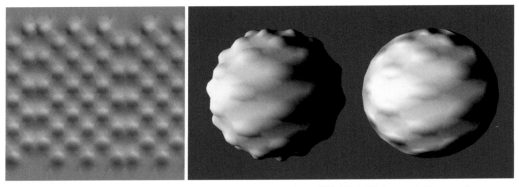

(Left) Normal map created with the Transfer Maps window. (Middle) High-resolution surface. (Right) Low-resolution surface with normal map bump.

You can create normal maps for multiple surfaces at a single time. To achieve this, you can add additional surfaces to the Target Meshes section of the Transfer Maps window by clicking the Add Selected button. By default, any surface that is not added to the Target Meshes section becomes a potential source for the normal mapping process. Each surface receives its own normal map.

To improve the quality of the normal maps, you can adjust the following attributes in the Transfer Maps window:

Display Controls whether the target surface and/or search envelope are displayed in the workspace view. The search envelope is an editable polygon "cage" that surrounds the target geometry. The envelope defines the volume in which the mapping process will search for source surfaces. When Smooth Shade All is checked in a workspace view, the search envelope appears transparent red. (The envelope is automatically assigned to a Lambert material.) You can transform the search envelope or its vertices. If a portion of a source surface is not enclosed by the search envelope, the envelope should be expanded or adjusted. The envelope is a polygon shape node that is parented to the target surface when **Display** is switched to Envelope. Initially, the search envelope is the same exact size as the target surface.

Search Envelope Increases the size of the search envelope. The value is a percentage of the search envelope's current size. If need be, you can leave this value at zero and manually scale the search envelope. **Display** and **Search Envelope** are located in the Target Meshes section.

Sampling Quality Sets the number of samples taken for each pixel of the normal map. This attribute serves as a supersampler. The higher the **Sampling Quality** value, the more accurate the resulting normal map.

Filter Type and Filter Size Sets the type of filter applied to the map. Gaussian creates slightly soft pixels. Triangular creates soft pixels. Box creates very soft pixels. The **Filter Size** attribute controls the strength of the filter. Higher values create blurry maps. **Sampling Quality**, **Filter Type**, and **Filter Size** are found in the Maya Common Output section.

Linking and Unlinking Shadows

With Maya 8.0, you can make or break shadow links between lights and surfaces. If a shadow link is broken, the surface no longer casts a shadow for that light. For a complex scene, the ability to pick and choose which lights cast shadows for which objects can save render time and improve the final look of the lighting.

By default, all objects cast shadows for lights that strike them. To break a shadow link for a surface when rendering with Maya Software, follow these steps:

1. Open the Render Settings window, switch to the Maya Software tab, and expand the Render Options section. In the Lights And Shadows subsection, change **Shadow Linking** to Shadows Obey Shadow Linking.

2. In a workspace view, select the surface and shadow-casting light. Switch to the Rendering menu set and choose **Lighting/Shading → Break Shadow Links**. Render a test frame. The selected surface no longer casts a shadow for the selected light. To restore a shadow link, select the surface and the shadow-casting light and choose **Lighting/Shading → Make Shadow Links**.

Breaking a shadow link does not prevent a surface from receiving a shadow from another object. If **Shadow Linking** is set to Shadows Obey Light Linking, then the surface will *not* cast a shadow *only* if it is unlinked from the light in the Relationship Editor (choose **Window → Relationship Editors → Light Linking → Light-Centric**). You can prevent a surface from casting shadows, regardless of its shadow or light linking settings, by unchecking **Casts Shadows** in the surface's Attribute Editor tab.

Demo Reels and Project Work Flow

10

ANIMATION DEMO REELS are an inescapable part of every student, independent, and professional animator's life. Creating high-quality footage involves careful planning and an attention to project management issues. This holds true for technical exercises as well as short animated films. Once you've completed your demo reel or short film, various distribution methods become available. Not only can you choose to transfer your work to video, but you have the option to burn it to DVD, post it on the Internet, or prepare it for the film festival circuit. Each of these formats requires different technical and logistical steps.

This chapter's topics are organized into the following techniques:

- Adding to Your Demo Reel
- Calibrating Your Monitor
- Creating 3D on Multiple Machines
- Estimating Project Requirements
- Industry Tip: Animation Project Management
- Prepping Animation for Video
- Prepping Animation for 35mm Film
- Finding an Audience for a 3D Short Film

Adding to Your Demo Reel

As an animator, your reel is never truly complete and must be updated periodically. Although 3D animation is a fairly young industry, enough reels have been created and watched to have spawned a "demo reel wisdom" that differentiates between a good and bad reel. Much of this wisdom is available on the Internet through animation websites. I've combined some of the critical elements of this wisdom with my own experiences reviewing reels as part of the animation hiring process:

- Avoid clichéd demo reel music. Techno music has been overused to the point that it has become a running joke in the industry. Overwrought symphonic music, such as *Flight of the Valkyries*, has also been abused and usually winds up sounding silly. Instead, choose unique, somewhat obscure music that adds excitement without becoming annoying to the viewer. If you're not sure what music fits, try cutting your reel with different pieces to see which one feels the best.

"Little Dead Girl"
Music Video
Texturing, Animation,
and Lighting
Maya

"Millennium Bug"
Short Film
Modeling, Texturing,
Animation, and Lighting
Alias PowerAnimator

"13 Ways To Die at Home"
Short Film
Animation and Lighting
Maya

"Weapons of Mass Destruction"
Short Film
Modeling, Texturing,
Animation, and Lighting
Maya

A breakdown sheet

- Use only your best work. If you're a professional with years' worth of experience, pick and choose the shots that are the most representative of your skills and toss the rest. In terms of demo reel length, keep it on the short side; 1 to 3 minutes tends to go over well. At the same time, keep your best, most breathtaking work at the front of the reel. If there are shots that are a little weaker, place them at the end. It's not unusual for a large animation studio to receive over a *thousand* reels in a year. Hence, the available time, and patience, of those reviewing the reels is very limited. If you're a student or are new to the industry, use the best work you have. If you can cut together a decent 1-minute reel, you will be better off than if you cut a mediocre 3-minute reel.

- It pays to specialize, at least in terms of your reel. When an animation company is hiring, they are usually trying to fill a specific niche, such as modeling, rigging, texturing, or lighting. As such, they want to see the best work available in that niche. If you are interested, or have experience, in more than one specific area, cut multiple versions of your reel. In fact, if you have the time, cut your reel for the specific job and specific company that you are sending it to.

- Always include a *breakdown sheet* with your reel. A breakdown sheet is a list of included shots, the software used, and what you did specifically on a shot. This is particularly critical if you include any shots from a group or professional project. The sheet can take the form of a printed piece of paper cut down to the size of a VHS case. The sheet can also be incorporated into the back cover artwork of a DVD case. The exact form can vary so long as the information is clear and easy to read.

Rendering Models for Your Reel

When including models on your reel, a separate set of tips apply:

- Avoid duplicating characters, vehicles, and props from fantasy or science-fiction shows. Although it might be fun to build Optimus Prime or the starship *Enterprise*, it will not bode well for the reel. Not only have such models been created over and over by other student and amateur animators, but it gives no indication of your own originality or diversity of thought.

- Models that replicate real-world objects are a plus so long as they are not toys or overly simplistic. Professional modeling jobs often require the modeler to work off photos or blueprints.

- When displaying your modeling skills, do not stick with a dull, 360-degree, gray-shaded spin. Add different camera moves to make the reel more diverse and interesting. For example, when showing off a character, start with a wide shot with a short, arced dolly, and then cut to a close-up, crane-up shot from the legs to the head. In addition, it always pays to add a wireframe render for each model, assuming the geometry is clean and neat. (For wireframe rendering tips, see Chapter 8.) Along those lines, it is generally a good idea to indicate the triangular polygon count through superimposed text. This is particularly critical for low-resolution game models.

- A textured model is always superior to a untextured one. A rigged and animated model is always superior to a static one. Even if your only interest is modeling, including a textured version of a model shows that you are aware of the texturing process and understand what detail should be geometry and what detail should be a color, bump, displacement, or normal map. At the same time, a model that is in motion shows that you are aware of rigging issues. For example, a character successfully doing jumping jacks demonstrates sound geometry at the upper arms, shoulders, and chest. That said, only include animation on your reel if the animation is polished. If you're not sure your animation skills are strong enough, ask fellow animators for their opinion.

- When showing off a textured, animated model, show it in steps. For example, start with the gray-shaded version, cut to the wireframe, cut to the textured version, then end on the animated version.

Preparing Animation for Your Reel

Animation examples require their own guidelines:

- When demonstrating animation, avoid common animation school projects (bouncing a ball, lifting a rock, dropping a weight on a foot, and so on). Although these scenarios are challenging, they have been animated countless times by other animators. Instead, choose unique scenes that show off advanced animation techniques, such as weight shifting, secondary action, follow-through, lip sync, and so on.

- Characters used to show off character animation need not be overly complex. Simple, blocky characters with no textures become very impressive when high-quality animation is applied to them. In fact, when the characters are simple, the animation is easier to see and study. In addition, avoid using characters that are widely distributed. For example, use an original character instead of the "short blue guy" that came with earlier versions of Maya. Rigged characters are available for purchase through online modeling sites such as www.turbosquid.com. If you're short on money, barter with a fellow animator who specializes in character modeling and rigging.

- Although animation cycles indicate your animation skill, they are not as impressive as noncycled animation. That is, having a character run from screen right to left in a believable fashion is superior to the same character at center screen going through a run cycle in place.

- Avoid space scenes. Unless you're a working professional who has spent time on projects set in space, such animation is not warmly accepted. In addition, avoid animations that are so fantastic that it's unclear what is going on. For example, glowing orbs flying through an indistinct tunnel will not add much value.

Editing and Outputting Your Demo Reel

Editing and output issues also require special attention:

- Fancy transitions are not necessary. That is, you do not have to fade in, fade out, or dissolve between shots. Hard cuts are fine. The point is to show off your skill as a 3D animator.

- Do not add a fancy logo for your name. A spinning, glowing, electric logo constructed from your initials is a turnoff. If you run a company (in your name) that is large enough to require a logo, odds are that you have no reason to mail your personal demo reel to other animation companies.

- VHS is still widely used as a demo reel format. DVDs, however, are quickly becoming a standard. VHS tapes have the advantage of playing on any and all VHS players. DVDs have the disadvantage of multiple codecs, whereby a DVD might not play on a particular

DVD player. Nevertheless, DVDs have the advantage of menus and submenus, which are preferred by some game companies. In any case, the format you choose should be desired by the company you're sending your demo reel to. When a company posts a job opening on its website, it almost always lists a required reel format and delivery method.

- When buying VHS tape for your reel, buy professional stock. Consumer stock is loaded with 2 hours worth of tape. Professional stock is loaded with as little as 5 or 10 minutes worth of tape. Not only is it cheaper to buy professional stock, but the end result looks more professional. (You can tell the difference between a consumer tape and a professional tape simply by its weight.) You can buy professional tape in bulk from Web vendors such as www.tapestockonline.com.

- When buying cases for VHS tapes or DVDs, make sure they are durable enough to hold up to the travails of the U.S. mail. For VHS tapes, clear plastic cases work well. For DVDs, flexible plastic jewel cases are extremely durable.

- Carefully label your reel with your contact information. DVD and VHS labels that you can print with an inkjet printer are available at numerous office supply stores.

Plastic cases for VHS tapes and DVDs. The DVD cases are manufactured by Disc Savers.

Ultimately, you should study the competition. You can find numerous demo reels on the Web by simply typing "3D animation demo reel" into a search engine.

Calibrating Your Monitor

Monitor calibration is an important step of 3D animation. However, it is often ignored or sidestepped by student and independent animators. There are several levels of calibration you can apply. Each is described in the following steps:

1. If you use graphics software published by Adobe, you have access to the Adobe Gamma program. When using Windows XP with the default taskbar settings, you can launch Adobe Gamma by choosing **Start → Control Panel** and double-clicking the Adobe Gamma icon. If you check the Step-by-Step (Wizard) radio button in the Adobe Gamma window, the program interactively steps you through a calibration process. The program allows you to set an appropriate brightness, contrast, and gamma; in addition, you can select

a phosphors set and choose a white point (a point in the monitor's color space that is considered white). Keep in mind that Adobe Gamma is designed for print work, and not video or film. Thus, while the program can help your calibration, it is by no means perfect.

2. Use chip charts. A grayscale chart reveals whether your monitor is *crushing* one part of the color range. For example, the following chart

Adobe Gamma Wizard window

possesses a smooth gradient and 11 steps running from pure black to pure white. If, when viewed on your monitor, the first three steps look pure black, your monitor is crushing the lower end of the range. Adjusting your monitor with step 1 can alleviate this problem to some degree. Although the crushing may be unpreventable on a particular monitor, an awareness of the crushing can at least allow you to adjust your animation, compositing, and digital painting habits. The chip chart is included as chip_chart.tif in the Chapter 10 images folder.

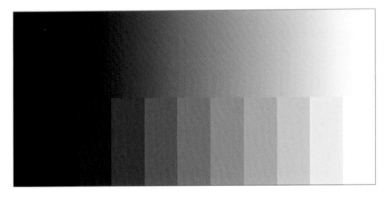

(Top) Grayscale chip chart with gradient and 11 tonal steps and (Bottom) Same chart on a miscalibrated monitor. The three leftmost steps are crushed.

3. If you are creating animation for video and color quality is critical, purchase a broadcast monitor. Broadcast monitors are constructed with higher-quality phosphors and electronic components that allow them to replicate color more accurately than a consumer television. In recent years, flat screen and HDTV broadcast monitors have also become available. For you to view your animation on a broadcast monitor, your PC or Macintosh must possess the ability to output full resolution video in real time. Numerous graphics cards, such as the ATI Radeon 9250, NVIDIA Quadro FX 540, and Matrox RT.X100, offer this ability. High-quality cards generally include a *breakout box*, which is an external case that carries video input and output connections.

(Left) A Sony PVM-14M2U broadcast monitor. (Right) A Matrox RTMac breakout box.

4. If you are creating animation for motion picture film or would like an additional layer of calibration for video, the best solution involves the use of monitor calibration hardware. These devices suction onto the computer monitor screen and are able to accurately read the current state of the monitor's dynamic (light to dark) and gamut (color) range. In turn, the associated software creates an International Color Consortium (ICC) color profile that is able to reprogram the look-up table (LUT) of the graphics card. As a result, at each startup, the monitor is accurately set for a particular project. Monitor calibration hardware manufacturers include ColorVision (www.colorvision.com) and LaCie (www.lacie.com).

If a broadcast monitor and monitor calibration hardware is beyond your budget, steps 1 and 2 will create a relatively accurate calibration. The trick, in this case, is to create tests along the way. For example, when prepping an animation for 35mm film, you can have 35mm slides created from still frames to test different film exposures.

Creating 3D on Multiple Machines

Animators often ask me what type of system they should buy to create their animations. I always suggest buying in bulk. Four $500 machines are usually superior to one $2,000 machine. With four machines, you can multitask more efficiently. Even if a $2,000 machine has dual processors, you are still limited by the number of separate tasks you can accomplish at one time. In comparison, if you have four machines, you can achieve the following:

Render shot A on machine 1

Composite shot B on machine 2

Edit the scene on machine 3

Animate shot C on machine 4

Even if the $2,000 machine has a faster processor and more memory, it is still less efficient than four slower machines. This is not to say that you can operate four machines simultaneously. However, many steps in the 3D animation process require downtime. For example, animation requires the creation of Playblasts. Texturing and lighting require the render of test frames. Editing requires the periodic rendering of footage for preview. Compositing requires the rendering of composites for export. Of course, batch-rendering eats up a huge amount of time. Thus, while one machine is stuck in downtime, you can switch to a second machine to do work.

The biggest disadvantage of multiple machines is the physical space requirement. After all, four monitors and four keyboards require a very long table! An easy way to avoid this, however, is to employ a KVM switch (KVM stands for Keyboard/Video/Mouse). For example, a Linksys ProConnect 4-station KVM switch is used on the system on which this book was written; the switch has the ability to take the PS/2 keyboard, PS/2 mouse, and VGA monitor output from four PCs and send a switched result to a single common keyboard, mouse, and monitor. Switching between PC outputs is as simple as pressing a button. USB switches are an inexpensive alternative that allow you to use a single USB mouse and USB keyboard with multiple PCs and/or Macintoshes. Audio switches also exist. I use a cheap GE Audio/Video Switch to send the audio output of multiple PCs to a single pair of headphones. Several manufacturers, such as Belkin, now offer KVM switches that can accept PS/2, USB, VGA, and audio connections within a single box.

KVM switches are not designed to network PCs together. However, since 10/100 Ethernet connections are standard on most PCs and wireless Ethernet cards are fairly inexpensive, it's easy enough to connect multiple PCs together with an Ethernet hub. Currently, I use a Linksys Ethernet Wireless Access Point.

(Left) A GE Audio/Video Switch stacked on top of a Linksys ProConnect 4-station KVM switch. (Right) Linksys Ethernet Wireless Access Point hub.

Setting Up a Render Farm

Once you have multiple machines linked together through a KVM switch and Ethernet hub, you can use the setup as a miniature render farm. To run Maya on multiple machines, you are legally required to purchase the appropriate site license (for more information, contact an authorized reseller or visit www.autodesk.com). Assuming your license is squared away, you can approach batch-rendering in one of two ways: install render farm management software or manually launch renders from a Windows Command Prompt or Macintosh Terminal window.

Render farm management software automates render queues and divvies up available CPU cycles on multiple machines. For example, Frantic Films Deadline software is available for Windows XP (software.franticfilms .com). Uberware Smedge 3 functions on Windows, Macintosh, and Linux systems (www.uberware.net).

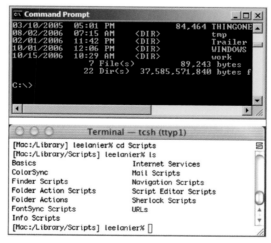

The manual method, on the other hand, requires the following steps:

1. Save a copy of your Maya scene to the machine on which you plan to render. Switch to that machine. If you are working in Windows XP with the default taskbar settings, open the Command Prompt window by choosing **Start → All Programs → Accessories → Command Prompt.** If you are working on a Macintosh, double-click the Terminal icon in the Utilities folder.

(Top) Windows XP Command Prompt window. (Bottom) Macintosh OS X Terminal window.

2. In the Command Prompt or Terminal window, change to the directory in which the scene file was saved. For example, if the scene file was saved to C:\Project, enter **cd c:\project** in the Command Prompt window. To launch a batch render, enter the following line and press Enter:

    Render *scene_name***.mb**

    If Maya has been installed on a Windows PC in a default fashion, the executable program Render.exe can be seen from all directories. If the prompt returns an error, the operating system is unable to find the program. With Windows, the error looks like this:

    ```
    'Render' is not recognized as an internal or
        external command, operable program or batch file.
    ```

    In this situation, you can change to the directory in which the render program is stored. For example, if Maya version 8.0 is running on Windows XP, enter the following:

    cd c:\Program Files\Alias\Maya8.0\bin

3. For a batch render to run, you don't need the Maya interface. The progress of the render is shown in the Command Prompt or Terminal window. By default, the various render settings are taken from the Render Settings window at the moment the scene file was saved in Maya. You can override these settings by using flags with the render program. For example, the following line renders only the first 10 frames of an animation:

    Render *scene_name*.mb -s 1 -e 10

    To see a complete list of available flags and their descriptions, enter **Render -h** in the Command Prompt or Terminal window.

Sharing Texture Libraries

Maya scene files do not store texture bitmaps. Instead, they hard-code a path to a particular directory in which a bitmap is stored. As such, when a scene file is moved to a different machine, the Maya renderer is unable to find the bitmap and will return an error. In this situation, you can apply one of two solutions: duplicating the texture library or updating the hard-coded path.

The first solution dictates that each machine carries identical texture libraries. That is, all the textures on machine A must be stored in an identical location on machine B. Although this solution is fairly straightforward, it requires that you periodically copy textures from one machine to the next so that each texture library is an exact match. This becomes difficult, however, when textures are constantly added or updated on a project. One way to manage this problem is to install file synchronizing software. File synchronization is the process by which the folder contents of two networked machines are compared. If a file on one machine is older, the newer version of the same file is copied from the other machine.

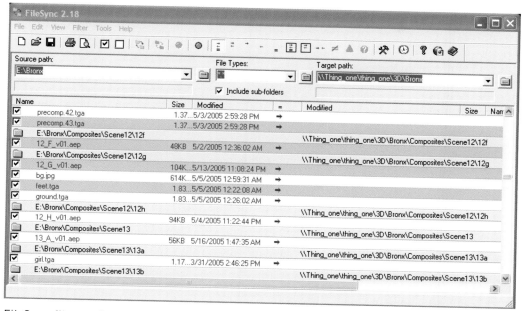

FileSync file synchronizer software compares the folder contents of two networked PCs (visit www.fileware.com for more information).

The second solution requires that you edit the Maya scene file and update the path. Although Maya .mb files are binary, Maya .ma files are text files that you can edit with a text editor. To change all the paths of a scene file on a Windows XP PC, follow these steps:

1. Save the file you plan to render as a .ma. You can select the .ma option in Maya by choosing **File → Save Scene As** ☐ and switching **File Type** to mayaAscii. Move the file to the PC on which you plan to render.

2. RMB click on the .ma file icon and choose Open With from the drop-down menu. In the Open With window, highlight WordPad and click the OK button.

3 Once the file is opened in WordPad, search for the first hard-coded path. If the PC has a single disk, you can choose **Edit → Find** in the WordPad menu, enter **C:/** in the Find What field of the Find window, and click the Find Next button. WordPad automatically scrolls to the first match. If there are bitmaps used by the scene, a line similar to the following is located:

```
setAttr ".ftn" -type "string""C:/TextureLib/Stucco/yellow_stucco.jpg";
```

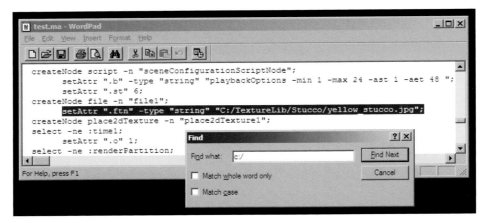

Hard-coded bitmap path in a .ma file, as seen in Windows XP WordPad

You can change the path to one that recognizes a networked location. For example, if you are running two PCs and the first one is named CompOne while the second one is named CompTwo, you can enter the following hard-coded path:

```
setAttr ".ftn" -type "string"

    "//CompOne/3DDisk/TextureLib/Stucco/yellow_stucco.jpg";
```

The //CompOne portion of the line tells Maya to search on the network for a PC named CompOne, even if the batch render is launched on CompTwo. The /3DDisk portion of the line indicates the name of the shared disk. With Windows XP, disks and folders on a remote PC must be set to share; otherwise, they will not be accessible. To set the sharing status, RMB click the disk or folder icon and choose Properties from the drop-down menu. Switch to the Sharing tab of the Properties window and check Share This Folder On The Network. Note that the disk/folder name is indicated in the Share Name field. If you are using Windows XP with the default taskbar settings, you can determine the name of a PC by choosing **Start → Control Panel**, double-clicking the System icon, switching to the Computer Name tab of the System Properties window, and noting the name entered into the Computer Description field.

You can search and replace all the hard-coded paths with WordPad by choosing **Edit → Replace** from the WordPad menu, entering **C:/** or the appropriate drive letter into the Find What field, entering **//CompOne/3DDisk/** or the appropriate remote PC and disk name into the Replace With field, and clicking the Replace All button. Once the .ma file is updated, choose **File → Save** and exit WordPad. You can then launch a batch render from the Command Prompt window.

If you are using a Macintosh, you can edit the .ma file with the TextEdit program. However, for a .ma file saved on a Macintosh, the path is listed in a slightly different way:

```
setAttr ".ftn" -type "string"("/TextureLib/Stucco/yellow_stucco.jpg");
```

In this case, the path is surrounded by parentheses. In addition, no drive letter is included.

Since OS X is based on a Unix kernel, navigating through the Terminal window requires a modified set of commands. For example, when changing directories, you must use forward slashes, /, while Windows requires the use of backward slashes, \. Linux systems, which also run a form of Unix, have requirements similar to OS X. Nevertheless, forward slashes are used to represent paths in both Macintosh and PC .ma files. To confuse things further, backward slashes appear in the **Image Name** field of the File texture's Attribute Editor tab.

Connecting a Macintosh to a PC presents additional challenges. For example, you must use the Macintosh SMB protocol, which defines a URL address by listing an IP address (for example, smb://192.168.1.101). For more information, see the Mac Help Center documentation.

The main disadvantage of the second solution is the need to transfer files back and forth over a network. When a batch render is launched, Maya must pull all the required textures from the remote machine to the local machine. Unless the network is fairly fast, this can slow the render process significantly. Nevertheless, this is the standard method of operation for large studios; a central texture library or texture server is made available to each machine in the studio's render farm.

Estimating Project Requirements

A calculator is a much-needed part of any animator's arsenal. Calculations are not limited to modeling tasks and scripting exercises; they're also needed to estimate a project's completion.

For example, you decide to output a 3-minute animation to video. How long will that take? In terms of rendering time, you can employ the following formula:

```
n seconds × n fps × n render passes × n seconds per frame
```

Although the shots of a simple project may be rendered in a single pass, a more complex one might require multiple render passes for each shot. Multiple render passes produce multiple sets of frames, which in turn become multiple layers in the composite. (For more information on render passes, see Chapter 8.) If the 3-minute animation averages three render passes for each shot, the formula looks like this:

```
180 seconds × 30 fps × 3 render passes × n seconds per frame
```

How long will each frame of each render pass take to render? Odds are, each frame will take a different amount of time. However, you can derive a reasonable average by rendering out test frames at different points in the animation. If no tests have been undertaken, you can estimate the time based on past projects. For example, on freelance animation projects, I find that frames take between 5 and 10 minutes. When estimating time requirements, I plug 7 minutes into the formula. Seven minutes (or 420 seconds) is a rough average of previous projects. Thus, the formula looks like this:

```
180 seconds × 30 fps × 3 render passes × 420 seconds per frame
```

```
180 × 30 × 3 × 420 = 6,804,000
```

If more than one machine is available, divide the total by the number of machines. For example, two render machines help drop the required time:

```
6,804,000 / 2 = 3,402,000
```

To determine the number of minutes, divide by 60:

```
3,402,000 / 60 = 56,700
```

To determine the number of hours, divide by 60:

```
56,700 / 60 = 945
```

To determine the number of days, divide by 24:

```
945 / 24 = 39 days and 9 hours
```

Of course, this formula does not take into account the time required to model, texture, rig, animate, or light the animation. Such estimation requires a look at project management issues, which are discussed in the next section.

Industry Tip: Animation Project Management

Project management concepts are not limited to the dry, dull, world of corporate business. You can apply them to any size animation project to help you meet your deadline goals. Tim Kelly, lead visual effects instructor at the Art Institute of Las Vegas, offers his advice in this area:

- Remember to constantly review your sketches, scripts, storyboards, and any other pre-production materials during production. Nothing is worse than finding out at the last minute that you missed a detail, causing you to have to go in and redo your work. If you're thinking of skipping preproduction planning, reconsider. Time spent up front can save you time on the back end.

- Start scheduling early, and continually check and update your schedule before and during your working sessions. Usually, your client will want a schedule before you start working, and you will be held to it. Be realistic with your schedule, but at the same time keep yourself under reasonable pressure to get the job done.

- Pad your time estimations, keeping Murphy's Law in mind. Build extra time into your schedule for revisions, glitches, bugs, errors, crashes, and so on. It is not unrealistic to add an extra 20 percent into your time estimations for unforeseen complications.

  As for items to include in your schedule, don't limit yourself to rendering. You'll probably want to include the time necessary for conceptual artwork, scripts, storyboards, animatics, modeling, texturing, rigging, character animation, lip sync, lighting, test renders, revisions, file management, system upgrades, backups, client correspondence, editing, color correction, video transfer, and so on.

- Keep your files organized. Create a single master folder for a project. Consider keeping your daily work sessions in a subfolder with a name and date on it. Within that folder, consider creating additional subfolders for scene files, reference, and so on. Consider building a project-specific texture library, in which each character, set, or prop has its own subfolder. Consider creating a separate folder for renders, with subfolders for each shot or element.

- Pick a naming convention at the beginning of a project and stick with it. If a texture is named `house_wall_v01.tif` at the beginning, you should follow the same naming convention at the end. Including a version number, *v01*, helps to differentiate between multiple copies of the same file.

- Whenever you make significant changes to anything in your project, save a new file and name it to reflect the change. Back up your project on multiple, physically separate mediums. For instance, you can make a copy of your project directory on a second system drive, and then make an additional copy on a DVD or external hard drive. If a project is particularly critical, consider storing your DVDs in a physically safe location, such as a fireproof safe. Whatever backup method you choose, never rely on a single backup. When a project is wrapped, create several master backups of all the project materials. It is not unusual to reuse parts of one project on a second project. Although such backups may seem a bit paranoid and time consuming, consider how much time you will be putting in on the project.

TIM KELLY

Tim is the lead instructor in the visual effects program at the Art Institute of Las Vegas. Before joining the school, he spent six years creating print, video, and interactive multimedia work for several firms in Michigan. Having served as an art director on many projects, he is intimately familiar with the pressures of production deadlines. To learn more about the Art Institute of Las Vegas, visit www.artinstitutes.edu/lasvegas.

Prepping Animation for Video

The transfer of 3D animation to video is a common task. Students must transfer their work during the preparation of demo reels. Professional animators must transfer their work for television commercials, series, and other projects. If you are undertaking the transfer yourself, the following steps are recommended:

1. Render square-pixel frames, preferably uncompressed Targas or TIFFs. Render out as large an image as time permits (for example, render 1440×1080 instead of 720×540). In the Render Settings window, activate multipixel filtering. For the Maya Software renderer, check on **Use Multi Pixel Filter** and set the **Pixel Filter Width X** and **Pixel Filter Width** Y to 1. For the mental ray renderer, set the **Filter Width** and **Filter Height** to 1. (With Maya 8.5, **Filter Width** and **Filter Height** are combined into a single attribute, **Filter Width**, with two fields.) Multipixel filtering blurs the rendered image as a post-process. This blurring helps to reduce anti-aliasing artifacts that plague 3D animation that is transferred to video. Lower pixel widths are recommended; higher pixel widths can lead to renders that are too soft.

2. Bring the frames for a single shot into a compositing program, such as After Effects. Fit the frames to a composite that uses the same resolution. Apply any compositing filters or techniques that help to improve the render. Fit the first composite into a second composite that is set to the video output format, such as 720×480 non-square pixel DV. (For more information on non-square pixels, see Chapter 8.) Export the second composite as an uncompressed movie (QuickTime works well).

3. Import the uncompressed movie into an editing program, such as Final Cut Pro or Premiere. (Ultimately, each shot of the animation will be imported as a separate uncompressed movie.) Apply any necessary color correction filters. Ideally, you should check the color quality of the movie through a broadcast monitor. Cut the various movies

together. When the edit is complete, export the cut animation to video through the PC's or Mac's video output or breakout box. If you decide to hand off the edit to a video transfer service or postproduction house, check to see what delivery formats they prefer (DVD, portable hard disc, and so on).

Prepping Animation for 35mm Film

For the presentation of 3D animation, nothing beats 35mm motion picture film. It has been the standard for motion pictures since the late 1800s, when Thomas Edison created 35mm film strips from stock supplied by George Eastman. For 3D animation to be captured in 35mm, digital files must be transferred to film stock. Large animation studios usually own their own transfer equipment in the form of film recorders. Film recorders are 35mm motion picture cameras mounted on specialized CRT screens or laser printers. Smaller studios often contract film labs to undertake their film transfers (also referred to as *digital to film conversions*). For an independent or student animator to transfer animation to 35mm, a film transfer service must also be used. Companies that offer such services include DVFilm in Austin, Texas (www.dvfilm.com), and Alpha Cine Labs in Seattle, Washington (www.alphacine.com).

When preparing animation for 35mm, there are several key items to keep in mind:

- Although proper resolution is critical, it is not out of the reach of an independent animator. Assuming that the images are carefully anti-aliased, renders as small as 1280×720 transfer successfully. Feature film productions generally transfer frames at 2K resolution, although resolutions as large as 4K have been used on films laden with visual effects, such as *Spiderman 2* (2004). At present, *digital intermediaries* are becoming common, whereby 35mm film is digitally captured for editing, color correction, and visual effects and is then transferred back to new 35mm film stock.

- The most difficult aspect of film transfer is the selection of proper exposure. A computer or broadcast monitor possesses a color space significantly different from motion picture film. Hence, it may be necessary to work through several exposure tests with the transfer service, either by filming out a short segment or creating 35mm slides from the 35mm film stock.

- Providing the transfer service with a series of uncompressed Targas or TIFFs, numbered from 1 to *n*, guarantees the best quality. That said, it has become relatively easy to transfer digital video footage to 35mm. Hence, you can choose to transfer your animation to video, and then transfer the video to film. If you do choose to transfer video to film, consult with the transfer service on the best way to prepare the video footage.

◼ In a large theater, 35mm will almost always look superior to video. However, such quality comes at a price. Transferring a 5-minute short film can easily cost between $3,000 and $6,000 for the first print (referred to as an *answer print*). Additional prints add to the price. 35mm reels are heavier than video and add to shipping costs.

The primary screening format for many film festivals remains 35mm. That said, preferences have softened over the last five years, and the majority of festivals now accept some form of professional video (DigiBeta, DVCAM, BetaSP, and so on).

◼ Finding an Audience for a 3D Short Film

Short films are a wonderful format with which to tell a story. At the same time, short films are well suited for animation, where length is difficult to achieve without a huge investment of time and energy. If you are toying with idea of creating a short film, it is worth investigating various means of distribution. After all, you want a find an audience that will appreciate your hard work and artistic vision.

The first place you may want to include a short is your demo reel. Although some human resource specialists prefer seeing animated shorts in place of standard technical exercises, this is not the general rule. A strong short film that you create as a solo project may be very impressive; however, it will probably fail to include a great deal of diversity. For example, if a company is hiring character animators, they usually prefer to see an animation demo reel with a wide range of character styles and animation styles. In contrast, a short film may include only a limited number of characters and a single visual style.

Distributing on the Internet

The Internet provides an inexpensive but far-reaching distribution method. It is relatively easy for any animator to post QuickTime, Windows Media, or RealPlayer versions of a short film on a website. New Web services such as YouTube (www.youtube.com) and MySpace (www.myspace.com) make the posting even easier.

The disadvantage of the Internet is its overwhelmingly large scope. There are over 100 million websites; 65,000 videos are uploaded to YouTube *each day*. Ultimately, this presents a tremendous amount of competition. To reduce the competition, you can submit your film to a recognized, online short film distributor, such as Atom Films (www.atomfilms.com). Although Atom Films hosts hundreds of shorts films of every style and genre, they pick and choose the shorts that they perceive to be the best. Thanks to the somewhat stringent selection process, films hosted by Atom Films sometimes receive *millions* of downloads and wind up with more viewers than any other medium can provide.

Screening at Film Festivals

Approximately 2,500 film festivals exist worldwide. Almost every major city in the world hosts at least one. Although a percentage of these only screen feature films, the majority show at least a handful of shorts. A small number of festivals specialize in animation. For example, the Ottawa International Animation Festival (`ottawa.awn.com`), Annecy Animation Festival (`www.annecy.org`), Hiroshima International Animation Festival (`www.urban.ne.jp/home/hiroanim/`), and Animafest World Festival of Animated Films (`www.animafest.hr`) are among the largest animation festivals. ACM SIGGRAPH, a computer graphics society with 8,000 members (`www.siggraph.org`), also hosts a 3D animation program at its annual convention. Although a small festival may screen as few as 12 short films, large festivals, such as Ottawa and Annecy, screen over a hundred shorts each year.

American film festivals, which are not subsidized by the government, charge submission fees for entering a film. The fees range from $10 to $40 per film. In contrast, European festivals are generally free. If you plan to submit your film worldwide, you will need NTSC and PAL copies. Submitting a film to a festival does not guarantee that it will be selected for screening. A small festival may receive 300 submissions in one year, and a large festival may receive as many as *three thousand*.

A short film usually has a limited lifespan on the film festival circuit. Once a short is older than two years, the majority of festivals will not program it. A finite number of distributors seek short films for DVD compilations, podcasts, mobile phone downloads, and website content, but the money earned rarely pays back the cost of the film. Regardless, distribution guarantees that the film will be accessible to many more people over a longer period of time.

In general, film festivals offer a fantastic means of getting your short film in front of an appreciative audience. Occasionally, such exposure can lead to industry interest in the filmmaker's skills. For example, the TV series *Tripping the Rift* (2000) started life as a short film. The short *9* (2005) caught the interest of director Tim Burton, who decided to develop it into a feature-length film.

For more information on film festivals, visit `www.filmfestivals.com` or `www.withoutabox.com`. I am also partial to the Dam Short Film Festival (`www.damshortfilm.org`), which I run in Boulder City, Nevada.

Index

Note to the Reader: Throughout this index **boldfaced** page numbers indicate primary discussions of a topic. *Italicized* page numbers indicate illustrations.